Body and Character in Luke and Acts

Body and Character in Luke and Acts

The Subversion of Physiognomy in Early Christianity

Mikeal C. Parsons

Baker Academic

Grand Rapids, Michigan

©2006 by Mikeal C. Parsons

Published by Baker Academic
a division of Baker Publishing Group
P.O. Box 6287, Grand Rapids, MI 49516-6287
www.bakeracademic.com

Printed in the United States of America

Library of Congress Cataloging-in-Publication Data
Parsons, Mikeal Carl, 1957–
    Body and character in Luke and Acts : the subversion of physiognomy in early Christianity /
Mikeal C. Parsons.
        p.   cm.
    Includes bibliographical references and index.
    ISBN 10: 0-8010-2885-X (pbk.)
    ISBN 978-0-8010-2885-4 (pbk.)
    1. Bible. N.T. Luke—Criticism, interpretation, etc. 2. Bible. N.T. Acts—Criticism, interpretation, etc. 3. Physiognomy—Religious aspects—Christianity. I. Title.
    BS2589.P36 2006
    226.4′06—dc22   2006018086

Dedicated to
my father, John Quincy Parsons, in his eighty-third year
and to his eight grandchildren:
John Thomas Parsons, Audrey Diane Parsons,
Lauren Mikeal Parsons, Thomas Drew Mabe,
Michael Keith Mabe, Kelsey Marie Parsons,
Mikeal Joseph Parsons, and Matthew Quincy Parsons

Contents

Acknowledgments

This book has had a rather long gestation period. I first published on the topic of Luke and physiognomy in an article on Zacchaeus for *New Testament Studies* in 2001, but I had worked on the topic since 1999. Before that, a passing comment about the curiosity of Zacchaeus's stature made in a seminary paper I graded as a graduate assistant in the early 1980s prompted a vague intuition that there was something "going on" in Luke's description of Zacchaeus as "short in stature" beyond what the commentary tradition told me (or didn't tell me). In the past several years I have had opportunity to work out some of these ideas in lectures and chapel addresses at Campbell University, Furman University, and Wingate University and in conference papers at regional and national meetings of the Society of Biblical Literature. I am grateful to all who have offered comment on this project, including especially my New Testament colleagues in the Department of Religion at Baylor University: Andy Arterbury, Sharyn Dowd, Naymond Keathley, and Charles Talbert. Some of those talks made it into print, and I gratefully acknowledge the editors and publishers of the following publications for permission to reuse some of those materials: "'Short in Stature': Luke's Physical Description of Zacchaeus," *New Testament Studies* 47 (2001): 50–57; and "The Lame Man in Acts 3–4," *Journal of Biblical Literature* 124 (2005): 295–312.

I wrote most of chapters 1 and 2 and revised the remaining chapters during a sabbatical semester in Cambridge, England. My family and I were residents at Tyndale House, and my wife and I were Visiting Fellows at St. Edmund's College, Cambridge University. I am most grateful for the reception and hospitality shown to us by the staff of the Tyndale

House, its readers and residents, and especially Dr. Bruce Winter, Warden. Thanks also to the Baylor University Sabbatical and Research Committees for providing the time and resources to complete this project. I also wish to thank several former and current research assistants who helped with various aspects of this book: Marty Culy (now of Briercrest Seminary), Jason Whitlark, Chad Hartsock, Josh Stigall, and Jim McConnell.

My editor at Baker Academic, Dr. James D. Ernest, is an accomplished scholar of New Testament and patristics in his own right. He has been a pleasure to work with on this and other projects, and I am honored to call him not only my editor but also, and more importantly, my friend. Last but by no means least, I must thank my wife, Heidi, for all the ways she has enriched my life, both personally and professionally.

Mikeal C. Parsons
Baylor University
Advent 2005

INTRODUCTION

The Prime Minister's first, foolish thought was that Rufus
Scrimgeour looked rather like an old lion. There were streaks
of gray in his mane of tawny hair and his bushy eyebrows; he
had keen yellowish eyes behind a pair of wire-rimmed spec-
tacles and a certain rangy, loping grace even though he walked
with a slight limp. There was an immediate impression of
shrewdness and toughness.

—J. K. Rowling, *Harry Potter and the Half-Blood Prince*

At the beginning of Jeffrey Ford's 1997 novel, *The Physiognomy*, the
protagonist, Physiognomist First Class Cley, is on his way out of
the Well-Built City on an assignment for his master, Drachton Below.
He muses over his career as a physiognomist:

After all my years of sweeping open the calipers to find the "soul," skin
deep, even a glimpse at a face could explode my wonder. A nose to me
was an epic, a lip, a play, an ear, a many-volumed history of mankind's fall.
An eye was a life in itself. . . .[1]

1. Jeffrey Ford, *The Physiognomy* (New York: Avon, 1997). In 1998, *The Physiognomy* won the World
Fantasy Award for novels.

While such language may be strange to the modern ear (and hence the book's categorization as "fantasy" literature), throughout history it has been commonplace to associate outer physical characteristics with inner qualities; it was assumed that you can, as it were, judge a book by its cover. The study of the relationship between the physical and the moral was known as "physiognomy."

Despite our unfamiliarity with the term "physiognomy," our contemporary culture is certainly not immune to the practice of it. One can purchase a Digital Physiognomy software package online that "determines a person's psychological characteristics and presents a detailed character analysis of that person in a graphic format."[2] A colleague of mine was told by his seminary professor that he would never be a great preacher because he had small hands! More seriously, contemporary practices such as "racial profiling" have their roots ultimately in the physiognomic consciousness.[3] The post–9/11 politics and ethics of racial profiling continue to be hotly debated.[4] The epigraph from Harry Potter at the beginning of this chapter shows that physiognomic categories are still effective in literary characterization.

Physiognomy was of intense interest in the eighteenth century. Johann Caspar Lavater (1741–1801), a Swiss pastor and theologian, is best remembered for his essays on physiognomy, published originally in German as *Physiognomische Fragmente zur Beförderung der Menschenkenntniss und Menschenliebe*.[5] Put simply, and as the epithet to the chapter shows, Lavater was convinced that the science of physiognomy, the study of a person's physical features, was the ABCs to understanding that person's character. He claimed, "Physiognomy, whether understood in its most extensive or confined signification, is the origin of all human decisions, efforts, actions, expectations, fears, and hopes from the cradle to the grave . . . from the worm we tread on to the most sublime of philosophers . . . physiognomy is the origin of all that we do and suffer."[6] Lavater's entire

2. See "Digital Physiognomy Software—Match a Person's Face to His or Her Character," http://www.uniphiz.com/physiognomy.htm.

3. See Kenneth Meek, *Driving While Black* (New York: Random House, 2000).

4. See for example the conflicting assessments in Amnesty International's report, *Threat and Humiliation: Racial Profiling, Domestic Security, and Human Rights in the United States* (New York: Amnesty International USA Publications, 2004) and Walter Williams, "Racial Profiling," *Capitalism Magazine* (April 21, 2004); http://www.capmag.com/article.asp?ID=3639.

5. Johann Caspar Lavater, *Physiognomische Fragmente zur Beförderung der Menschenkenntniss und Menschenliebe* (Leipzig and Winterthur, 1775–1778).

6. Johann Caspar Lavater, *Essays on Physiognomy: For the Promotion of the Knowledge and the Love of Mankind*, trans. Thomas Holcroft, 3 vols. (London, 1789–1793), 1:16–17; cited by Lucy Hartley,

"scientific" theory was based on the premise that the mind (and soul) of an individual could, uniquely among God's created order, be divined by a proper understanding of the individual's actions, gestures, expressions, and physicality. Put simply, according to Lavater, you can—and should—judge a book by its cover.[7]

The collection of Lavater's writings on physiognomy became one of the most influential books of the eighteenth and nineteenth centuries, partly due to its lavish illustrations and fine printing. By the middle of the nineteenth century there were more than 150 editions, including German, French, American, Russian, Dutch, and English. While the original edition was a very expensive folio, many later editions were pocket-sized paperbacks. These inexpensive editions won wide popularity and assisted in the widespread dissemination of Lavater's theories.[8] The broad acceptance of Lavater's ideas in the popular culture of his day is attested in the eighth edition of the *Encyclopaedia Britannica*, published some seventy years after the original edition of Lavater's work:

> Its publication created everywhere a profound sensation; admiration, resentment, and fear were cherished towards the author. The discoverer of the new science was everywhere flattered or pilloried; and in many places, where the study of human character from the face became an epidemic, the people went masked through the streets.[9]

This acclamation has been confirmed by modern assessments as well. Graeme Tytler claims that "it would be scarcely an exaggeration to say that his name was once a household word and that he enjoyed the kind of adulation nowadays bestowed on film stars and 'pop' idols."[10]

Physiognomy and the Meaning of Expression in Nineteenth-Century Culture (Cambridge: Cambridge University Press, 2001), 1.

7. On Lavater's influence especially on nineteenth-century British culture, see Hartley, *Physiognomy and the Meaning of Expression*; more generally on its influence on early modern European culture, see Martin Porter, *Windows of the Soul: Physiognomy in European Culture 1470–1780* (Oxford: Oxford University Press, 2005). It is worth noting that Sir Thomas Browne, the English physician whose work influenced Lavater, is credited with introducing the word "caricature" into the English language and has obvious ties with the "science" of physiognomy.

8. On the influence of Lavater in England, see John Graham, "Lavater's Physiognomy in England," *Journal of the History of Ideas* 22 (1961): 561–72.

9. *The Encyclopaedia Britannica*, 8th ed., 22 vols. (Edinburgh: Archibald Constable, 1853–1860), 18:576; cited by Hartley, *Physiognomy and the Meaning of Expression*, 42.

10. Graeme Tytler, *Physiognomy in the European Novel: Faces and Fortunes* (Princeton, NJ: Princeton University Press, 1982), 6. For more on Lavater, see Ellis Shookman, ed., *The Faces of Physiognomy: Interdisciplinary Approaches to Johann Caspar Lavater* (Columbia, SC: Cambden House, 1993).

Lest we dismiss the then wildly popular views of Lavater as an eccentric or anomalous moment in the intellectual history of Western civilization, let us note that Lavater was simply building upon, or in some cases reviving, a very ancient "science" associated with the likes of Aristotle, Hippocrates, Galen, and Cicero. Lavater was quite aware of this indebtedness. Consider his comments on comparing the similarities between humans and eagles found in the U.S. edition cited above in the epigraph:

> According to Aristotle's opinion on Physiognomy, he whose nose is curved from the root of the forehead, and strongly marked like the beak of an eagle, must be a brave man. It was also observed by Polemon and Adamantius that such a nose denotes courage; and Albert, upon the authority of Loxus, conveys the same idea. Noses thus formed are commonly distinguished by the term aquiline, or Roman, and seem to bear the character of something royal or majestic; for the eagle, whose bill is so formed, is the king of birds: from this it may be inferred that an aquiline nose denotes a dignified mind, capable of magnificent conceptions.[11]

Lavater here cites four of the major sources of authority for physiognomists, the "physiognomic scriptures": pseudo-Aristotle, Adamantius, Polemo, and Loxus (partially preserved in a later anonymous treatise).

The author of one of the tractates mentioned by Lavater, the pseudo-Aristotelian tractate, *Physiognomonica*, claims: "The physiognomist takes his information from movements, shapes, colors, and traits as they appear in the face, from the hair, from the smoothness of the skin, from the voice, from the appearance of the flesh, from the limbs, and from the entire stature of the body" (806a28–34). This method is based on the assumption that "soul and body react on each other; when the character of the soul changes, it changes also the form of the body, and conversely, when the form of the body changes, it changes the character of the soul" (808b12–15). This is the gist of physiognomy as understood and practiced in the ancient world.

This book is concerned with the impact and influence of the practice and principles of ancient physiognomy on the writings of Luke and Acts. We will argue that Luke at times employs physiognomic categories in his literary presentation of certain characters, usually for the purpose of subverting them. This is especially true of those texts that seek to estab-

---

11. *The Physiognomist's Own Book: An Introduction to Physiognomy Drawn from the Writings of Lavater* (Philadelphia: James Kay Jun. & Brother, 1841), 83–84.

lish Luke's vision of the eschatological community, established around the person of Jesus Christ and grounded on the Abrahamic covenant (Genesis 12). For Luke this is a radically inclusive community, comprised not only of sinners and social outcasts but also of the physically disabled and disfigured who, on the basis of the appearance of their physical body, have been ostracized as misfits from the body politic (or religious). Much of the prejudice and bias of Luke's day was grounded in this pervasive physiognomic consciousness that presumed one's outer appearance determined one's moral character. In at least four texts that deal in some fashion with the fulfillment of the Abrahamic covenant, Luke presumes physiognomic principles only to overturn them by story's end.

The plan of this book is to explore this pervasive physiognomic consciousness in the larger Greek and Roman cultures (chapter 1), the Jewish and Christian subcultures (chapter 2), and Luke's own symbolic world (chapter 3). The remaining four chapters will consider the stories of the bent woman (Luke 13), Zacchaeus (Luke 18), the lame man (Acts 3–4), and the Ethiopian eunuch (Acts 8). An epilogue returns to the question of what it means to read these ancient stories in light of our contemporary setting.

I

SOUL AND BODY REACT ON EACH OTHER

Body and Character in Greek and Roman Literature

In the ancient Greek and Roman world it was commonplace to associate outer physical characteristics with inner qualities. The study of the relationship between the physical and the moral was known as *physiognomics* and was widely practiced in late antiquity by philosophers, astrologers, and physicians. Elizabeth Evans has convincingly demonstrated that from Homer through at least the third century CE, physical descriptions of characters in epic, history, drama, and fiction, as well as in medical writings, were used by writers to explain the character's actions. The physiognomic consciousness that developed permeated the Greco-Roman thought world.[1]

1. Elizabeth Evans "*Physiognomics in the Ancient World,* Transactions of the American Philosophical Society 59, part 5 (Philadelphia: American Philosophical Society, 1969). Evans's argument for a pervasive "physiognomic consciousness" was originally resisted by classicists but recently has received confirmation in a variety of writings on ancient drama, theater, and art: see G. Raina, "Il verosimile in Menandro e nella Fisiognomica," in *Il meraviglioso e il verosimile tra antichità e medioevo,* ed. D. Lanza and O. Longo (Florence: L. S. Olschki, 1989), 173–85; G. Krien, "Der Ausdruck der antiken Theatermasken nach Angaben im Pollux-Katalog und in der pseudo-aristotelischen 'Physiognomik,'" *Jahreshefte des*

The Origins of Physiognomy

The origins of the "science" of physiognomy are obscure. Some recognize the philosopher Pythagoras as the inventor of physiognomy (Hippolytus, *Haer*. 1.2; Porphyry, *Vita Pyth*. 13; Iamblichus, *Vit. Pyth*. 17).[2] Aulus Gellius, a second-century CE writer who followed this tradition, describes the admissions examination administered by Pythagoras for entrance into his school:

> It is said that the order and method followed by Pythagoras, and afterwards by his school and his successors in admitting and training their pupils were as follows: At the very outset he "physiognomized" the young men who presented themselves for instruction. That word means to inquire into the character and dispositions of men by an inference drawn from their facial appearance and expression, and from the form and bearing of their whole body. Then, when he had thus examined a man and found him suitable, he at once gave orders that he should be admitted to the school. (*Noct. Att*. 1.9)[3]

Galen, on the other hand, credited his "master" Hippocrates with founding the science of physiognomy (*Anim. mor*. 7; cf. Kühn, 4, 797–98). Indeed, the first occurrence of the verb φυσιογνωμονέω is found in Hippocrates' *Epidemics*, and that treatise contains several instances of physiognomic thinking. For example, Hippocrates wrote, "Those with a large head, large black eyes and a wide, snub nose are honest" (*Epid*. 2.6.1; cf. 2.5.1; 2.5.16; 2.6.14, 19; 6.4.19).

Zopyrus (fifth century BCE) is one of the first persons known to have been a practitioner of the art of physiognomy. He purportedly diagnosed Socrates as stupid and fond of women. Cicero reports, "Do we not read how Socrates was stigmatized by the 'physiognomist' Zopyrus, who professed to discover men's entire characters from their body, eyes, face and brow? He said that Socrates was stupid and thick-witted because he had not got hollows in the neck above the collarbone—he used to say that these portions of his anatomy were blocked and stopped up; he also

---

Österreichischen Archäologischen Instituts in Wien (1955): 84–117; B. Kiilerich, "Physiognomics and the Iconography of Alexander," *Symbolae Osloenses* 63 (1988): 5–28.

    2. See Elizabeth Evans, "Descriptions of Personal Appearance in Roman History and Biography," *Harvard Studies in Classical Philology* 46 (1935): 47.

    3. Unless otherwise noted, English versions of classical texts are from the Loeb Classical Library editions. Regarding entrance examinations, see R. A. Pack, "Physiognomical Entrance Examinations," *Classical Journal*, 31 (1935): 42–43.

added that he was addicted to women—at which Alcibiades is said to have given a loud guffaw" (*Fat.* 5.10). Thus one of the earliest recorded attempts at physiognomy was met with ridicule because the reading did not match what Socrates' followers knew to be true of their leader.

Elsewhere, however, Cicero notes that Socrates came to the defense of Zopyrus: "when he [Zopyrus] was ridiculed by the rest who said they failed to recognize such vices in Socrates, Socrates himself came to his rescue by saying that he was naturally inclined to the vices named, but had cast them out of him by the help of reason" (*Tusc.* 4.37).[4] While many in the ancient world thought the relationship between outer appearance and inner character was fixed and determined, Socrates here sides with those who believed that this relationship, however natural and true, was subject to transformation. In Socrates' case one's innate nature, reflected in outer physical appearance, could be changed by philosophical reflection and study.[5]

A certain Eusthenes was another of the earliest named practitioners of physiognomy. Among the epigrams attributed to Theocritus is an epitaph of Eusthenes, who was "skilled to infer the character of the mind from the eye."[6]

Antecedents in Medicine and Philosophy

Given that the "honor" of founding physiognomy is shared by a physician and a philosopher, we are not surprised to find that the subject held

4. For Lavater's critique of Zopyrus's reading of Socrates, see Lavater, *Essays on Physiognomy*, trans. Thomas Holcroft, 4th ed. (London, 1844), plate XV and accompanying text, in which Lavater asserts that "the declaration of Zopyrus, that he was stupid, was incontrovertibly erroneous nor was Socrates less mistaken when he was so ready to allow that he was, by nature, weak. It may have been, and perhaps was, an inevitable effect of the weight of these features, that the perspicuity of his understanding was, sometimes, as if enveloped by a cloud. But had Zopyrus, or any true physiognomist, been accustomed accurately to remark the permanent parts of the human face, he never could have said Socrates was naturally stupid."

5. For an excellent overview of the role of physiognomy in ancient philosophy and among the medical writers, see George Boys-Stones, "Physiognomy and Ancient Psychological Theory," in *Seeing the Face, Seeing the Soul: Polemon's Physiognomy from Classical Antiquity to Medieval Islam*, ed. Simon Swain (Oxford: Oxford University Press, 2006). Limiting himself to texts that reflect theoretical discussions of physiognomy, Boys-Stones reaches the largely negative conclusion that most philosophers did not view the body-soul relationship in strictly physiognomic categories. In this study, we are interested in the way the physiognomic consciousness shaped characterization in ancient narrative and the ways in which physiognomy was used as a rhetorical tool in invective and encomium to judge the moral quality of one's foes and friends, regardless of whether the philosophical roots of those presentations ran very deep or not. Appreciation is expressed to Professor Boys-Stones for making his material available to me in a prepublication format.

6. See A. S. T. Gow, *Theocritus*, 2nd ed. (Cambridge: Cambridge University Press, 1952), 11.

a place in the repertoire of both, even if that place was not as central as is sometimes thought.[7]

Hippocratic Medicine

Hippocrates wrote: "We must not fail to observe that there is a difference in places, and that some beget better men and others worse; and we must legislate accordingly. Some places are subject to strong and fatal influences by reason of diverse winds, or again, from the character of the food given by the earth, which not only affects the bodies of men for good or evil, but produces similar results in their souls" (*Lex* 188a). The sentiment expressed here is similar to the ethnographic method of physiognomy described in the later handbooks (see below). Galen, a second-century physician in the Hippocratic tradition, approached physiognomy through the doctrine of the humors.[8] In fact he wrote a handbook that evidently bore a title something like "That the faculties of the mind follow the mixtures or temperaments of the body."[9] According to Evans, it was Galen who "first of all skillfully combined the Aristotelian parallelisms of men and animals in the study of physiognomy with the theory of the humours circulating in the body, and thus laid the foundations for what have become commonplaces through the centuries in the interpretation of the character of a man from his physique."[10]

Aristotelian Philosophy

As noted above, Galen often drew on Aristotle's writings for his understanding of physiognomic convention, especially in his understanding of the humors, or bodily fluids. Although they were not a driving force in his thought, Aristotle did comment on the humors: "The thicker and hotter the blood is, the more conducive it is to strength, while in proportion to its thinness and coldness is its suitability for sensation and intelligence" (*Part. an.* 2.2.648a).

7. See Evans, *Physiognomics*, 17–28; also Evans, "Galen the Physician as Physiognomist," *Transactions and Proceedings of the American Philological Association* 76 (1945): 287–98. For a more restrained approach to the question of the place of physiognomy in the thought of ancient philosophers and medical writers, see Boys-Stones, "Physiognomy and Ancient Psychological Theory."

8. Galen, however, shared with Hippocrates an ethnographical interest in the ways in which a region's climate and topography affect the character of the inhabitants.

9. *Claudii Galeni Pergameni Scripta Minora*, ed. I. Müller et al. (Leipzig: Teubner, 1891), 2:32–79; See Evans, "Galen the Physician as Physiognomist," 294.

10. Evans, "Galen the Physician as Physiognomist," 298.

But neither Aristotle's nor Galen's interests were limited to "ethno-graphical" physiognomy, as it would later be labeled. One finds in Aristotle's writings also an interest in physiognomic signs derived from the animal world: "When men have large foreheads, they are slow to move; when they have small ones, they are fickle; when they have broad ones, they are apt to be distraught; when they have foreheads rounded or bulging out, they are quick tempered" (*Hist. an.* 1.8.491b).

Platonic and Stoic Philosophy

Philosophic interest in the science of physiognomy was not limited to Aristotle, as the following quotations demonstrate. Plato wrote, perhaps somewhat tongue in cheek:

> Is not this a way you have with the fair; one has a snub nose, and you praise his charming face; the hooked nose of another has the grace of regularity; the dark visage is manly, the fair are children of the gods; and as to the "honey pale," as they are called, what is the very name but the invention of a lover who talks in diminutives, and is not averse to paleness, if appearing on the cheek of youth? (Plato, *Resp.* 5.19.474d)

Zeno, the founder of Stoicism, in a passage preserved by Clement of Alexandria, describes the desired physical attributes of the virtuous man:

> Let the face be open, the eyebrows neither drooping, nor the eyelids wide apart nor turned back. The neck should not be stretched up stiffly, nor the parts of the body be loosely jointed together. Let the limbs be held by a proper tautness. The mind should be keen and well keyed for discussion, and in firm possession of what has been said. Let the gestures and movements give no hope to the intemperate, but rather let modesty rest upon the countenance, and firmness be evident in the face. (*Paed.* 3.11.74)

Marcus Aurelius likewise reflects the Stoic interest in physiognomy current in the second century CE: "The intention will reveal itself; it ought to be graven on the forehead; the tone of the voice should give that sound at once; the intention should shine out in the eyes at once, and as the beloved at once reads the whole in the glances of lovers" (*Med.* 11, 15).

Physiognomic Handbooks

While Antisthenes reportedly wrote a treatise on physiognomy in the classical period, the extant systematic studies devoted to the topic all come from the third century BCE and later. Among the best known are a third-century BCE document, *Physiognomica*, attributed (inaccurately) to Aristotle;[11] *On Physiognomy*, a work by the second-century CE rhetorician, Polemo of Laodicea; the fourth-century CE *Physiognomonica* by Adamantius the sophist; and an anonymous fourth-century Latin handbook, *De physiognomonia*.[12] Here the physiognomic conventions as they have developed over several centuries are set down. The treatise of pseudo-Aristotle is generally recognized to be the epitome of two different works.[13] In chapters 1–34 the first author criticizes previous physiognomic methods and then sets forth twenty-two characters (e.g., the "flirt," the "well-born," the "irascible," and the "debaucher") along with the signs by which they can be recognized. In chapters 35–74 the second author details aspects of the body, both as a whole and in its individual parts, and what these physical signs reveal about the inner character.[14]

According to the author of the pseudo-Aristotelian tractate *Physiognomonica*: "The physiognomist takes his information from movements, shapes, colors, and traits as they appear in the face, from the hair, from the smoothness of the skin, from the voice, from the appearance of the flesh, from the limbs, and from the entire stature of the body" (806a). This method is based on the assumption that "soul and body react on each other; when the character of the soul changes, it changes also the form of the body, and conversely, when the form of the body changes, it changes the character of the soul" (808b12–15).

Pseudo-Aristotle mentions three kinds of physiognomic analysis: what we might call the anatomical method, the zoological method, and the

---

11. See Pliny, *Hist. nat.* 11.273–74; Diogenes Laertius, *Vit.* 5.25.

12. These texts were collected, edited, and published by Richard Foerster in *Scriptores Physiognomonici Graeci et Latini*, 2 vols. (Leipzig: Teubner, 1893). A major project to translate these texts into English is under way, *Seeing the Face, Seeing the Soul: Polemon's Physiognomy from Classical Antiquity to Medieval Islam*, headed by Simon Swain of the Department of Classics and Ancient History at the University of Warwick. Appreciation is expressed to Professor Swain for making some of these translations available to me in prepublication form. To avoid confusing the similar titles of these works by using similar abbreviations, I will reference the anonymous treatise as "*De physiogn.*" and the others as "ps.-Aristotle," "Polemo," and "Adamantius."

13. See *Scriptores Physiognomonici* 1:xiii–xiv.

14. See Tamsyn S. Barton, *Power and Knowledge: Astrology, Physiognomics, and Medicine under the Roman Empire* (Ann Arbor: University of Michigan Press, 1994), 101.

ethnographical method.[15] In the anatomical method, the physiognomist looks at a facial feature (e.g., the scowl or the furrowed brow) and identifies its corresponding emotion.[16] Whenever the expression is subsequently observed on a different person, the corresponding character trait can be inferred.

The zoological method seeks to determine a person's character by observing similarities in appearance between the person and features of various kinds of animals.[17] While humans might seek to mask their inner moral character, animals have no such pretensions. Rather, the character traits of animals are fixed and transparent for all to observe: all deer and hares are timid, all lions are courageous, all foxes are wily and cunning. When a physical feature is peculiar to a particular animal and that animal is characterized by certain character traits, the physiognomist may infer that persons with similar physical features share the inner nature of the corresponding animal.

The ethnographical or racial method, according to A. MacC. Armstrong, "amounts to an application of the zoological method to human races and peoples."[18] The physiognomist considers the collective behaviors of a particular race of people and links those behaviors to their distinctive physical features. Polemo discusses geographic stereotypes, grouping them in terms of Northerners (chapter 32), Southerners (chapter 33), Easterners (chapter 34), Westerners (chapter 35), and Greeks (chapter 36).[19] He introduces the discussion thus:

> It follows from the indices and signs of this discipline that as often as you judge any race or a people of the world on the basis of these indices, you will judge them correctly. However you will find that some signs typical of a people are negative and lead them to deviance, while others are positive, correcting the deviance. For example you will scarcely find

15. Here I am following the suggestion of Jacques André, ed. and trans., *Anonyme Latin: Traité de Physiognomonie* (Paris: Belles Lettres, 1981), 12, who speaks of the three methods as "l'anatomique, la zoologique et l'ethnologique." A. MacC. Armstrong, "The Methods of the Greek Physiognomists," *Greece and Rome* 5 (1958): 53, however, refers to "the expression method, the zoological method, and the racial method."

16. Armstrong, "The Methods of the Greek Physiognomists," 53.

17. Ibid., 53–54.

18. Ibid., 55; on these three methods, see also J. Mesk, "Die Beispiele in Polemos Physiognomonik," *Wiener Studien* 50 (1932): 51–67; Bruce J. Malina and Jerome H. Neyrey, *Portraits of Paul: An Archaeology of Ancient Personality* (Louisville: Westminster John Knox Press, 1996), 113–25. Since we will deal with the zoological and expression methods in more detail in chapter 3, we will spend a bit more space on the racial method in this chapter and return to it in chapter 7.

19. See Malina and Neyrey, *Portraits of Paul*, 119.

keen insight and excellence in letters among the Egyptians; on the other hand keen insight is widespread among the Macedonians; and you will find among Phoenicians and Cilicians the pursuit of peace and pleasure; and finally you will be offended by Scythians, a treacherous and devious people. (Polemo 31.236)

Interest in ethnography was not limited to the physiognomists but was rather commonplace in ancient thinking about the relationship of persons to their places of origin. Hippocrates, for example, writes:

Inhabitants of a region which is mountainous, rugged, high and (not) watered, where the changes of season exhibit sharp contrasts are likely to be of big physique, with a nature well adapted for endurance and courage, and such possess not a little wildness and ferocity. The inhabitants of hollow regions that are meadowy, stifling, with more hot than cold winds, and where the water is hot, will be neither tall nor well made, but inclined to be broad, fleshy, and dark-haired; they are dark rather than fair, less subject to phlegm than to bile. Similarly bravery and endurance are not by nature part of their character, but the imposition of law can produce them artificially. . . . Such as dwell in a high land that is level, windy, and watered, will be tall in physique and similar to one another, but rather unmanly and tame in character. As to those who dwell on thin, dry and bare soil, and where the changes of the seasons exhibit sharp contrasts, it is likely that in such country people will be hard in physique and well-braced, fair rather than dark, stubborn and independent in character and temperament. For where the changes of the season are most frequent and most sharply contrasted, there you find the greatest diversity in physique, in character, and in constitution. . . . [Where] the land is bare, waterless, rough, oppressed by the winter's storms and burnt by the sun, there you will see men who are hard, lean, well articulated, well braced and hairy. Such natures will be found energetic, vigilant, stubborn, and independent in character and temper wild rather than tame, of more than average sharpness and intelligence in the arts, and in war of more than average courage. (*Aër.* 24.1–40)[20]

Common examples from the ancient world would include the stereotypes of Cretans as liars and Corinthians as promiscuous.

In addition, a kind of geocentrism, expressed in antiquity in various forms of the "omphalos" myth (the notion that one's city or country of origin lay at the center or "navel" [ὄμφαλος] of the world) is related to

20. Cited ibid., 117.

geographical stereotyping.[21] This geocentrism is found in both pagan and Jewish sources. To the Greeks, Delphi was the center or navel of the universe. Strabo recounts the commonly held view that "Delphi was the center of the inhabited world, and people called it the navel of the earth" (*Geogr.* 9.3.6; cf. also Pindar, *Pyth.* 4.74, 6.3; Pausanias, *Descr.* 10.16.3). The author of Jubilees makes the same claim for Jerusalem: "Mount Zion was in the midst of the navel of the earth" (*Jub.* 8.12; cf. *Tanh. Qed.* 10). Philo of Alexandria makes a similar claim for Jerusalem as the "mother city, not of one country, Judea, but of most of the others in virtue of the colonies sent out at different times to the neighboring lands" (*Legat.* 281).[22] From there it was only a small step to marginalize or vilify the "barbarian" races that lived at the edges of the Roman Empire while elevating the status of the Romans (or Greeks).

Furthermore, the body of the Roman male citizen was considered normative; races or ethnic groups exhibiting real or presumed deviations from that body type would be subject to denigration. Often the farther away a group lived from the political center of the empire the more that group was given monstrous and exotic attributes (dwarfism, giantism, etc.) to underscore their "otherness."[23] The underlying conviction that the body of the Roman male free citizen was the normative body, physically and politically, is critical to understanding the bias against slaves, women, and "inferior" men and races that permeates so much of physiognomic thinking in the ancient world. We will return to this point

---

21. Ibid., 120–24; Samuel Terrien, "The Omphalos Myth and Hebrew Religion," *Vetus Testamentum* 20 (1970): 315–38; Mikeal C. Parsons, "The Place of Jerusalem on the Lukan Landscape: An Exercise in Theological Cartography," in *Literary Studies in Luke-Acts*, ed. Richard P. Thompson and Thomas E. Phillips (Macon, GA: Mercer University Press, 1998), 155–72.

22. Early and medieval Christians continued to place Jerusalem at the center of the known world; cf. the earliest extant Christian map, the Madaba map, a sixth-century mosaic that places Jerusalem at the center. For more on "Christian" cartography, see Daniel J. Boorstin, *The Discoverers* (New York: Random House, 1983), 100–101; cf. Parsons, "The Place of Jerusalem," 156–58, where I argue that Luke and Acts resist the notion of making Jerusalem the center of its narrative world, preferring rather to depict it as a beginning point or "beachhead for the Gentile mission" (p. 168).

23. The racial or ethnographical interest in marginalizing other races as monstrous existed in a symbiotic relationship with the Greco-Roman fascination, even obsession, with deformity and disability. Robert Garland has detailed this phenomenon in *The Eye of the Beholder: Deformity and Disability in the Greco-Roman World* (Ithica, NY: Cornell University Press, 1995). Since all of the characters in the texts we treat in Luke/Acts had deformities or disabilities (in the ancient sense), we will need to return to Garland's work (as well as studies on Jewish views of disability) later in this study. For a critique of the work of Garland and others, see Sharon V. Betcher, "Rehabilitating Religious Discourse: Bringing Disability Studies to the Theological Venue," *Religious Studies Review* 27 (2001): 341–48.

in our treatment of the physiognomic (or antiphysiognomic) passages in Luke and Acts.

Pseudo-Aristotle criticizes aspects of each of these three methods (see below); he makes little use of the racial method (mentioning specifically only the Corinthians and Ethiopians in his physiognomic analysis) and most use of the expression method (rightly understood).

The work by Polemo was composed during the first third of the second century CE and survives intact only in a fourteenth-century Arabic translation.[24] Polemo was a native of Laodicea and a descendant of the kings of Pontus, though he spent much of his adult life as a leading citizen of Smyrna.[25] He was both a sophist and a physiognomist.[26] Much (about one-third) of his tractate on physiognomy focuses on traits of the eyes, followed by a discussion on zoological physiognomy that considers traits of more than ninety animals (1.170–98, ed. Foerster), followed by a section on the signs of the various parts of the body, in which Polemo moves from the extremities of fingernails, fingers, and feet up through the torso to the neck, head, and face (1.198–236). The next section deals with ethnographical physiognomy (1.236–44) and continues with a discussion of eye and skin color (1.244–48), body and hair (1.248–56), and the signs associated with movement and voice (1.256–68). The last section (1.268–92) lists the physical signs by which one may detect various character traits (brave, effeminate, ambitious, etc.). Polemo made effective rhetorical use of physiognomy for both encomium and invective, viciously attacking his arch rival, Favorinus.[27]

The anonymous fourth-century Latin handbook seems to summarize the writings of Aristotle, Loxus, and chiefly Polemo.[28] The Latin author does not usually reproduce Polemo's individual character sketches; the description of the "criminally stupid man" is an exception.[29]

---

24. One sentence of the Greek original survives. The Arabic was translated into Latin by A. Schmoelders and revised by G. Hoffman for the Teubner edition (see Foerster, *Scriptores*, 1:lxxxiiff.). For the problems with Polemo's text, see Barton, *Power and Knowledge*, 102.

25. Philostratus, *Vit. soph.* 530, 532, 611. See G. W. Bowersock, *Augustus and the Greek World* (Oxford: Clarendon, 1965), 51–53, 143–44.

26. For a summary of Polemo's life and work, see Maud W. Gleason, *Making Men: Sophists and Self-Presentation in Ancient Rome* (Princeton, NJ: Princeton University Press, 1995), 21–37. Adamantius the Sophist produced a Greek paraphrase of Polemo's work that is occasionally useful in clarifying the Arabic text.

27. Gleason, *Making Men*, 46–48, discusses Polemo's polemical invectives against Favorinus, a point to which we shall return in our chapters on the lame man of Acts 3–4 and the Ethiopian eunuch in Acts 8.

28. This work is also available in André, ed. and trans., *Anonyme latin*.

29. Gleason, *Making Men*, 31.

Rhetorical Handbooks

Physiognomy was part and parcel of rhetorical theory. Evans says of rhetorical delivery, "All of these suggestions, set down to ensure that the speaker is saying exactly what is in his heart, reflect the 'physiognomic consciousness' of the later Greek world, wherein the physical appearance deliberately displays the inner emotions of the mind. These ideas are consonant with Roman rhetorical practice, and Cicero himself pursues the subject at some length."[30] For example, Cicero claims that "everything rests with the face, and the face in turn is under the power of the eyes. . . . and the eyes are the index of the emotions . . . No one can achieve the same end with eyes closed" (*De or.* 3.221–22).

Elsewhere Cicero maintains that nature "has so formed his [human] features as to portray therein the character that lies hidden deep within him; for not only do the eyes declare with exceeding clarity the inner-most feelings of our hearts, but also the countenance, as we Romans call it, which can be found in no other living being, save man, reveals the character" (*Leg.* 1.9.26).

Physiognomy was especially useful in rhetorical invective, a speech of condemnation or blame. Cicero employs this device in his invective against L. Calpurnius Piso Caesonius, a Roman consul at the time of Cicero's exile in 58 BCE. Cicero focuses on Piso's countenance:

> We were not deceived by your slavish complexion, your hairy cheeks, and your discolored teeth; it was your eyes, eyebrows, forehead, in a word, your whole countenance, which is a kind of silent speech of the mind that pushed your fellow-men into delusion. This was how you tricked, betrayed, inveigled those who were unacquainted with you. There were but few of us who knew of your filthy vices, the crassness of your intelligence, and the sluggish ineptitude of your talk. Your voice had never been heard in the forum; never had your wisdom in council been put to the test; not a single deed had you achieved either in peace or war that was, I will not say famous, but even known. You crept into office by mistake, by the recommendation of your dingy family bust, with which you have no resemblance save color. (*Pis.* 1)[31]

---

30. Evans, *Physiognomics*, 41.

31. On this text, see J. Albert Harrill, "Invective against Paul (2 Cor 10:10), the Physiognomics of the Ancient Slave Body, and the Greco-Roman Rhetoric of Manhood" in *Antiquity and Humanity: Essays on Ancient Religion and Philosophy Presented to Hans Dieter Betz on His 70th Birthday*, ed. Adela Yarbro Collins and Margaret M. Mitchell (Tübingen: Mohr Siebeck, 2001), 201–4. See also D. M. MacDowell, "Piso's Face," *Classical Review* 14 (1964): 9–10; Joseph J. Hughes, "Piso's Eyebrows," *Mnemosyne* 45 (1992): 235–36.

The use of physical features to draw moral conclusions was a common rhetorical strategy in the ancient Mediterranean world.

Physiognomy in Practice

Interest in things physiognomic in ancient medicine, philosophy, and rhetoric is so widespread that Elizabeth Evans rightly speaks of a pervasive physiognomic consciousness in the ancient world. Evans also documents interest in physiognomy in other genres of literature as well, including biography, drama, epic, poetry, and (to a slightly lesser extent) historiography. Dominic Montserrat has also shown that physiognomy influenced even notices for runaway slaves. He cites a third-century CE notice from Oxyrhynchus:

> An Egyptian from the village of Chenres in the Arthribite nome, utterly ignorant of Greek, tall, skinny, clean-shaven, with a [small] wound on the left side of the head, honey-complexioned, rather pale, with a wispy beard—in fact, with no hair at all to his beard—smooth-skinned, narrow in the jaws, long-nosed. By trade a weaver, he swaggers around as if he were someone of note, chattering in a shrill voice. He is about 32 years old. (*P.Oxy.* 51.3617)[32]

Montserrat concludes:

> Naturally some of the bodily details are included here for entirely practical purposes, but there is a sub-text to their inclusion. Because he is a slave, he cannot be a "real man," and the adjectives applied to the body of this anonymous slave serve both to set him physically apart and render him ridiculous. He is ugly and beardless, and thus infantile, although 32 years old; and like a child he goes around jabbering away as though he has delusions of grandeur.[33]

Our concern in this study is with the literary practice of using physical descriptions to interpret and reveal the "inner person"—the morality and spirituality—of characters in ancient narrative. Thus, while the physiognomic theories of philosophers, physicians, and rhetoricians is indispens-

---

32. Dominic Montserrat, *Sex and Society in Graeco-Roman Egypt* (London: Kegan Paul International, 1996), 56.

33. Ibid., 56. Harrill, "Invective against Paul," 201, counts references such as this as evidence of a "somatic hierarchy" based on physiognomy.

able for understanding the categories and conventions of physiognomy, it is crucial to see this physiognomic consciousness at work in the literary presentation of characters in various kinds of writing from antiquity. Evans has provided a huge database of physiognomic references in literature that ranges from epic to drama. We will consider in some detail two examples[34] of literary portraits of characters that utilize aspects of the physiognomic consciousness, in order to develop the characterization of certain antagonists or protagonists in their narratives.[35]

Suetonius on Tiberius

Suetonius's description of Tiberius is certainly susceptible of a physiognomic interpretation, as are many of Suetonius's descriptions:[36]

> He was large and strong of frame, and a stature above the average; broad of shoulders and chest; well proportioned and symmetrical from head to foot. His left hand was the more nimble and stronger, and its joints were so powerful that he could bore through a fresh, sound apple with his finger, and break the head of a boy, or even a young man with a flip. He was of fair complexion and wore his hair rather long at the back, so much as even to cover the nape of his neck; which was apparently a family trait. His face was handsome, but would break out on a sudden with many pimples. His eyes were unusually large and, strange to say, had the power of seeing even at night and in the dark, but only for a short time when first opened after sleep; presently they grew dim-sighted again. He strode along with his neck stiff and bent forward, usually with a stern countenance and for the most part in silence, never or very rarely conversing with his companions, and then speaking with great deliberation and with a kind of supple movement of his fingers. All of these mannerisms of his, which were disagreeable and signs of arrogance, were remarked by Augustus, who often tried to excuse them to the senate and people by declaring that they were natural failings and not intentional. (*Tib.* 69)

34. A third, Thersites in Homer, will be discussed in chapter 7.

35. It is certainly possible that the flow of influence between physiognomic theory (preserved in the handbooks) and practice (seen in various genres) moved in both directions, and not necessarily from theory to practice, as Evans suggests. In other words, Homer's (and others') descriptions of characters may very well have shaped development of physiognomic canons; on this, see Philip DeLacy, review of *Physiognomics in the Ancient World*, by Elizabeth C. Evans, *American Journal of Philology* 92 (1971): 508–10.

36. See, e.g., the description of Augustus (*Aug.* 79) and Caligula (*Cal.* 50). For a comparison of these descriptions with the physiognomic handbooks, see Evans, *Physiognomics*, 54–55. See also J. Coussin, "Suétone physiognomiste dans les vies des XII Césars," *Revue des études latines* 31 (1953): 234–56.

Evans comments that there is a remarkably "close correspondence between his [Tiberius's] physical merits and defects and the known virtues and vices of his character."[37] One of Tiberius's positive features was a body "large and strong" (*corpore fuit amplo atque robusto*), which was a sign of courage (Polemo 268; Adamantius 408–9; *De physiogn.* 2.119). Furthermore, like a lion, Tiberius was broad of shoulder and chest (*latus umeris et pectore*), part of the signs of a character that "is generous and liberal, magnanimous and with a will to win" (ps.-Aristotle 809b). Tiberius was also "well proportioned and symmetrical from head to foot" (*ceteris quoque membris usque ad imos pedes aequalis et congruens*). This, too, fits well with physiognomic canons. The "well-proportioned" (σύμμετροι), according to pseudo-Aristotle, "are naturally just and courageous" (814b; cf. Adamantius 411; *De physiogn.* 2.131).

Certainly Suetonius portrays Tiberius as a strong and effective military leader (cf. *Tib.* 9; 14; 16; 17; 18), but these virtues seem confined to his role as a military leader because Tiberius's physical description also betrays many weaknesses in moral character. His "fair complexion" (*colore erat candido*) suggests a tendency toward cowardice ("the very fair are cowardly; witness women," ps.-Aristotle 812a; cf. Polemo 244; Adamantius 386; *De physiogn.* 2.106). His "unusually large eyes" (*praegrandibus oculis*) are reminiscent of cattle and therefore, according to pseudo-Aristotle, are a sign of "sluggishness" (ps.-Aristotle 812b; cf. Polemo 108; *De physiogn.* 2.138), and his temporary nocturnal vision was, according to Polemo, a sign of "unjust behavior" (*iniustitiam adiudica*; Polemo 152, cf. 156, 160; Adamantius 331–32; *De physiogn.* 2.52). Tiberius's gait was especially revealing. "He strode along with his neck stiff and bent forward" (*incedebat cervice rigida et obstipa*). Suetonius notes that these mannerisms were "disagreeable and signs of arrogance." Pseudo-Aristotle asserts that one mark of the "shameless" (ἀναιδής) man is that "his figure is not erect but inclines to stoop forward" (807b; cf. Polemo 220, 234; Adamantius 368; *De physiogn.* 2.75–76; 2.99). Polemo even suggested that a "neck bent forward" (*cervice obstipa*) suggested that its possessor was not "free from insanity" (Polemo 222). A stern countenance (*adducto fere vultu*) such as Tiberius possessed signified a gloomy or morose disposition (ps.-Aristotle 812a; *De physiogn.* 2.28) or even a treacherous or faithless spirit (Polemo 156; Adamantius 378). Suetonius comments elsewhere, "I am also aware that some have written that Augustus so openly and

---

37. Evans, *Physiognomics*, 55.

unreservedly disapproved of his austere manner that he sometimes broke off his freer and lighter conversation when Tiberius appeared" (*Tib.* 21).[38]

These weak character traits are reflected at the end of this passage where Augustus is reported to have tried to excuse them before the Senate and the whole people. Earlier Suetonius reported the conflicting traditions regarding Augustus's opinion of Tiberius and offered his own conclusion: "It is my opinion that after weighing the faults and merits of Tiberius, he [Augustus] decided that the latter preponderated" (*Tib.* 21). But this passage is probably aimed more at defending Augustus's reputation than Tiberius's. Although Augustus struggled with his decision he ultimately—reluctantly, according to Suetonius—gave his approval to this conflicted character. For surely Augustus would not have knowingly thrown the Roman people into "jaws that crunched so slowly" (*Tib.* 21). At the end, Suetonius sums up Tiberius's career in a way that confirms this negative physiognomic reading: Tiberius "did so many other cruel and savage deeds under the guise of strictness and improvement of the public morals but in reality rather to gratify his natural instincts" (*Tib.* 59).

This extended discussion of the physiognomic implications of the physical description of Tiberius demonstrates Suetonius's familiarity and use of the physiognomic categories in his literary characterization. Suetonius's audience, likewise familiar with these conventions, would have understood this characterization.

Lucius in Metamorphoses

When Lucius's aunt, Byrrhena, sees Lucius for the first time in many years, she offers the following description: "He inherited that well-bred behaviour from his pure and virtuous mother Salvia. And his physical appearance is a damnably precise fit too: he is tall but not abnormal, slim but with sap in him, and of a rosy complexion; he has blond hair worn without affectation, wide-awake bluish-grey eyes with flashing glance just like an eagle's, a face with a bloom in every part, and an attractive and unaffected walk" (Apuleius, *Metam.* 2.2). Byrrhena claims that there is a "precise fit" (*amussim congruentia*) between Lucius's actions and his

---

38. Pseudo-Aristotle, however, suggests that the signs of the "orderly man" (κόσμιος) includes being "deliberate in movement and speech" (807b). The difference between deliberate speech (as in pseudo-Aristotle) and reticence in speech is presumably of degree and not of kind.

physical appearance, a judgment with which the physiognomist, no doubt, would agree.[39]

This ecphrasis lends itself well to a physiognomic interpretation and is thus an excellent example of the physiognomic consciousness at work. The physiognomist was interested in stature (taller being preferred to shorter, and symmetry in proportion to be preferred above all). Pseudo-Aristotle comments at the end of his tractate, "If the ill-proportioned are scoundrels the well-proportioned would naturally be just and courageous" (814a). The observation that Lucius is tall but not abnormal (*inenormis*) is important also from a physiognomic point of view, for "the excessively large are slow [-witted]; for as the blood travels over a large area the impulses arrive slowly at the seat of the intelligence" (813b). Being of a "rosy complexion" (*rubor temperatus*) echoes the handbook's assertion that those whose "complexion is ruddy (ἐρυθρός) are keen (ὀξεῖς), because all parts of the body grow red when they are heated up by movement" (ps.-Aristotle 812a; cf. 806b, 807b; Polemo 244, 246). Likewise, "Those with golden hair (ξανθοί) are brave (εὔψυχοί); consider the lions" (ps.-Aristotle 812a; cf. Polemo 250).

"Bluish-grey eyes" (*oculi caesii*) were a sign of those who were "brave" (εὔψυχοί), like the lion or eagle (cf. ps.-Aristotle 812b). A "flashing glance like an eagle's" is also a positive physiognomic attribute: "Those whose eyes are not grey but bright are stouthearted; witness the lion and the eagle" (ps.-Aristotle 812b). Lucius also has a "face that is blooming in every part" (*os quoquoversum floridum*). This feature, too, is significant from a physiognomic perspective for "forms and affections appearing in the face are considered according to their likeness to the affection. For when one experiences anything, one becomes as if one has the kind of expression" (ps.-Aristotle 806b). Clearly, Lucius's blooming face reflected a character in full moral bud.

Finally, Byrrhena's closing comment that Lucius's walk was "attractive and unaffected" (*speciosus et immeditatus incessus*) echoes the physiognomic concern for gait and deportment. In the anonymous Latin physiognomic handbook we read:

---

39. The passage is discussed in Evans, *Physiognomics*, 72–73. F. Opeku, "Physiognomy in Apuleius," in *Studies in Latin Literature and Roman History*, ed. Carl Deroux (Brussels: Latomus, 1979), 1:469, denies any physiognomic import is found in *Metam.* 2.2. H. J. Mason, "Physiognomy in Apuleius' *Metamorphoses* 2.2," *Classical Philology* 79 (1984): 307–9, defends the physiognomic reading but departs from Evans's interpretation at one significant point; see note 47 below.

He whose feet and hands move in harmony with all the rest of his person, who moves forward with shoulders calm and carefully controlled, with his neck but slightly inclined—he is the one whom men call brave and magnanimous, for his is the walk of the lion. (*De physiogn.* 76.2.99–100, ed. Foerster; cf. Polemo 50.1.262, ed. Foerster)

By contrast, Polemo describes the gait of the effeminate or cowardly:

You may recognize him by his provocatively melting glance and by the rapid movement of his intensely staring eyes . . . his loins do not hold still, and his slack limbs never stay in one position. He minces along with little jumping steps. (Polemo 2.52.1.415–16, ed. Foerster)

Dio Chrysostom confirms the significance of deportment for understanding character: "Walking is a universal and uncomplicated activity, but while one man's gait reveals his composure and the attention he gives to his conduct, another's reveals his inner disorder and lack of self-restraint" (*Or.* 35.24).[40] Clearly Lucius's gait, according to his aunt, raised no concern regarding her nephew's conduct.

The cumulative effect of Byrrhena's description of Lucius is to paint a thoroughly positive portrait of the protagonist's moral character, an assessment that could not be missed by any reader steeped in the physiognomic consciousness that was so prevalent among Apuleius's second-century readers.

Mason notes that the description is "more than a collection of such 'signs' (*semeia*) of several virtues"; rather, "it corresponds to the description of ethical 'types' (e.g., the brave man) to which large sections of the treatises are devoted. Lucius's features all exemplify the Golden Mean: he is tall but not disproportionately so, slender but with some flesh on him, moderately red in complexion. This mean is frequently praised in the treatises."[41] He comments further:

This mean is best exemplified by the εὐφυής or *ingeniosus*. He is described in the Latin treatise (*Phy. Lib.* 92): "ingeniosus esse debet non satis procerus nec breuis, coloris albi, cui sit permixtus etiam rubor, capillo flauo . . . habens . . . oculos humidos, splendidos χαροπούς." Polemo uses almost identical language to describe the "pure Greek" ethnic type (Foerster, *Scriptores*, 1:242–44). The portrait of Lucius corresponds in many details (medium

---

40. For more on the importance of deportment in physiognomy, see chapter 7 on the lame man in Acts 3–4.

41. Mason, "Physiognomy," 307–8.

height, partially red complexion, blond hair, bright eyes) to the εὐφυής of the physiognomists, and it seems reasonable to suppose that Apuleius meant his readers to associate Lucius with that type.[42]

Mason, however, argues that Lucius's eyes do not fit the golden mean. He suggests that *caesii* is the equivalent of γλαυκοί, which is associated with cowardice in pseudo-Aristotle (812b14), and concludes that:

> Lucius's unusual eyes, suggesting cowardice, rashness, and impudentia, are more significant for his character than are his other, ostensibly praiseworthy, features. Lucius's appearance is thus like his noble birth, which is much praised in early sections of the work but which turns out (*Metam.* 11.15) to be of little moral or practical worth and to have given him a false sense of his own value.[43]

According to Liddell-Scott-Jones, however, χαροποί is the Greek equivalent to *caesii*.[44] Pseudo-Aristotle uses χαροποί "bluish-grey" (which the Loeb translator renders "bright") in distinction from "grey" (γλαυκοί) to signify the "brave" (see above). Furthermore, Loxus describes χαροπός as the *optimus* and mean between *niger* and *glaucus* (*De physiogn.* 81). Hence, the feature of the eyes is also positive and comports well with the view that Lucius fits the golden mean.[45]

Greco-Roman Critiques of Physiognomy

Not all ancients thought the physical body was a reliable indicator of moral quality. In Euripides' play, Medea laments:

> O God, you have given to mortals a sure method
> of telling the gold that is pure from the counterfeit;
> Why is there no mark engraved on men's bodies
> By which we could know the true one from the false one.

> (*Medea* 516–19)

42. Ibid., 309. We agree further with Mason's comment (308 n. 12) that Apuleius's readers "need not have read the [physiognomic] treatises. Physiognomical explanation must have been a normal part of rhetorical training."

43. Mason, "Physiognomy," 309.

44. See LSJ, 1980. According to C. T. Lewis and C. Short, *A Latin Dictionary* (Oxford: Clarendon, 1896), 265, the term "bluish-grey" is rare in Latin literature and refers only to the eyes ("cat-eyed").

45. Nonetheless, this positive portrait of Lucius may ultimately be overthrown, as Mason suggests, by subsequent events in the narrative. See H. J. Mason, "The Distinction of Lucius in Apuleius' *Metamorphoses*," *Phoenix* 37 (1983): 135–43.

Even though physiognomy was an integral part of his medical repertoire, Galen could be critical of certain physiognomic practices: "When
they say that he has a chest like a lion and is therefore spirited, but legs
like a goat, and is lascivious, they describe that they have observed, but
they have omitted the reason for these characteristics."[46]

The physiognomic handbooks themselves caution against relying too
heavily on any one physiognomic method. This criticism is obviously at
the level of practice and execution and is not a philosophical attack on
the principles of physiognomy per se. Pseudo-Aristotle writes:

> Those who proceed in their science entirely by characteristics are wrong;
> first of all, because some men, who are in no sense alike, have the same
> facile expressions (for instance the brave and the shameless man have the
> same expressions), but are widely different in disposition; secondly, be-
> cause at certain times they do not have the same expressions but different
> ones; for the low-spirited sometimes spend a happy day and conversely
> the high-spirited may be suffering grief, so that the expression in the face
> changes. . . .
>
> But those who base this science of physiognomics on wild beasts do not
> make their selection of signs correctly. For it is impossible to go through the
> forms of each of the beasts and say that, whosoever resembles this beast in
> body, will also be similar in soul. For first of all, no one would find it possible
> to say simply that a man was really like a beast, but only that he resembled it
> to a certain extent. Again, in addition to this only a few animals have peculiar
> characteristics, but most have common ones. So that, when a man resembles
> an animal not in a peculiar but in a common characteristic, why should he be
> more like a lion than a deer? . . . Common characteristics would then give no
> clear sign to the student of physiognomics. (805b)

Pseudo-Aristotle then notes the kinds of data that can properly be collected and the correct way to assess them (see above).

Epictetus expresses concerns about certain physiognomic practices:
"Surely everything is not judged by its outward appearance only, is it?
Therefore, neither are the nose and the eyes sufficient to prove that one
is a human being, but you must see whether one has the judgments that
belong to a human being" (*Diatr.* 4.5.19–21). Pliny the Elder criticizes
Aristotle for placing credence in physiognomy: "For my own part, I am
surprised that Aristotle not only believed but also published his belief
that our bodies contain premonitory signs of our career," and concludes,

---

46. *Mixt.* 2.6 (Kühn 1.624), cited by Evans, *Physiognomics*, 25.

"I think this view unfounded" (*Hist. nat.* 11.273–74). Plutarch, in his discussion of Marcus Cato in *Parallel Lives*, notes, "I shall now record a few of his [Cato's] famous sayings, believing that men's characters are revealed much more by their speech than, as some think, by their looks" (*Cat. maj.* 7.2).[47]

Seneca wrote:

> Virtue is just as praiseworthy if it dwells in a sound free body, as in one which is sickly or in bondage. Therefore, as regards your own virtue also, you will not praise it any more, if fortune has favored it by granting you a sound body, than if fortune has endowed you with a body that is crippled in some member, since that would mean rating a master low because he is dressed like a slave. (*Ep.* 66.23)

Seneca attempts to dissuade his reader from drawing conclusions regarding one's character from outward appearance since matters of Fortune—"money, person, position"—are transitory and prone to change (see *Ep.* 66.23). Even those who, like Galen and Seneca, criticize the practice of physiognomy bear witness to its appeal.[48]

Conclusion

The evidence for a pervasive physiognomic consciousness in the larger Greco-Roman world is impressive, both in theory and in practice. Evans concludes that physiognomy "enjoyed a far greater popularity among Greek and Roman writers, especially those of the later Greek society and Roman Empire, than has generally been supposed. As a quasi-science, it always bore a close relationship to the science of medicine; as an art, to the practice of rhetoric."[49] The conclusion that this physiognomic consciousness was pervasive in the ancient pagan world seems beyond dispute. Of course not all writers were equally enthusiastic in their support of physiognomy nor, as Socrates reminds us, did all of them think

47. Plutarch may have felt forced into this conclusion, since earlier he had acknowledged that his subject, Marcus Cato, was red-headed and gray-eyed, which Plutarch knows is understood negatively: "red-haired, snapper and biter, his grey eyes flashing defiance" (*Cat. maj.* 1.3; LCL). Even though he thus prefers to interpret Cato's character by his words, he is forced to refer to "his discourse" as "a second body, as it were" (1.4; LCL).

48. Harrill, "Invective against Paul," 207.

49. Evans, *Physiognomics*, 5.

that the physiognomic connection between the outer and inner self was predetermined and irreversible. What impact, if any, did the physiognomic consciousness (and its critique) have on the presentation of characters in Jewish and Christian sources? We turn our attention to this question in the next chapter.

2

THE MOVEMENT OF THE BODY
IS A VOICE OF THE SOUL

Body and Character in Early Jewish and Christian Literature

E arly Jewish and Christian writings demonstrate awareness—but not uncritical acceptance—of physiognomic ideas. We turn now to the evidence.

Jewish Literature

Physiognomy is not a dominant theme in ancient Judaism, but one does see an interest in how inner qualities are reflected in outer characteristics, beginning with the scriptures of Israel. Several examples are found in the Deuteronomistic History, the authors of which had presumably ingested some physiognomic theories of Babylonian origin.[1]

Scriptures of Israel

Saul is described as "a handsome young man. There was not a man among the people of Israel more handsome than he; he stood head and

---

1. See F. R. Kraus, *Die physiognomischen Omina der Babylonier* (Gräfenhainichen: C. Schulze, 1935) and *Texte zur babylonischen Physiognomatik,* Archiv für Orientforschung, Beiheft 3 (Berlin, 1939).

shoulders above everyone else" (1 Sam. 9:2; cf. 10:23b). One thinks also of David who "was ruddy, and had beautiful eyes, and was handsome" (1 Sam. 16:12). About Absalom the narrator writes, "Now in all Israel there was no one to be praised so much for his beauty as Absalom; from the sole of his foot to the crown of his head there was no blemish in him" (2 Sam. 14:25).

In addition to these examples taken from Hebrew narrative, the priestly restrictions regarding the temple cult also lend themselves to physiognomic interpretation. The need for unblemished sacrifices is well known. Consider the following example:

> The LORD spoke to Moses, saying: Speak to Aaron and his sons and all the people of Israel and say to them: When anyone of the house of Israel or of the aliens residing in Israel presents an offering, whether in payment of a vow or as a freewill offering that is offered to the LORD as a burnt offering, to be acceptable in your behalf it shall be a male without blemish, of the cattle or the sheep or the goats. You shall not offer anything that has a blemish, for it will not be acceptable in your behalf. When anyone offers a sacrifice of well-being to the LORD, in fulfillment of a vow or as a freewill offering, from the herd or from the flock, to be acceptable it must be perfect; there shall be no blemish in it. Anything blind, or injured, or maimed, or having a discharge or an itch or scabs—these you shall not offer to the LORD or put any of them on the altar as offerings by fire to the LORD. An ox or a lamb that has a limb too long or too short you may present for a freewill offering; but it will not be accepted for a vow. Any animal that has its testicles bruised or crushed or torn or cut, you shall not offer to the LORD; such you shall not do within your land, nor shall you accept any such animals from a foreigner to offer as food to your God; since they are mutilated, with a blemish in them, they shall not be accepted in your behalf. (Lev. 22:17–25)

Considerations of unblemished bodies extended from the sacrifice to the one offering the sacrifice.[2] It is required that "priests must not shave their heads or shave off the edges of their beards or cut their bodies" (Lev. 21:5). The following is particularly noteworthy:

---

2. Jacob Milgrom, *Leviticus 17–22: A New Translation with Introduction and Commentary*, AB 3A (New York: Doubleday, 2000), 1875–82, notes that the blemishes of sacrificial animals correspond roughly with those listed for priests. He concludes, "*mutatis mutandis*, the same blemishes that invalidate officiating priests also invalidate animal sacrifices" (p. 1877).

For no one who has a blemish shall draw near, one who is blind or lame, or one who has a mutilated face or a limb too long, or one who has a broken foot or a broken hand, or a hunchback, or a dwarf, or a man with a blemish in his eyes or an itching disease or scabs or crushed testicles. No descendant of Aaron the priest who has a blemish shall come near to offer the LORD's offerings by fire; since he has a blemish, he shall not come near to offer the food of his God. (Lev. 21:16–18)

Many interpreters are struck by the fact that the list of physical blemishes for priests is not accompanied by a parallel list of moral "blemishes" that would exclude a priest from service. One solution is to see a connection between the outward and inward. As Samuel Balentine has noted, "In Israel's priestly system the concern for wholeness and integrity of the physical body is an extension of the understanding that God's holiness is perfect and complete. Holy and unblemished persons (and sacrifices) are external expressions of the requirement to be holy as God is holy."[3] Certainly there may be a physiognomic correlation between the outward, unblemished physical attributes of the priest (and sacrificial animal) and the inner holiness or purity that the physical state manifests.[4]

Whether or when these restrictions extended beyond the temple priests to the temple worshipers is debated and perhaps irresolvable. The subscript in verse 24—"Thus Moses spoke to Aaron and his sons and to all the Israelites"—could be taken to suggest that this list applied to worshipers as well as priests. Most commentators, however, have taken the subscript to refer to the fact that issues of priestly disqualifications should be the concern of the entire community.[5]

3. Samuel E. Balentine, *Leviticus* (Louisville: Westminster John Knox, 2002), 169. On the priest's role in examining animals for blemishes, see also Mal. 1:13–14a. Furthermore, the common denominator of these blemishes (with the exception of a "crushed testicle") is that they are outward and easily perceived by any observer. Milgrom, *Leviticus 17–22*, 1876, argues on this basis that the priestly blemishes derived from the list of animal blemishes, since in the case of the latter a "crushed testicle" would be readily observable. He reverses an earlier opinion and argues that it is the "appearance" of a blemish, rather than its reality that is crucial.

4. Here I agree with Milgrom (*Leviticus 17–22*, 1843), who, in his section "Blemished Priests: A Comparative Survey," notes the "absence of any moral requirements in amply attested Mesopotamian texts.... Still, in view of the same silence of Lev. 21, we should not be too hasty in concluding that moral qualities were not required of Babylonian priests." I disagree, however, with the explanation of the silence as due to "the fact that both lists, Mesopotamian and biblical, were written by priests who may have taken moral requirements for granted." More plausible is the explanation that in both cases the priestly writers assumed that unblemished bodies were indicative of pure moral character; physiognomy was practiced in Babylonia during the time of the final redaction of these texts (see the studies listed in note 61).

5. See *Sipra Emor* 3.12; Milgrom, *Leviticus 17–22*, 1833.

It is clear that in Qumran in addition to those holding offices (cf. 1QSa 2:409) worshipers with deformities or disabilities were precluded from entering the assembly: "The maimed, the lame, the deaf, and minors, none of these may enter the midst of the community" (4QD 171:6–9). The LORD's promises in Isaiah 56:4–5 regarding the inclusion of eunuchs in the cultus are in an eschatological context and cannot be interpreted as evidence of historical reality:

For thus says the LORD:

> To the eunuchs who keep my sabbaths,
> who choose what pleases me
> and hold fast my covenant,
> I will give, in my house and within my walls,
> a monument and a name
> better than sons and daughters;
> I will give them an everlasting name
> that shall not be cut off.[6]

Returning to Hebrew narrative, the rather difficult passage in 2 Samuel 5:8 is tantalizing in this regard: "The blind and the lame shall not come into the house." To this phrase some Greek translators add "of the Lord." Some take this text to demonstrate that at least Hellenized Jews in the second century BCE assumed that the blind and the lame are excluded from entering the temple precincts.[7]

Postbiblical Judaism

The priestly interest in unblemished bodies is detectable also in post-biblical Judaism, especially at Qumran. In addition to the concern for whole bodies in worship, note the following passage from Qumran:

[...] a man of [...] secrets. And his thighs are long and slender, and the toes of his feet are slender and long. And he is in the second position. His spirit has six (parts) in the house of light and three in the pit of darkness. And this is the sign in which he was born: the foot of Taurus. He will be poor. And his animal is the bull. (4Q186, Frag 1. col. II.3–8)

---

6. For more on this, see chapter 7 on the Ethiopian eunuch.

7. See especially, Saul M. Olyan, "'Anyone Blind or Lame Shall Not Enter the House': On the Interpretation of Second Samuel 5:8b," *Catholic Biblical Quarterly* 60 (1998): 218–27.

His eyes are of a colour between black and stripy. His beard is ... [...] and frizzy. The sound of his voice is simple. His teeth are sharp and well aligned. He is neither tall nor short, and like that from his birth. Then the fingers of his hands are slender and long. His thighs are smooth and the soles of his feet [...] are even. His spirit has eight (parts) [in the house of light] in second position, and one [in the house of darkness ...] And the sign in which he was born is [...] And his animal is [...] this [...] ... (4Q186, Frag. 2 col. I.1–11)[8]

As Philip Alexander has demonstrated, this text "is not, as has been widely supposed, a horoscope but a physiognomy."[9] These texts combine physiognomy and astrology in an effort to predict a person's character and perhaps also his destiny. Since astrology required knowledge of one's birth sign (often not accessible), physiognomy was the "science" of choice to evaluate someone's character.[10] Not all the elements are drawn from physiognomic or astrological symbolism. The "house of light," for example, is contrasted with the "pit of darkness" and has a "strongly sectarian meaning, which is related ... to some of the central theological ideas of the Qumran community."[11] Likewise, the use of a nine-point scale to assess the degree to which a person is ruled by the cosmic forces of "light/good" and "darkness/evil" appears to be sectarian.[12] The number nine, however, does not seem to have any special astrological or physiognomic significance, but it does mean that no one can have equal parts of light and evil; "one is either predominantly good or predominantly bad."[13]

Nonetheless, Alexander points out two significant features about these passages that are shaped by physiognomic concerns. First, the physiog-

8. The translation is taken from Florentino García Martínez, *The Dead Sea Scrolls Translated: The Qumran Texts in English*, trans. Wilfred G. E. Watson (Leiden: E. J. Brill, 1992), 456. For the original text (and a slightly different English translation), see Florentino García Martínez and Eibert J. C. Tigchelaar, eds., *The Dead Sea Scrolls Study Edition*, vol. 1, *1Q1–4Q273* (Leiden: Brill, 1997), 380–84.

9. Philip S. Alexander, "Physiognomy, Initiation, and Rank in the Qumran Community," in *Geschichte—Tradition—Reflexion: Festschrift für Martin Hengel zum 70. Geburtstag*, vol. 1, *Judentum I*, ed. Hubert Cancik, Hermann Lichtenberger, and Peter Schäfer (Tübingen: J. C. B. Mohr, 1996), 385. Alexander goes on to argue that 4Q186 should be renamed "4QAstrological Physiognomy" to replace its persistent misnomer "4QHoroscopes." Even Lawrence Schiffman, who continues to refer to 4Q186 as a "horoscope," admits that "physiognomy and chiromancy played an important role in the sect's thought and practice": *Reclaiming the Dead Sea Scrolls: The History of Judaism, the Background of Christianity, the Lost Library of Qumran* (Philadelphia: The Jewish Publication Society, 1994), 364.

10. Alexander, "Physiognomy," 386.

11. Ibid., 386–87.

12. Ibid., 390. Which of these forces are found and to what degree one is ruled by them "appears to be totally predestined and beyond one's control" (390).

13. Alexander, "Physiognomy," 388.

nomy "appears to be based on the whole body from head to toe."[14] Some of the observations fit what we know of Greek physiognomy: interest in moderation (eyes between dark and striped), symmetry (neither tall nor short), and unaffected voice and gesture ("simple" voice). The text also draws on a kind of "zoological method"; here the person who is in the "house of light" has as his animal a bull. Importantly, most of the description is available from observation, meaning that the person being examined does not have to cooperate with the examination or even be aware of it.[15] Alexander further cites Josephus as an example from antiquity who drew parallels between the Essenes and the Pythagoreans: "those we call Essenes, a group which employs the same daily regime as was revealed to the Greeks by Pythagoras" (*Ant.* 15:371). Alexander suggests that physiognomy was used in evaluating candidates for entrance into the community, much like the Pythagoreans.[16]

Another text from Qumran, 4QElect of God (=4Q534 [4QMess ar]), suggests a physiognomic interpretation, this time with regard to a "messianic figure." The text reads: "From the hand two [. . .] a mark; red is his hair and he has moles upon [. . .] and tiny marks upon his thighs [. . .] different from each other."[17]

Alexander comments upon this fragment:

> The text is not, of course, strictly a physiognomy, nor does it involve astrology. But it presupposes physiognomy and uses physiognomy for literary ends. It provides further evidence for interest in physiognomy at Qumran. The possibility cannot be ruled out that some members of the Qumran set would have seen physiognomy as playing a role not only in admitting members to the community, and, possibly, in determining rank within it, but also in helping to identify at the end of history the Sons of Light in general and the Messiah in particular.[18]

Jewish interest in physiognomy was not limited to the Qumran community. Josephus approvingly recounts an instance of it in the Jewish War. Caesar Augustus had sent one Celadus to determine whether someone posing as a prince was an impostor. Celadus exposed the

---

14. Ibid., 387. This approach stands in contrast to some forms of physiognomy that focused on a particular part of the body: chiromancy (palm-reading), metoposcopy (reading the lines of the forehead), or phrenology (reading the shape of the cranium).

15. Alexander, "Physiognomy," 387.

16. Ibid., 392.

17. Martínez, *Dead Sea Scrolls Translated,* 263.

18. Alexander, "Physiognomy," 394.

plot in language reminiscent of a physiognomist reading the features of the face and body: "Celadus had no sooner set eyes on him than he detected the points of difference in the face, and noting that his whole person had a coarser and servile appearance, penetrated the whole plot" (*Bell.* 2.107).[19]

The inner coherence between body and spirit is also acknowledged in the *Testaments of the Twelve Patriarchs*, a second-century BCE Jewish document (with some later Christian interpolations).[20] In the *Testament of Naphtali*, we have perhaps the fullest expression of what the translator has termed "psychophysiology":[21]

> For just as a potter knows the pot, how much it holds, and brings clay for it accordingly, so also the Lord forms the body in correspondence to the spirit, and instills the spirit corresponding to the power of the body. And from one to the other there is no discrepancy, not so much as a third of a hair, for all the creation of the Most High was according to height, measure, and standard. And just as the potter knows the use of each vessel and to what it is suited, so also the Lord knows the body to what extent it will persist in goodness, and when it will be dominated by evil. . . . As a person's strength, so also is his work; as is his mind, so also is his skill. As is his plan, so also is his achievement; as is his heart, so is his speech; as is his eye, so also is his sleep; as is his soul, so also is his thought . . . for God made all things good in their order: the five senses in the head; to the head he attached the neck, in addition to the hair for the enhancement of appearance; then the heart for prudence; the belly for excretion from the stomach; the windpipe for health; the liver for anger; the gallbladder for bitterness; the spleen for laughter; the kidneys for craftiness; the loins for power . . . and so on. (*T. Naph.* 2.2–9)

The author identifies this coherence between outer appearances and inner character and between internal organs and human behavior as gifts bestowed by God, who functions in this text as the Master Potter (perhaps even the Master Physiognomist!); God knows the correspondence between body and spirit because he created it.

---

19. The parallel passage in *Jewish Antiquities* (17.333–34) is not as explicitly "physiognomic."

20. On the Christian interpolations, see H. C. Kee, "Testament of the Twelve Patriarchs: A New Translation and Introduction," in *The Old Testament Pseudepigrapha*, ed. James Charlesworth, 2 vols. (London: Darton, Longman & Todd, 1983), 1:777; for bibliography, 1:781.

21. See Kee, "Testament of the Twelve Patriarchs," 1:811 n. 2a. Elsewhere Kee speaks of the relationship of human organs to human behavior as "a kind of somatic psychology" and lists *T. Sim.* 2.4; *T. Zeb.* 2.4; *T. Gad* 5.11; and *T. Jos.* 15.3 as examples (1:778–79). The translation is from Kee, "Testament of the Twelve Patriarchs," 1:811.

Later Jewish Apocalyptic Texts

Jewish apocalyptic texts also show interest in physiognomy. Alexander argues, "In certain apocalyptic traditions, in the context of 'signs of the end,' physiognomy was applied to the identification of the Messiah, and, indeed, of the 'anti-Christ' as well."[22] We mention three such texts dating between the first and the ninth centuries.[23]

> The appearance of his [the antichrist's] face is as of a wild man. His right eye is like a star rising at dawn and the other is unmoving. His mouth is one cubit, his teeth are a span long, his fingers like scythes, the soles of his feet two span, and on his forehead an inscription "Antichrist." (*Gk. Apoc. Ezra* 4.29–32)

The *Apocalypse of Elijah* (first–fourth centuries CE) has a description of the antichrist:

> For behold I will tell you his signs so that you might know him. He is a . . . of a skinny-legged young lad, having a tuft of gray hair at the front of his bald head. His eyebrows will reach to his ears. There is a leprous bare spot on the front of his hands. He will transform himself of those who see him. He will become a young child. He will become old. He will transform in every sign. But the signs of his head will not be able to change. Therein you will know that he is the son of lawlessness. (3.15–18)[24]

Finally in the ninth-century CE *Apocalypse of Daniel* we read:

> The height of his stature (will be) fifteen feet. And the hairs of his head (will reach) as far as his feet. And he (will be) large and three-crested. And the track of his feet (will be) large. His eyes (will be) like the star which rises in the morning, and his right (eye will be) like a lion's. His lower teeth (will be) iron and his lower jaw diamond. And his right arm (will be) iron

22. Alexander, "Physiognomy," 393. Alexander claims that these "traditions are, on the whole, late." While this may be true for the identification of messianic figures, we argue that the physiognomic interpretations of the antichrist figure (and his followers, see Rev. 9:7–11) are much earlier and more widespread. See W. Bousset, *The Antichrist Legend: A Chapter in Christian and Jewish Folklore*, trans. A. H. Keene, introd. D. Frankfurter, Texts and Translations Series 24 (Atlanta: Scholars Press, 1999), 156.

23. For more on these and other texts, see J. Massyngbaerde Ford, "The Physical Features of the Antichrist," *Journal for the Study of the Pseudepigrapha* 14 (1996): 23–41.

24. The translation is taken from O. S. Wintermute, "Apocalypse of Elijah," in *The Old Testament Pseudepigrapha*, ed. James Charlesworth, 2 vols. (London: Darton, Longman & Todd, 1983), 1:745–46.

and his left copper. And his right hand (will be) four and a half feet (long). (He will be) long-faced, long-nosed and disorderly. (9.16–24)[25]

Mention of just a few of the physical features that have physiognomic symbolism will suffice to make our point here. We can see that these various traditions present the antichrist as grotesquely or abnormally tall, a negative feature according to physiognomic tradition (ps.-Aristotle 813b). Furthermore, he is "disproportionate" (cf. ps.-Aristotle 814a: "ill-proportioned men are scoundrels"), an asymmetry that extends to the hands and eyes, otherwise canceling out what might have been viewed as a positive feature ("one eye like a lion"). Likewise, an "unmoving" eye may refer to blindness and hence a covering over the window to the soul, the eye being one of the favored regions for examination (ps.-Aristotle 814b).

According to *Apocalypse of Daniel*, the antichrist is a composite of metals and jewels, a kind of monstrous figure. The anonymous *De physiognomonia* equates such composite figures with monsters and labels them "evil" (44). A "wild" or "gloomy" countenance is either immoral or foolish (cf. Polemo 31). Thin legs are a sign of salaciousness (ps.-Aristotle 810a). Hands like scythes and large feet are both ill omens (cf. Polemo 53; 72).

Jewish interest in the way physical description revealed one's character was not limited to eschatological speculation about the antichrist, however.[26] At times, physical features indicate a positive moral quality. Adam's beauty, before the fall, makes his face shine (*Eccles. Rab.* 8.1). Likewise, Methusalam's face is radiant as the midday sun when he offers sacrifice to God (*2 En.* 69.10).

More often the physical attributes symbolize a negative moral quality. Nebuchadnezzar, though ruler of the world, is as small as a dwarf, "smaller than a handbreath," indicating his relative insignificance and meanness of spirit (*Gen. Rab.* 16.4). After the fall, Adam's body is reduced to "one hundred ells" (*Num. Rab.* 13.2; *Gen. Rab.* 12.6; 19.8). Esau's hairiness is a sign of the demonic (*Gen. Rab.* 65.15; cf. ps.-Aristotle 812b); in other places his reddishness and hairiness are signs of his violent and bestial nature (*Gen. Rab.* 63.6, 8, 12).

25. The translation is taken from G. T. Zervos, "Apocalypse of Daniel," in *The Old Testament Pseudepigrapha*, ed. James Charlesworth, 2 vols. (London: Darton, Longman & Todd, 1983), 1:767–68. For other apocalyptic traditions regarding the physical attributes of the antichrist, see especially, J.-M. Rosenstiehl, "Le Portrait de l'Antichrist," in *Pseudépigraphes de l'Ancien Testament et manuscrits de la Mer Morte*, ed. M. Philonenko, Cahiers d'Histoire et de Philosophie Religieuses 41 (Paris: Presses Universitaires de France, 1967), 45–60.

26. On this point, see Lynn Holden, *Forms of Deformity* (Sheffield: Sheffield Academic Press, 1991), esp. part 2, section 3, "Abnormality, Deformity or Disability as a Symbol," 326–47.

This interest in physiognomy is continued by the medieval Qabbalists. Philip Alexander mentions the following texts that are devoted to later Jewish meditation on physiognomy: "The Physiognomy of R. Ishmael," "The book of the Reading of the Hands by an Indian Sage," "The Secret of Physiognomy," and Genizah Fragments A, B, and C.[27] While it would be misleading to suggest that physiognomy per se was a central or leading theme in exilic or postbiblical Judaism, we detect a sustained interest in the subject, perhaps rooted in the by now largely theoretical priestly custom of examining sacrificial animals for blemishes (and examining worshipers for physical defects before allowing entrance into the temple). Interest in physiognomy is seen in various streams of Judaism from the Second Temple period through the Middle Ages, and is consistent with Greco-Roman physiognomy as examined in the last chapter.[28]

Early Christian Literature

We find also in the early Christian writings varying levels of interest in and critique of physiognomic conventions.

The Writings of Paul

The study of physiognomy in relation to the New Testament is in its infancy. We shall point to three Pauline studies that offer initial soundings in this area.[29] Several times in his writings, the Apostle Paul apparently alludes to some physical ailment or weakness that was a potential source of shame rendering him vulnerable to opponents' attacks (cf. e.g., Gal. 4:13–14; 1 Cor. 2:3; 2 Cor. 10:1; 12:7). A variety of explanations have been offered to explain Paul's physical weakness. Recently Dale Martin

27. Alexander, "Physiognomy," 367–68.

28. One need not argue for a continuity in tradition in Jewish interest in physiognomy from Qumran to the *merkabah* mystics to note the role it played in various streams of Jewish thought, though I. Gruenwald does in fact argue for this: see "Further Jewish Physiognomic and Chiromantic Fragments," *Tarbiz* 40 (1971): 304–6.

29. We may mention also a work on the physiognomy of blindness in John 9: Michael L. Humphries, "The Physiognomy of the Blind: The Johannine Story of the Blind Man," in *Reimagining Christian Origins: A Colloquium Honoring Burton L. Mack*, ed. Elizabeth A. Castelli and Hal Taussig (Valley Forge, PA: Trinity Press International, 1996), 229–43. Humphries, a professor of comparative literature, is less interested in examining the physiognomy of the blind man than in the history of its interpretation. He asks, "Should we not consider the possibility of a scholarship released from the hegemony of the Johannine *Logos*, a scholarship of blind men and women who continue to see precisely because they confess their own blindness?" (p. 239).

has argued that "we would do well to assume that Paul is ... referring to an actual condition: a physical deficiency that adversely affected his rhetorical performance." Drawing on the canons of physiognomy, Martin points out that there was a sense in the ancient world that "strength and beauty of the body are reflections of nobility of character." Conversely, the rhetor who betrayed a "discrepancy between the content of the speech and the embodiment of the speaker" was a "target of ridicule."[30]

Martin cites Quintilian (*Inst.* 12.11.2–3) as an example of a rhetor who understands the risks involved for older men to continue their declamation despite their more frail physical conditions:

> For the orator depends not merely on his knowledge, which increases with the years, but on his voice, lungs, and powers of endurance. And if these be broken or impaired by age or health, he must beware that he does not fall short in something of his high reputation as a master of oratory, that fatigue does not interrupt his eloquence, that he is not brought to realize that some of his words are inaudible, or to mourn that he is not what he once was.

Martin points out, "Quintilian is not simply addressing the practical problems of being heard; rather, he is expressing the Greco-Roman sense that ... the speaker's message may be admirable, but if it is belied by his body, his message will be impugned because it does not match 'reality.'"[31]

This was the criticism to which Paul responded in 2 Corinthians 10–13: "His critics point to his weakness of body (whether due to illness, disfigurement, or simply constitutional infirmity) as irrefutable evidence of weakness of character. His letters (strong) do not match his presence or speaking ability (weak)." Paul recognizes this problem, according to Martin, and responds by offering "himself as an instance of the surprising action of God, who works strength in weakness and overcomes the strong by means of the weak."[32] Paul both recognizes and challenges existing physiognomic conventions as embodied and employed by those rhetorically trained.

J. Albert Harrill has refined Martin's argument regarding Paul's weakness,[33] focusing especially on the charge by Paul's opponents, "For they say, 'His letters are weighty and strong, but his bodily presence is weak, and his speech contemptible'" (2 Cor. 10:10). Harrill rejects the conventional

---

30. Dale B. Martin, *The Corinthian Body* (New Haven, CT: Yale University Press, 1995), 54.
31. Ibid., 54.
32. Ibid., 55.
33. Harrill, "Invective against Paul," 189–213.

interpretation of this passage as a "neutral description of Paul's physical appearance."[34] Rather, Harrill notes how the physiognomic handbooks hold up the freeborn male as the ideal body and engage in "negative stereotyping" of the body of the slave, or "the slavish freeborn body" (signifying moral corruption). Polemo describes "flatterers" who say one thing while doing the opposite in secret as having "thick legs and heels" signifying "stupidity, insufficiency of understanding, and the natural character of slaves" (*servorum mores*).[35]

Harrill argues that "physiognomic distinctions between slave and free, therefore, had little to do with social descriptions of actual slaves and more to do with the Greco-Roman rhetoric of manhood. The servile/free-looking dichotomy served as a mask for disputes about manhood in Greco-Roman thinking across the board, from oratory and history to moral philosophy, comedy, and satire."[36] Harrill then interprets 2 Corinthians 10:10 against the backdrop of the physiognomy of the slavish body and concludes:

> Rather than neutral description of Paul's physical appearance, or evidence of so-called gnostic influences on Pauline Christianity, the reference to Paul's "weak bodily presence" and "contemptible speech" in 2 Cor 10:10 is best interpreted as slave physiognomics. The charge is rhetorical and attacks Paul's moral character as a servile flatterer. The invective draws on commonplace character-assassination techniques . . . which typecast an enemy as "looking" and "talking" like a natural slave. . . . Paul quoted this invective to expose the fallacy of its logic. In effect, he wanted the charges to backfire, exposing his rivals as the true religious frauds.[37]

Karl Sandnes[38] has explored physiognomic texts on the stomach to see whether they shed any light on the Pauline passages that refer to persons whose "god is the belly" (Phil. 3:19) and who "serve . . . their own appetites (lit. 'belly')" (Rom. 16:18).[39] Polemo comments on the "signs" of the stomach:

> The thinness and leanness of the stomach are marks of a healthy mind, greatness in spirit as well as zeal. Excessive slenderness and thinness of

---

34. Harrill, "Invective against Paul," 190.

35. Polemo 7; cited by Harrill, "Invective against Paul," 196 n. 28; cf. Barton, *Power and Knowledge*, 213 n. 115. Unless otherwise noted, citations of Polemo are from Foerster, *Scriptores*, vol. 1.

36. Harrill, "Invective against Paul," 201.

37. Ibid., 212.

38. Karl Olav Sandnes, *Belly and Body in the Pauline Epistles* (Cambridge: Cambridge University Press, 2002).

39. See also the Pauline tradition that claims "Cretans are . . . gluttons (lit. 'bellies')" (Titus 1:12).

the stomach indicate a timid and distorted mind as well as gluttony. A big and fleshy belly, and especially if it is soft and extending downwards, indicates that the lively sexual appetite has been damaged by drunkenness. If it really has a lot of flesh and is solid, leading a vicious life, it is a sign of imitation, dishonest conduct, cunning and no understanding. (14.1)[40]

Sandnes quite rightly notes that "nothing suggests that Paul considered the outward appearance or form of the belly, nor the rest of the body, to be signs of spiritual significance. But in some way the stomach was to him a codeword, too, revealing an identity which endangered true faith in Christ." In other words, "although Paul shows no traces of putting these theories into practice, his body-theology subscribes to a correlation between body and spiritual qualities."[41] Paul's critique of "belly-worshipers" is a warning for Christians not to return to their former life by indulging the passions and physical desires. Sandnes concludes:

Indeed, the power of the belly outweighs the question of its size and form. However, Paul has retained one basic insight of physiognomics. Body and character do belong together, not in the sense that the depths of human character can be inferred from outward appearance of the body, but in the sense that lifestyle, which also includes matters of food, drinking, and sex, represents a yardstick by which the spiritual life may be measured, judged or corrected. Faith was to Paul not purely a matter of the heart, invisible to all but God. Faith worked itself out also in body and stomach.[42]

These works indicate the potential value of examining Paul's writings against the prevailing backdrop of the pervasive physiognomic consciousness.

Noncanonical Christian Writings

Some early Christian texts reflect physiognomic consciousness. *The Acts of Paul*, a second-century early Christian writing, contains a section titled *The Acts of Paul and Thecla*, in which a certain Onesiphorus went out to meet Paul. He had been told "what Paul looked like," by Titus and so compared passers-by with Titus's description.

40. This translation is found in Sandnes, *Belly and Body*, 28.
41. Ibid., 34.
42. Ibid., 269–70.

[Paul] a man small of stature, with a bald head and crooked legs, in a good state of body; with eyebrows meeting and nose somewhat hooked, full of friendliness; for now he appeared like a man, and now he had the face of an angel. (*Acts Paul Thec.* 3)

For earlier commentators, this text has often been taken as a literal description of Paul's features and as confirmation of the Pauline texts (including 2 Cor. 10:10 discussed above), which suggest that Paul was physically unattractive.[43] Many were content with Sir William Ramsay's argument that the description of Paul goes back to a first-century document and is essentially a historically accurate portrayal: "This plain and unflattering account of the Apostle's personal appearance seems to embody a very early tradition."[44]

There are, however, features of this text that suggest more is going on than a simple, straightforward, and unflattering description of Paul's physique. Onesiphorus recognizes Paul and welcomes him, "Greetings, thou servant of the blessed God!" (*Acts Paul Thec.* 3:4). At the same time, Onesiphorus refuses to greet Demas and Hermogenes, Paul's two deceitful traveling companions, as servants of the Blessed One, but rather admonishes them, "I do not see in you any fruit of righteousness." Thus Onesiphorus not only sees these physical features but also understands from them that Paul is a "righteous person."[45] Several writers have explored this text's possible physiognomic dimensions and have drawn widely differing conclusions. In one of the first such assessments, Robert Grant denied that the description of Paul in *The Acts of Paul and Thecla* corresponded to any extant description found in the physiognomic handbooks.[46] He also refuted the idea that the description was to be taken as a literal and negative characterization. Rather, Grant found the basis

---

43. One writer even suggested Paul was depicted as the "antichrist"! See E. Preuschen, "Paulus als Antichrist" *ZNW* 2 (1901): 169–201, esp. pages 191–93.

44. Sir William Ramsay, *The Church in the Roman Empire Before A.D. 170* (London: Hodder and Stoughton, 1903), 32. See also T. Zahn, "Paulus der Apostel," *RE* 15 (1904): 70; J. Geffcken, *Christliche Apokryphen* (Tübingen: Mohr, 1908), 27. This line of interpretation in conjunction with 2 Cor. 10:10 continues right into the modern period; see, among many, Ernest Best, *Second Corinthians* (Louisville: John Knox, 1987), 96–97. For a slightly more balanced view, see E. Margaret Howe, "Interpretations of Paul in the Acts of Paul and Thecla," in *Pauline Studies: Essays Presented to Professor F. F. Bruce on His 70th Birthday*, ed. Donald A. Hagner and Murray J. Harris (Grand Rapids: Eerdmans, 1980), 44, who writes, "The canonical material parallels the *Acts of Paul and Thecla* in its suggestion that Paul's personal appearance was not outstandingly attractive, although the evidence is sometimes slight and open to other interpretations."

45. See Malina and Neyrey, *Portraits of Paul*, 128.

46. Robert M. Grant, "The Description of Paul in the *Acts of Paul and Thecla*," *Vigiliae Christianae* 36 (1982): 1–4, esp. 1.

for *The Acts of Paul and Thecla* description in ancient Greek poetry and rhetoric. He cites as especially relevant a fragment of Archilochus (eighth or seventh century BCE): "I love not a tall general nor a straddling one, nor one proud of his hair nor one part-shaven; for me a man should be short and bowlegged to behold, set firm on his feet, full of heart."[47] From this and other texts Grant concludes that the author of *The Acts of Paul and Thecla*, an admirer of Paul, chose to depict him as a military figure, or more specifically as a "general of God."[48]

Grant's essay has prompted several responses challenging Grant's dismissal of the physiognomic handbooks as relevant for understanding the description of Paul in the Acts. The first, by Abraham Malherbe, suggests that Paul is being depicted as a hero and claims that the description of Paul in *The Acts of Paul and Thecla* is to be understood positively rather than negatively.[49] He cites two texts in particular, first a description of Augustus found in Suetonius:

> His teeth were wide apart, small, and ill-kept; his hair was slightly curly and inclining to golden; his eyebrows met. His ears were of moderate size, and his nose projected a little at the top and then bent slightly inward. His complexion was between dark and fair. He was short of stature . . . but this was concealed by the fine proportion and symmetry of his figure. (*Aug.* 2.79.2)[50]

The second text, also cited by Grant, runs as follows:

> His hair grew evenly on his head, his eyebrows were bushy and they met as though they were but one, and his eyes gave out a brilliant gleam which betrayed his impulsive temperament; he was hook-nosed, and had a solidly built neck, which was due rather to work than to diet. His chest, too, was well formed and beautifully slim, and his legs were slightly bowed outward, which made it easy from him to stand firmly planted. (Philostratus, *Vit. soph.* 552)

Unlike Grant, Malherbe sees that many of the features mentioned in this text (and others) have parallels in the physiognomic handbooks. Meeting

47. Cited by Grant, "The Description of Paul," 2. The translation can be found in J. M. Edmonds, trans., *Elegy and Iambus*, 2.127; LCL.

48. Grant, "The Description of Paul," 4.

49. Abraham J. Malherbe, "A Physical Description of Paul," *Harvard Theological Review* 79 (1986): 170–75.

50. Cited ibid., 173.

eyebrows were a sign of beauty;[51] a hooked nose was a sign of royalty or magnanimity;[52] symmetry in body was to be preferred over excessive height or small stature.[53] He concludes, "This short excursion into the world of ancient physiognomy may cast some light on how Paul was represented as a hero among the Greeks. It calls for further attention to the description in the interpretation of the *Acts*."[54]

More recently, Bruce Malina and Jerome Neyrey have explored the physical description of Paul in *The Acts of Paul and Thecla* from a physiognomic perspective.[55] They conclude, from a comparison of this description and surrounding narrative, that Paul is portrayed not in the role of a general (Grant) or Heracles-like hero (Malherbe), but as the "ideal male" in ancient Mediterranean culture. Certainly the character traits that befit an "ideal male" would well serve a military or other public figure. For example, we are told that "Paul feared nothing but comported himself with full confidence (παρρησία) in God" (*Acts Paul Thec.* 3.18). The term "confidence" or "boldness" (παρρησία) is one of the marks of the ideal male, according to Malina and Neyrey.[56]

In addition to emphasizing that Onesiphorus is trying to determine what kind of person Paul was, they point out that Thecla herself had "only heard his word" but had not yet seen the character (χαρακτῆρα) of Paul (3.7). They argue that in context this means that because she has not yet "seen" Paul's thorn in the flesh Thecla has not drawn conclusions about his moral character.[57] They argue:

> In *The Acts of Paul*, when Thecla hears Paul's voice, although she has not yet seen his "character," the author is concerned with his physical appearance. This physical appearance will offer clear indication of his behavioral or "ethical" qualities as a virtuous person. The narrator has already given the reader both a physical description of Paul and indications of the kind

51. Pollux, *Onom.* 2.73; ed. Foerster, 2.281.26–27.

52. Ps.-Aristotle 811a36–38; *De physiogn.* 51.

53. Here, Malherbe, "Physical Description of Paul," 173 n. 27, cites Evans, *Physiognomics*, 10, 53.

54. Malherbe, "Physical Description of Paul," 175. Malherbe ends with an invitation that has not been taken up: "The basic assumption of physiognomics was that 'dispositions follow bodily characteristics and are not themselves unaffected by bodily impulses.' It remains to be determined whether there is such a correlation between the description of Paul's physical appearance and his deeds in the *Acts*" (p. 175).

55. Bruce J. Malina and Jerome H. Neyrey, "Physiognomics and Personality: Looking at Paul in *The Acts of Paul*," chap. 4 in *Portraits of Paul*, esp. 127–52.

56. Ibid., 131.

57. Ibid., 133.

of person he is, and so it remains for Thecla to see and appreciate what the readership already knows.[58]

Although Paul's eyes and voice are not mentioned in the actual description in *The Acts of Paul and Thecla*, there are allusions to their qualities elsewhere in the narrative, and Malina and Neyrey begin their consideration of Paul's character with these features. At the beginning of chapter 3 we read, "Paul, who had eyes only for the goodness of Christ, did them no evil but loved them greatly" (3.1). Eyes, of course, are one of the keys to reading a person's character (ps.-Aristotle 811b15–28; 812a38–812b13; Polemo 1.107–70; also see the discussion in the previous chapter). Thus, while we are not given the color of Paul's eye, clearly "his gaze is benevolent and full of benefaction."[59] Likewise, Paul's voice is not described per se, but the narrator does comment that Paul "sought to make sweet to them all the words of the Lord" (3.1), a description consistent with the deep voice of the "brave," as opposed to the annoying high pitch of the cowardly (ps.-Aristotle 807b18–22; cf. 807a13–18).[60]

Malina and Neyrey then proceed to examine the physical features of Paul detailed in the *Acts* passage in light of physiognomic conventions. They conclude that Paul's stature, baldness, bowed legs, "good state of body," meeting eyebrows, hooked nose, and "friendly face," interpreted in light of physiognomic conventions, are consistent with the portrayal of Paul as the "ideal male."[61]

> What kind of person is Paul, then? He is clearly an ideal male figure. The composite of his various physical features suggests a certain kind of person. His benevolent eyes are fixed on goodness; his voice, with a conversational tone, evokes sincerity, kindness and truthfulness. His stature, although short, is that of an active person who accomplishes much; he has "balanced" humours, a sign of excellence. His shaved head denotes piety to God. His crooked legs, although ideal for a military figure, suggest a fearless person who stands his ground. Paul's body is in good shape and healthy, which may suggest a relatively high status associated with gymnastic training. His meeting eyebrows suggest manliness and beauty; his longish nose, virtuousness and handsomeness. Being full of grace indicates a favored

---

58. Ibid., 134.

59. Ibid., 135.

60. Ibid., 135–36.

61. This conclusion is consistent with the importance placed by physiognomists on the freeborn Roman male as possessing the "ideal body"; cf. Harrill, "Invective against Paul," 201, and Gleason, *Making Men*, esp. chap. 3, "Deportment as Language: Physiognomy and the Semiotics of Gender," 55–81.

person suitable for a public role. His physical features, then, indicate the kind of person he is: masculine, fearless, pious, virtuous, truthful, benevolent, but above all, fit for public life. . . . The physiognomic description of Paul, then, serves as the only information about him in *The Acts of Paul*, yet by contemporary standards, it is more than adequate. This is all the ancients thought necessary to know about him, providing all the vital clues to the kind of person he was.[62]

Grant, Malherbe, and Malina and Neyrey differ in their specific conclusions, primarily due to their differing use of the physiognomic handbooks. They agree, however, that Paul's physical description in *The Acts of Paul and Thecla*, read within the cultural context of the ancient Mediterranean world, is a positive rather than a negative portrayal, thus correcting the critical consensus of a hundred years.[63]

Patristic Examples

A number of texts from patristic writers demonstrate physiognomic interests. Clement of Alexandria, for example, wrote, "'A fool raises his voice in laughter,' says the Scripture [Eccles. 21:23]; but a clever man smiles almost imperceptibly" (*Paed.* 2.5; cf. 2.7, 46; 3.3, 5, 11).[64] We will focus our attention on a widely popular Christian document, the *Physiologus*, that reflects physiognomic concerns, and Ambrose, whose

62. Malina and Neyrey, *Portraits of Paul*, 148.

63. This positive reading also confirms, in a curious way, Tertullian's judgment that the author of *The Acts of Paul and Thecla* had written out of "love for Paul" (*Bapt.* 17.5). János Ballók, "The Description of Paul in the Acta Pauli," in *The Apocryphal Acts of Paul and Thecla*, ed. Jan N. Bremmer (Kampen: Pharos, 1996), 1–15, has also interpreted the physical description of Paul from a physiognomic perspective, but concludes that the description is mixed, leaning toward the negative. Ballók's reading of much of the evidence is flawed because he does not "triangulate" the physiognomic theory with its practice. That is, while the theorists present mixed ideas on some of these physical features, when examined in actual practice, a more coherent picture emerges, consistent with the positive interpretation proposed by Grant, Malherbe, and Malina and Neyrey. We do, however, applaud his effort and agree with his assertion that "the effect of physiognomy must have been much wider than has been supposed on the basis of modern research" (p. 13). Nor has Paul been the only character in *The Acts of Paul and Thecla* recently examined in light of physiognomic convention; see also Willi Braun, "Physiotherapy of Femininity in the *Acts of Thecla*," in *Text and Artifact in the Religions of Mediterranean Antiquity: Essays in Honour of Peter Richardson*, ed. Stephen G. Wilson and Michel Desjardins (Waterloo, Ont.: Wilfrid Laurier University Press, 2000), 209–30, who notes that Thecla is described in terms of "masculinized femininity." Read in the light of physiognomy, the text presents a "female-to-male conversion story" wherein Thecla "takes flight from femininity so that masculinity and all the positive values attached to masculinity would 'prevail,'" to use Polemo's term" (p. 222).

64. See also Tertullian, *Cult. fem.* 2.1, 8, 13; *An.* 5, 20, 25, 32; Gregory of Nazianzus, *Or.* 7.5, 8.10, 18.5; Basil, *Ep.* 1.2, 20–21, 132–35.

reflections on bodily gestures and movements sound very similar to pseudo-Aristotle.[65]

The *Physiologus*, an anthology from the second through fourth centuries CE, catalogs traits of various animals and draws moral and theological lessons from their behavior.[66] The anonymous work was so widely popular that it was at times (wrongly) attributed to Jerome and Ambrose. Some of the animals discussed in the *Physiologus* (lions, panthers, and eagles) are also prominent in the physiognomic handbooks. Others are drawn from the biblical tradition (e.g., snakes, doves) and Christian mythological sources (e.g., unicorns, hippocentaurs, the phoenix). Although not, strictly speaking, a Christian physiognomic handbook, the similarities between the *Physiologus* and the zoological method of physiognomy are readily apparent. The comments in the *Physiologus* about the viper and the fox will serve to illustrate the connection.[67]

About the viper, the *Physiologus* says (chapter 10):

> Well did John say to the Pharisees, "Generation of vipers, who showed you how to flee from the wrath to come?" (Matt. 3:7; Luke 3:7). The Physiologus said of the viper that the male has the face of a man, the female, the face of a woman. To the navel they have a human form, but they have the tail of a crocodile. The female has no vagina, just the eye of a needle; the male expels his sperm in her mouth. If she swallows it she cuts off his testicles and he dies immediately. As the offspring grow they eat the mother's stomach and come out; thus they are patricides and matricides.
>
> Well, then, did John compare the Pharisees with the viper; as the viper kills the father and mother, so they killed their spiritual fathers, the prophets (he said) and our Lord Jesus Christ and the church. How then will they flee from the wrath to come? The father and mother live forever, but these died.[68]

65. Gleason, *Making Men*, 61, briefly discusses this passage.

66. For a critical edition of this text, see D. Offermanns, *Der Physiologus nach den Handschriften G und M*, Beiträge zur klassichen Philologie 22 (Meisenheim am Glan: Hain, 1966). An English translation is available in Robert M. Grant, *Early Christians and Animals* (London: Routledge, 1999), 52–72. In addition to animals, the qualities of certain plants (e.g., the fig tree) and inanimate objects (e.g., Indian stone, magnet stone, pearl, etc.) are also discussed.

67. These two animals are chosen from among the nearly fifty examples because, as we shall see in the next chapter, the viper and fox (along with the wolf) function symbolically in Luke's narrative.

68. Cited from Grant, *Early Christians and Animals*, 56. Grant's volume is primarily a collection of translations with little or no added comment, a strategy that has received mixed reviews (positive, Frederick W. Norris in *Journal of Early Christian Studies* 8 [2000]: 312–13; negative, Margaret Atkins in *Journal of Ecclesiastical History* 51 [2000]: 774–75).

Thus, like the physiognomic handbooks, the *Physiologus* cites a destructive behavior of the viper, widely known in the ancient world (cf. Herodotus, *Hist.* 3.109; Pliny, *Hist. nat.* 10.169), in order to explain John the Baptist's labelling as "vipers" those who had come out to receive his baptism.[69] Consider also the comments about the fox (chapter 15):[70]

> The Physiologus said of the fox that it is a crafty animal, for when it is hungry and does not find an animal to eat, it seeks to find a pond or a shelter for chaff and throws itself in, looking upward, and holds it breath and blows hard. The birds think it is dead and settle on it to eat it, and thus it rises, seizes them and eats them.
>
> So also the devil is completely crafty, as are his deeds. He who wants to share in his flesh will die. For these are his flesh; acts of fornication, avarice, pleasure, murder.
>
> This is why Herod resembled a fox (Luke 13:22) and the scribe heard the Savior, "The foxes have holes and the birds of the heaven have nests" (Matt. 8:20). And in the Canticles (2:15) Solomon says, "Catch for us the little foxes, for they destroy the vineyards." And David says in the Psalms (62:11), "They will be the portions of foxes," etc. The Physiologus spoke well about the fox.[71]

Again the *Physiologus* uses the animal's behavior (in this case the fox's craftiness) to explain why Herod, for example, is called a "fox" by Jesus.[72] The *Physiologus* enjoyed popularity throughout the late antique and early medieval periods, despite its condemnation as heretical by Pope Gregory. It laid the groundwork for the later bestiaries, which reflected the fascination of medieval Christian thought with the moral implications of behaviors in the natural world and continued the zoological method's interest in drawing parallels between animal and human action.[73] Evidence of physiognomic consciousness can also be found in the works of Ambrose. He writes:

69. It should be noted that in identifying the "vipers" as Pharisees, the *Physiologus* is following Matthew's account (which speaks of the Pharisees and Sadducees) and not Luke's (which simply refers to the crowds that had come out for baptism).

70. The translation is taken from Grant, *Early Christians and Animals*, 59.

71. The refrain, "The Physiologus spoke well about the . . . ," occurs regularly throughout the text. It should be understood to mean that the Physiologus spoke "truly" about the animal in question, not that he was complimenting its behavior.

72. This explanation is echoed by Irenaeus (*Haer.* 4.41.3).

73. As further evidence of this claim, we may cite the writings of Basil the Great and Isidore of Seville (excerpts from both are found in Grant, *Early Christians and Animals*, 78–106 and 123–62). Isidore of Seville also employed the "ethnographical method" to speak of "monstrous" races of persons (see Grant, *Early Christians and Animals*, 117–22).

Modesty must further be guarded in our very movements and gestures and gait. *For the condition of the mind is often seen in the attitude of the body.* For this reason the hidden man of our heart (our inner self) is considered to be either frivolous, boastful, or boisterous, or, on the other hand, steady, firm, pure, and dependable. *Thus the movement of the body is a sort of voice of the soul.* (*Off.* 1.18.71; my emphasis)[74]

Compare this with pseudo-Aristotle's assertion: "Dispositions follow bodily characteristics and are not in themselves unaffected by bodily impulses" (805a).

Ambrose goes on to give two examples of how moral character is reflected in bodily movements.

Ye remember, my children, that a friend of ours who seemed to recommend himself by his assiduity in his duties, yet was not admitted by me into the number of the clergy, because his gestures were too unseemly. Also that I bade one, whom I found already among the clergy, never to go in front of me, because he actually pained me by the seeming arrogance of his gait. That is what I said when he returned to his duty after an offence committed. This alone I would not allow, nor did my mind deceive me. (*Off.* 1.18.72)

In the first case, Ambrose refuses ordination to a candidate on account of his "unseemly gestures." Unseemly gestures, according to Ambrose, would include those that consciously imitate "the gestures of actors," presumably because they are forced and artificial "as though they were bearers in the processions, and had the motions of nodding statues, to such an extent that they seem to keep a sort of time, as often as they change their step" (*Off.* 1.18.73).

In the second case, Ambrose refuses fellowship with one already ordained because of the "arrogance of his gait." In the subsequent paragraphs, Ambrose details what he deems appropriate and inappropriate movements:

Nor do I think it becoming to walk hurriedly, except when a case of some danger demands it, or a real necessity. For we often see those who hurry come up panting, and with features distorted. But if there is no reason for the need of such hurry, it gives cause for just offence. I am not, however,

---

74. For a critical edition (with French translation) of Ambrose's *De officiis*, see Saint Ambroise, *Les Devoirs: Introduction,* ed. and trans. Maurice Testard (Paris: Belles Lettres, 1984), 1.1. The translations given here are from *NPNF*[2] 10.

talking of those who have to hurry now and then for some particular reason, but of those to whom, by the yoke of constant habit, it has become a second nature. In the case of the former I cannot approve of their slow solemn movements, which remind one of the forms of phantoms. Nor do I care for the others with their headlong speed, for they put one in mind of the ruin of outcasts.

A suitable gait is that wherein there is an appearance of authority and weight and dignity, and which has a calm collected bearing. But it must be of such a character that all effort and conceit may be wanting, and that it be simple and plain. Nothing counterfeit is pleasing. Let nature train our movements. If indeed there is any fault in our nature, let us mend it with diligence. And, that artifice may be wanting, let not amendment be wanting. (*Off.* 1.18.74–75)

Ambrose takes some satisfaction in noting that his intuitions about both of these men proved true.

Both have left the Church. What their gait betrayed them to be, such were they proved to be by the faithlessness of their hearts. The one forsook his faith at the time of the Arian troubles; the other, through love of money, denied that he belonged to us, so that he might not have to undergo sentence at the hands of the Church. In their gait was discernible the semblance of fickleness, the appearance, as it were, of wandering buffoons. (*Off.* 1.18.72)

Ambrose does not limit his remarks to movements and gestures but comments also about the voice.

The voice, too, should not be languid, nor feeble, nor womanish in its tone, such a tone of voice as many are in the habit of using, under the idea of seeming important. It should preserve a certain quality, and rhythm, and a manly vigour. For all to do what is best suited to their character and sex, that is to attain to beauty of life. This is the best order for movements, this the employment fitted for every action. But as I cannot approve of a soft or weak tone of voice, or an effeminate gesture of the body, so also I cannot approve of what is boorish and rustic. Let us follow nature. The imitation of her provides us with a principle of training, and gives us a pattern of virtue. (*Off.* 1.19.84).

In this passage, Ambrose makes clear what is only implied in the case of the two clergy. Having a "womanish voice" or an "effeminate body" is against nature and not acceptable for Christian clergy. Traditional physiognomic masculinity has taken on Christian garb.[75]

Jewish Critiques of Physiognomy

If a physiognomic consciousness is detectable in the Deuteronomistic History, Israel's scriptures also warn against placing too much emphasis on physical appearances. In the same text that gives a physical description of David, Samuel, who is looking for Saul's replacement among David's older siblings, is warned by God, "Do not look on his appearance or on the height of his stature, because I have rejected him; for the LORD does not see as mortals see; they look on outward appearance, but the LORD looks on the heart" (1 Sam. 16:7).[76] Lyle Eslinger provides a sharp critique of the apparently contradictory actions of God in choosing tall Saul (1 Sam. 9:2; 10:23) and God's rebuke of Samuel for his interest in Eliab, presumably also because of his stature. Taking into account also David and Absalom's checkered careers, one may say that the procedure of using physical attributes to measure a king's potential for success, much less his heart, were less than successful in this portion of the Deuteronomistic History.[77] Furthermore, the fact that Saul's career is depicted as something of a failure points not only to the much-recognized "anti-monarchy critique" in the Deuteronomistic History, but also a more general critique of the physiognomic

75. The usual approach to this work is to look to Cicero's *De officiis* (as do M. Winterbottom, "The Text of Ambrose's *De Officiis*," *Journal of Theological Studies* 46 [1995], 559–66, and M. Testard, "Étude sur la composition dans le 'De officiis ministrorum' de saint Ambroise," in *Ambroise de Milan: XVIe centenaire de son élection épiscopale: Dix études*, ed. Y.-M. Duval [Paris: Etudes Augustiniennes, 1974], 155–97) as the rhetorical and methodical inspiration for Ambrose's articulation of Christian ethics. Ambrose is thought to be mirroring the philosophical life, which is of course not untypical for early Christian writers when addressing the Christian lifestyle, and physiognomy, as we have seen, does play a role in the philosophical life.

76. Difficulties with this text have led some scholars to offer conjectural emendations based on versional evidence: see Jan Joosten, "1 Samuel 16:6,7 in the Peshitta Version," *Vetus Testamentum* 41 (1991): 226–33; and Frank Cross and Emmanuel Tov, "The Composition of 1 Samuel 16–18 in the Light of the Septuagint Version," in *Empirical Models for Biblical Criticism*, ed. J. H. Tigay (Philadelphia: University of Pennsylvania Press, 1985), 97–130.

77. Lyle Eslinger, "'A Change of Heart': 1 Samuel 16," in *Ascribe to the Lord: Biblical and Other Studies in Memory of Peter C. Craigie*, ed. Lyle Eslinger and Glen Taylor, JSOTSup 67 (Sheffield: JSOT Press, 1988), 341–61. See also Bastiaan Jongeling, "La préposition L dans 1 Samuel 16:7," in *Scripta signa vocis*, ed. H. L. J. Vanstiphout (Groningen, Netherlands: Egbert Forsten, 1986), 95–99; Ashley S. Rose, "The 'Principles' of Divine Election: Wisdom in 1 Samuel 16," in *Rhetorical Criticism*, ed. J. J. Jackson and M. Kessler (Pittsburgh: Pickwick, 1974), 43–67.

tendency to view physical beauty as a sign of divine favor and moral uprightness.[78]

In this regard, we might also mention the Servant Song of Isaiah 53, which offers this physical description of the servant:

> See, my servant shall prosper; he shall be exalted and lifted up, and shall be very high. Just as there were many who were astonished at him—so marred was his appearance, beyond human semblance, and his form beyond that of mortals—so he shall startle many nations; kings shall shut their mouths because of him; for that which had not been told them they shall see, and that which they had not heard they shall contemplate.... he had no form or majesty that we should look at him, nothing in his appearance that we should desire him. He was despised and rejected by others; a man of suffering and acquainted with infirmity; and as one from whom others hide their faces he was despised, and we held him of no account. (Isa. 52:13–53:2)

Scholars differ as to the cause of the servant's physical unattractiveness,[79] but agree that these physical features have caused him to be despised and ostracized. His rejection, based on physical appearance, led to the conclusion that the servant was "of no account" (53:2). Joseph Blenkinsopp notes the assumption that this person was of no moral consequence: "Presupposed is the relation of moral causality between sin and physical affliction. This is a diagnostic based on experience: misfortune and sickness are symptomatic of moral failure."[80]

78. For a close reading which attends to the rhetorical function of the rebuke in regard to the Saul tradition, see Martin Kessler, "Narrative Technique in 1 Sam 16:1–13," *Catholic Biblical Quarterly* 32 (1970): 543–54. As Kessler rightly points out, the rebuke is partially muted by the fact that Saul's successor, however small in stature he is in comparison to Saul, is nonetheless "ruddy . . . and handsome" (1 Sam. 16:12). On Saul's failure as a king, see David Gunn, *The Fate of King Saul* (Sheffield: JSOT Press, 1984), 27; Kenneth Cohen, "King Saul: A Bungler from the Beginning," *Bible Review* 10 (1994): 34–39, 56–57; Daniel Hawk, "Saul as Sacrifice: The Tragedy of Israel's First Monarch," *Bible Review* 12 (December 1993): 20–25, 56; Howard Cooper, "'Too Tall by Half'—King Saul and Tragedy in the Hebrew Bible," *Journal of Progressive Judaism* 9 (November 1997): 8–9.

79. Walter Brueggemann, *Isaiah 40–66* (Louisville: Westminster John Knox, 1998), 142, 145, speaks of a "disfigured" or even "disabled" person, while John Watts, *Isaiah 34–66*, WBC 25 (Waco, TX: Word, 1987), 230, refers to the servant's "executed body" that was "mutilated." Jerome assumed the affliction was leprosy and gave the Latin *leprosum* in translating Isa. 53:4.

80. Joseph Blenkinsopp, *Isaiah 40–55*, AB 19 (New York: Doubleday, 2002), 352. Blenkinsopp also suggests relocating 52:14b ("so marred was his appearance . . . his form beyond human likeness," in his translation) to just before 53:3, to highlight the "contrast between the former humiliation and the future glorification of the servant" (p. 346).

Of course, this passage assumes the same perspective as that of 1 Samuel 16:7.[81] The marred figure of Isaiah 52:14 becomes the awesome figure of verse 15, not by a transformation of his physical appearance—that remains the same—but "by the powerful resolve of Yahweh, who transposes this figure with an inexplicable firmness. Thus the theme is not simply humiliation and exaltation, but rather that the humiliated one becomes the exalted one by the intention of Yahweh. The will of Yahweh, nothing else, transforms and transposes."[82] The efficacy of the servant figure comes not despite his disfigurement but as a result of it. Conventional physiognomy breaks down at this point.[83]

Later rabbinic tradition also breaks the inner coherence between the unblemished human body and the holy heart, which lies at the root of the priest's participation in the sacrificial system: "R. Abba b. Judah said, 'Whatever the Holy One, blessed be He, declared unfit in the case of an animal, he declared fit in the case of man. In animals he declared unfit 'blind, has a broken limb, is maimed . . .' (Lev. 22:22), whereas in man he declared fit 'a broken and contrite heart' (Ps. 51:19 [MT; = 51:17 ET]). R. Alexandrini said, 'If an ordinary person makes use of broken vessels, it is a disgrace for him, but the vessels used by the Holy One blessed be He, are precisely broken ones, as it is said, 'the Lord is nigh unto them that are of a broken heart' (Ps. 34:18)" (*Lev. Rab.* 7:2).

Philo of Alexandria also expresses ambivalence. He writes:

> Indeed, some of those thus bought and sold reverse the situation to such an extreme extent that they become the masters of their purchasers instead of their slaves. I have often myself seen pretty little slave girls with a natural gift for wheedling words, who with these two sources of strength, beauty of face and charm of speech, stormed the hearts of their owners. . . . If selling constitutes slavery we should have to assert that a person who had bought some lions is master of the lions, whereas if the beasts do but turn menacing eyes upon him, the poor man will learn at once by experience the cruel and ferocious lordship of those whom he has purchased. Well then must we not suppose that if lions cannot, still less can the wise man be enslaved, who has in his free and unscathed soul a greater power of

---

81. So Klaus Baltzer, *Deutero-Isaiah: A Commentary on Isaiah 40–55*, Hermeneia, trans. Margaret Kohl (Minneapolis: Fortress, 2001), 404.

82. Brueggemann, *Isaiah 40–66*, 142.

83. Blenkinsopp, *Isaiah 40–55*, 352–53, concludes that "the consciousness of communal guilt combined with reflection on the Servant's career made it impossible at a certain point to sustain this interpretation" (i.e., that the servant's suffering was the result of his own sin).

resistance to the yoke than any he could make with the naturally slavish body and all the vigour of its physical strength? (*Prob.* 38–40)

On the one hand, Philo can speak of a "naturally slavish body" (σώματι φύσει δούλῳ) as though the spirit of a slave were inscribed in the body itself. On the other hand, he resists the idea that the body determines one's status as free or slave.[84]

Christian Critiques of Physiognomy

Martin, Sandnes, and Harrill all agree that Paul is no supporter of physiognomics. Martin argues that Paul, while aware of the prevailing assumption of the connection between rhetorical effectiveness and physical wholeness, nonetheless wished to guide the Corinthians to a different view. "Paul's wish to convince the Corinthian church of the validity of his own theological and ethical opinions would necessitate both appropriating and modifying their assumptions regarding the body—each of their bodies and their communal body."[85] Sandnes agrees: "Physiognomics does not appear as a point of departure in Paul's letters."[86] Harrill expresses the point more strongly: "Not all ancient thinkers agreed with this use of physiognomics, however, and Paul was one of them."[87]

Hippolytus also rejected physiognomy, which he equated with pagan astrology, demonstrating that not all Christians in late antiquity were as taken with physiognomy as was Ambrose:

But since, also, there is another more profound art among the all-wise speculators of the Greeks—to whom heretical individuals boast that they attach themselves as disciples, on account of their employing the opinions of these (ancient philosophers) in reference to the doctrines tempted (to be established) by themselves, as shall a little afterwards be proved; but this is an art of divination, by examination of the forehead, or rather, I should say, it is madness: yet we shall not be silent as regards this (system). There are some who ascribe to the stars figures that mould the ideas and dispositions of men, assigning the reason of this to births (that have taken place) under particular stars; they thus express themselves: Those who are born

---

84. See Harrill, "Invective against Paul," 200; Peter Garnsey, *Ideas of Slavery from Aristotle to Augustine* (Cambridge, England: Cambridge University Press, 1996), 157–72.

85. Martin, *Corinthian Body*, 37.

86. Sandnes, *Belly and Body*, 269.

87. Harrill, "Invective against Paul," 213.

under Aries will be of the following kind: long head, red hair, contracted eyebrows, pointed forehead, eyes grey and lively, drawn cheeks, long-nosed [ἐπίρρινοι], expanded nostrils, thin lips, tapering chin, wide mouth. These, he says, will partake of the following nature: cautious, subtle, perspicuous, prudent, indulgent, gentle, over-anxious, persons of secret resolves, fitted for every undertaking, prevailing more by prudence than strength, deriders for the time being, scholars, trustworthy, contentious, quarrellers in a fray, concupiscent, inflamed with unnatural lust, reflective, estranged from their own homes, giving dissatisfaction in everything, accusers, like madmen in their cups, scorners, year by year losing something serviceable in friendship through goodness; they, in the majority of cases, end their days in a foreign land. (*Haer.* 4.15; trans. *ANF* 5)

The attempt to exclude the *Physiologus* from the list of accepted Christian reading is a serious form of criticism, though the failure of official channels to curtail its popularity supports the conclusion that, at least at a popular level, many early Christians had difficulty resisting the temptation to read one's outward physical characteristics as commentary on one's inner moral character.

Conclusion

There is sufficient evidence to conclude that some Jews and Christians reflect the physiognomic consciousness even though it is not a major theme in their writings. Like their pagan counterparts, some Jewish and Christian thinkers objected to some or all of the conventions associated with physiognomic practices in antiquity. We turn now to the writings of one specific early Christian author, Luke, to ask what, if anything, we may learn of ancient physiognomic thought, and its critique, from the Luke/Acts corpus.

3

YOUR EYE IS THE LAMP OF YOUR BODY

Luke and the Body-Soul Relationship

It is tempting in a study such as this one, once a line of approach has been established, to search for evidence in every textual nook and cranny. By doing so, one can almost always find what one is looking for. As we search for evidence of ancient physiognomy in the Lukan writings, we will do well to make a crucial distinction between topics on which Luke *touches* and subjects about which Luke *teaches*. In the case of physiognomy, Luke does both. That is to say, in certain passages of Luke and Acts, knowledge of ancient physiognomic convention will shed additional light on the text. But that does not mean that these conventions represent what Luke thinks about the subject. So we begin by examining places where Luke touches on ancient physiognomy and conclude with a summary of what Luke teaches about the subject. That summary will then serve as an introduction to the second half of the book, where we treat passages in which Luke instructs his readers about the limitations of physiognomy.

Incidental Uses of Conventional Animal Imagery

We focus here especially on the zoological and anatomical methods. Interest in the racial or ethnographical method of physiognomy, however, is not entirely missing from Luke/Acts. Luke frequently identifies characters by reference to some location. See for example, Jesus of Nazareth (Acts 10:38); Jesus the Nazarean (Luke 18:37; Acts 2:22); Peter the Galilean (Luke 22:59); Judas the Galilean (Acts 5:37); Disciples called Galileans (Acts 1:11; 2:7); Saul/Paul of Tarsus (Acts 9:11; 21:39; 22:3); Simon of Cyrene (Luke 23:26); Corinthians (Acts 18:8); Romans (Acts 2:10; 16:21, 37; 28:17); Samaritans (Luke 17:16); Aquila the Judean, native of Pontus (Acts 18:2); and Lydia of Thyatira (Acts 16:14).[1]

We cannot rule out the possibility that some of these places would have held symbolic meaning for Luke's audience in the same way that references to animals and physical features resonated with certain stereotypes. The term "Samaria" (or Samaritan) is a good example. Enmity between Samaritans and Jews in the ancient world is well known. The writer of John states simply, "Jews do not share things in common with Samaritans" (John 4:9). The ancient Jewish historian, Josephus, identifies the Samaritans as "apostates from the Jewish nation" who still "profess themselves Jews" when it is to their advantage (*Ant.* 11.340–41). An audience already accustomed to this kind of geographical stereotyping could easily accept the stereotyping of ethnic groups new to them. Thus Gentile readers who previously had no knowledge of the Samaritans could readily adopt the ethnic stereotyping assumed in the Jewish milieu that underlies the Gospels. Only one of the places named in Luke/Acts—Ethiopia—receives any appreciable attention in the handbooks *and* functions symbolically in Acts. In contrast, Corinthian and Leucadian ethnicity are mentioned in the handbooks, but take on no figurative meaning in Acts. We will deal with the symbolic meaning of "Ethiopian" in chapter 7. We turn now to the function of Lukan echoes of the zoological and anatomical methods.

Pseudo-Aristotle observes, "It is also evident that the forms of the body are similar to the functions of the soul, so that all the similarities in animals are evidence of some identity" (808b27–30). The lion was a favorite animal when discussing the ideal "male type" (809b15). After discussing his bodily characteristics, pseudo-Aristotle draws inferences from those features: "in character he [the lion] is generous and liberal,

---

1. Cited by Malina and Neyrey, *Portraits of Paul*, 114.

magnanimous and with a will to win; he is gentle, just, and affectionate toward his associates" (809b34–36). Of course, not all animals conveyed such positive features. Three in particular—the fox, the viper, and the wolf—figure in Luke's narrative. We focus on these three because each one is used figuratively in Luke to refer to a person or group of people. Luke is not suggesting (at least not explicitly) that these characters physically resemble the animals whose moral character they imitate. Nonetheless, it is instructive to read these texts in the light of the cultural symbolism of antiquity, of which the physiognomic consciousness formed an important part.[2]

These texts do not teach the reader about physiognomic concerns related to foxes, wolves, or vipers. Nor is it necessary to consult the physiognomic treatises to understand the cultural connotations of each term. The handbooks, however, reveal the ways in which the zoological method uses these animals to describe and condemn specific human behaviors. Furthermore, they provide another angle onto the culturally conditioned ways in which these animals function figuratively for human behavior. Thus, while they may not teach us much about what Luke (or Jesus) thought about physiognomic conventions, they do demonstrate how familiarity with the physiognomic consciousness of late antiquity further illuminates our reading of these texts.

Herod the Fox

"Some Pharisees" approach Jesus and warn, "Get away from here, for Herod wants to kill you" (Luke 13:31). To this Jesus replies, "Go and tell that fox for me, 'Listen, I am casting out demons and performing cures today and tomorrow, and on the third day I finish my work'" (13:32).

Pseudo-Aristotle remarks rather briefly that, in contrast to lions who are "brave," foxes, because they are "reddish," are of "bad character" (πανοῦργοι; 812a17), a comment that echoes Aristotle's point that the fox is cunning and of evil disposition (*Hist. an.* 1.1.488b20). Polemo is more expansive: "The fox is wily, deceitful, coy, evasive, rapacious, shrewd" (174). What they lack in physical strength, foxes make up for with cunning and deceit.

---

2. It would be a mistake to think that every animal mentioned in Luke and Acts has symbolic or figurative meaning. We will limit ourselves to places where animals are used figuratively or metaphorically to stand for a person or group (as in the examples that follow) or where mention of an animal is in the context of a text with physiognomic significance (see the discussion of oxen and asses in chap. 4). On the place of animals in early Christian thought, see Grant, *Early Christians and Animals.*

This judgment is confirmed throughout ancient Mediterranean litera-ture, where foxes are depicted in a mostly negative manner.[3] Epictetus, musing over the mixed human and divine nature of humanity, suggests that most of us succumb to the view that we are mainly flesh and behave accordingly: "Most of us become foxes, that is to say, rascals (ἀτυχήματα) of the animal kingdom. For what else is a slanderous and malicious man but a fox, or something even more rascally and degraded?" (*Arrian's Dis-courses of Epictetus*, 1.3.7–9).[4]

We find some confirmation of this negative view in Israel's scriptures as well. In Ezekiel, false prophets are compared to carnivorous foxes: "Like foxes in the deserts are your prophets, O Israel; they have not stood steadfast; and they have gathered flocks against the house of Israel" (Ezek. 13:4–5 [LXX]). By nature foxes are destructive. In the Song of Songs, we read, "Catch us the little foxes that are destroying the vineyards" (Song 2:15a [LXX]). *First Enoch* lists foxes along with dogs and wild boars as those who "devour" sheep (*1 En.* 89.42). They are inferior creatures, a view consistently expressed in later Jewish literature. According to the Babylonian Talmud, it is more honorable to be the tail of a lion than the head of a fox (*Sanh.* 37a; cf. also *Eccles. Rab.* 11.2.1, where foxes are depicted as inferior to lions).[5]

In the Talmud we read a parable by Rabbi Akiba suggesting that even the fox's cunning is not immune to critique:

> A fox was once walking alongside of a river, and he saw fishes going in swarms, from one place to another. He said to them: From what are you fleeing? They replied: From the nets cast for us by men. He said to them: Would you like to come up on to the dry land so that you and I can live together in the way that my ancestors lived with your ancestors? They replied: Art thou the one that they call the cleverest of all animals? Thou art not clever but foolish. If we are afraid in the element in which we live,

3. In Aesop's fables, however, the fox is often associated with sagacity, although the fox's use of wis-dom is often self-serving and undisciplined; see L. W. Daley, trans., *Aesop without Morals* (New York: T. Yoseloff, 1961). Some thirty-nine of the corpus of 420 fables deal with the fox. Many of the references in the following paragraphs are taken from "Appendix XI: The Meaning of 'Fox,'" in Harold Hoehner, *Herod Antipas*, SNTSMS 17 (Cambridge: Cambridge University Press, 1972), 343–47.

4. Unlike pseudo-Aristotle, however, Epictetus has little good to say about lions either, characterizing them as "wild and savage and untamed" (1.3.7).

5. Hoehner's conclusion (*Herod Antipas*, 346–47) seems correct: "When a fox is contrasted with another animal, it is for the most part with the lion. The lion is pictured as the one who had its position because of its power, whereas the fox only gained a high position by the deceitful means of outwitting the other animals. . . . Therefore, one can conclude that a person who is designated a fox is an insignificant or base person. He lacks real power and dignity, using cunning deceit to achieve his aims."

how much more in the element in which we would die! So it is with us.
If such is our condition when we sit and study the Torah, of which it is
written, For that is thy life and the length of thy days, if we go and neglect
it how much worse off we shall be! (*b. Ber.* 61b)

It is not necessary to introduce the lion/fox contrast as the primary
context of Jesus' saying, as some do,[6] in order to understand how the
imagery would have impacted the reader familiar with the cultural symbolism of foxes echoed in the zoological method of physiognomy. To be
sure, as John Darr has demonstrated, the primary image of "Herod the
Fox" must be seen within the developing characterization of Herod in
the Lukan narrative, from Luke 3–Acts 13. Darr rightly suggests that
it is Herod's foxlike trait of destructiveness that is most likely in the
mind of the Lukan audience, a metaphor that is continued in Jesus' next
statement about Jerusalem: "How often have I desired to gather your
children together as a hen gathers her brood under her wings, and you
were not willing" (Luke 13:34b). Darr concludes, "The image is that
of the hen defending her chicks against attack by a predator. Although
the predator is not specified, the reader very likely understands it to be
a fox, for the fox was known as a common predator of chickens and
this animal imagery lay close at hand in the passage."[7] This conclusion,
however, should not exclude the metaphor from having a "surplus" of
meaning, some of which is provided by the zoological method of the
physiognomists. Thus the negative portrayal of Herod is reinforced by
an appeal to the physiognomic repertoire that would have held foxes
as essentially destructive creatures whose only virtue—cleverness—was
self-serving.

Opponents as Wolves

Jesus commissions seventy(-two) and sends them out with the warning,
"Go on your way. See, I am sending you out like lambs into the midst of
wolves" (Luke 10:3). Paul uses similar imagery in his farewell address to

---

6. See W. Grimm, "Eschatologischer Saul wider eschatologischen David: Eine Deutung von Lc.
xiii 31ff," *Novum Testamentum* 15 (1973): 114–33, esp. 114–16, and R. Buth, "That Small-Fry Herod
Antipas, or When a Fox Is Not a Fox," *Jerusalem Perspective* 40 (1993): 7–9, 14, esp. 8. But neither is it
necessary to dismiss this comparison too quickly, as does John Darr, *Herod the Fox: Audience Criticism
and Lukan Characterization*, JSNTSup 163 (Sheffield: Sheffield Academic Press, 1998), 181–82. Note
the pervasiveness of this contrast in the physiognomic handbooks and ancient literature (e.g., twelve of
Aesop's thirty-nine fables with foxes as their subject also mention lions).

7. Darr, *Herod the Fox*, 182–83.

the Ephesian elders: "I know that after I have gone, savage wolves will come in among you, not sparing the flock" (Acts 20:29). Although neither the Lukan Jesus nor the Lukan Paul is suggesting that the opposition physically resembled wolves, the physiognomists once again provide some background as to the culturally conditioned meaning of the imagery of the wolf in the ancient world.[8]

According to Polemo, the wolf is "bold, treacherous, vicious, plundering, greedy, harmful, deceitful, offering help in order to harm" (172). Similarly in the anonymous tractate we read:

> The wolf is a rapacious animal, irascible, deceitful, bold, violent. . . . Men of this type are crafty, impious, blood-thirsty, quick to anger, vicious to the extent that they refuse what is given or offered them, but steal what is not given. (*De physiogn.* 126; ed. André, 136–37)

This view finds confirmation in the larger Greco-Roman world even as early as Homer, who in a particularly vivid passage compares the Myrmidon warriors with wolves:

> But Achilles went to and fro throughout the huts and let harness in their armour all the Myrmidons, and they rushed forth like ravening wolves in whose hearts is fury unspeakable—wolves that have slain in the hills a great horned stag, and rend him, and the jaws of all are red with gore; and in a pack they go to lap with their slender tongues the surface of the back water from a dusky spring, belching forth the while blood and gore, the heart in their breasts unflinching and their bellies gorged full; even in such wise the leaders and rulers of the Myrmidons sped forth round about the valiant squire of the swift-footed son of Aeacus. And among them all stood warlike Achilles, urging on both horses and men that bear the shield. (*Il.* 16.156–66; cf. *Il.*4.472)

8. We could also explore the use of "lambs" or "flock" to stand for God's people, but again lambs are not as suggestive in the physiognomic literature; neither "lamb" (ἀρήν; Luke 10:3) nor "flock" (ποίμνιον; Acts 20:29) occurs in the physiognomic corpus (see index of terms in Foerster, *Scriptores*, 2:398–432). For figurative uses of "flock" in reference to a sophist's pupils, see Libanius, *Or.* 58.36; in reference to the people of Israel, see Jer. 13:17 (LXX); Zech. 10:3 (LXX); in reference to the church, see 1 Pet. 5:3; *1 Clem.* 44.3; 54.2; 57.2 (in addition to these citations in Acts 20). The defenselessness of lambs against the wolf is well known (Homer, *Il.* 22.263; *Epig. Gr.* 1038.38 [in *Anth. Gr.* 105]; Philostratus, *Vit. Apoll.* 8.22; Justin, *1 Apol.* 58.2; Didymus, *In Gen.* 86.18). Certainly the metaphor is common in Jewish litera-ture (cf. Isa. 11:6; 40:11; Ezek. 34:11–31; Philo, *Praem.* 86). "What does a wolf have in common with a lamb? No more has a sinner with the devout" (Sir. 13:17). "The devout of God are like innocent lambs among them" (*Pss. Sol.* 8.23; cf. *4 Ezra* 5.18). "Hadrian said to Rabbi Jehoshua: 'There is something great about the sheep [Israel] that can persist among the seventy wolves [the nations]'" (*Tanh. Tol.* 5; cited by Str-B 1:574).

To quote Epictetus again, wolves are "faithless and treacherous and hurtful" (*Arrian's Discourses of Epictetus*, 1.3.7). Of course, the imagery of lambs and wolves also echoes Isaiah's "the wolf shall live with the lamb" (11:6; cf. 65:25), though that eschatological vision does not quite seem fulfilled in Jesus' and Paul's warnings.[9]

These descriptions help circumscribe how the metaphor would have been heard as culturally conditioned symbols within the ancient Mediterranean thought world. Wolves connote people who behave badly in particular ways: they are, among other things, faithless, treacherous, impious, and blood-thirsty. Paul adds the chilling note that such fierce opposition may come from within the community as well as from without. Luke communicates an environment of danger and hostility that awaits his followers and presumes that the symbol of the wolves will communicate that picture effectively. Knowledge of the place of wolves in the physiognomic consciousness helps considerably in filling out that picture.

When we do not seek to understand the cultural context of writings that are removed from ours in space and time we will inevitably read those texts against our "default" cultural contexts. This brief exercise shows that the physiognomic handbooks (along with other texts) help us to place the references to wolves in the sayings of Jesus and Paul within their ancient cultural context. Without such help we are likely to hear such sayings against the backdrop of "Little Red Riding Hood" and "The Boy Who Cried Wolf." Certainly such more recent stories form part of the intertext that lies between scripture and the modern hearer of the Bible, but they should not hold an elevated place in our understanding of the biblical text.

The Brood of Vipers

The multitudes that come out to be baptized by John the Baptist are greeted with angry words: "You brood of vipers! Who warned you to flee from the wrath to come?" (Luke 3:7). In typical physiognomic thinking we find that the serpent "is a cruel, harmful, insidious animal, terrible when it decides to be, quick to flee when afraid, gluttonous. . . .

9. This certainly seems to be the concern of Peter expressed in an apocryphal account cited in *2 Clement*: "For the Lord said, 'You will be like sheep in the midst of wolves.' But Peter replied to him, 'What if the wolves rip apart the sheep?' Jesus said to Peter, 'After they are dead, the sheep should fear the wolves no longer. So too you: do not fear those who kill you and then can do nothing more to you; but fear the one who, after you die, has the power to cast your body and soul into the hell of fire" (*2 Clem.* 5.2–4). Note that here, too, wolves are used figuratively for destructive and evil people who oppose the followers of Jesus.

Such men are murderers, bold, timid, devoted to evil-doing" (*De physi-ogn.* 128; ed. André, 137). Polemo concurs: "The serpent is hypocritical, wise, harmful, fearful, quick to flee, often friendly, quick to change, of baser character" (188).

These negative connotations are likewise reflected in the larger literary environment.[10] Aeschylus has Orestes muse over the "abhorrent deed" done to his father, Agamemnon, by his mother, Queen Clytemnestra, and in the course of his monologue refers to her as a viper:

> But she who devised this abhorrent deed against her husband, whose children she had conceived . . . what thinkest thou of her? Had she been born seasnake or viper, methinks her very touch without her bite had made some other to rot, if shamelessness and wickedness of spirit could do it. (*Cho.* 991–96)

Note that Orestes equates "shamelessness" and "wickedness of spirit" with the activity of a viper, similar in concept if not specific language to that of Polemo.

In his oration against Aristogeiton, Demosthenes offers the following invective against the accused, comparing him to (among other things) a viper:

> Just consider. There are something like twenty thousand citizens in all. Every single one of them frequents the market-place on some business (you may be sure) either public or private. Not so the defendant. He cannot point to any decent or honourable business in which he has spent his life; he does not use his talents in the service of the State; he is not engaged in a profession or in agriculture or in any other business . . . but he makes his way through the market-place like a snake (ἔχις) or a scorpion with sting erect, darting hither and thither, on the look-out for someone on whom he can call down disaster or calumny or mischief of some sort, or whom he can terrify till he exhorts money from him. (*1 Aristog.* 1.25.52)

Later, Demosthenes explains how to deal with a person who acts like a viper:

> Perhaps none of you has ever been bitten by an adder or a tarantula, and I hope he never may be. All the same, whenever you see such creatures, you

10. In Sophocles' play *Trachiniae*, the three-headed hound who guards Hades is called "dread Echidna" (δεινῆς Ἐχίδνης) or "dreaded Viper" (1099). The term "dread" often accompanies the word for "serpent" or "viper" (cf. Hesiod, *Theog.* 299).

promptly kill them all. In just the same way, men of Athens, whenever you see a false accuser, a man with the venom of a viper (ἔχιν) in his nature, do not wait for him to bite one of you, but always let the man who comes across him exact punishment. (*1 Aristog.* 1.25.96)

Herodotus attests to the consistently negative portrayal of vipers and people who imitate them in this graphic description, demonstrating that they are dangerous and destructive even to their own kind:

> It is so too with vipers and the winged serpents of Arabia; were they born in the natural manner of serpents no life were possible for men; but as it is, when they pair, and the male is in the very act of generation, the female seizes him by the neck, nor lets go her grip til she has bitten the neck through. Thus the male dies; but the female is punished for his death; the young avenge their father, and gnaw at their mother while they are yet within her; nor are they dropped from her till they have eaten their way through her womb. (*Hist.* 3.109)

In his parallel to Luke 10:3, Matthew combines the imagery of wolves and vipers, albeit not using the same word for serpent as that in Luke 3:7: "See, I am sending you out like sheep into the midst of wolves; so be wise as serpents (ὄφεις) and innocent as doves" (Matt. 10:16). Here, in a passage omitted by Luke (if he knew it), the audience is admonished to follow the example of serpents. The oxymoronic nature of this command is reflected well in Augustine's comments:

> Now if the simplicity of doves be enjoined us, what has the wisdom of the serpent to do with that? What I love in the dove is that she is without gall; what I fear in the serpent is his poison. But *do not fear the serpent altogether* for he has . . . something for you to imitate. For when the serpent is weighted down with age and feeling the burden of his many years he contracts and forces himself into a hole, and casts off his old coat of skin that he may spring forth into new life. . . . And the Apostle Paul says to you also, "Put ye off the old man with his deeds, and put ye on the new man" [Col. 3:9–10; Eph. 4:22–24]. So you do have something in the serpent to imitate. Die not for the "old man," but for the truth. (*Serm.* 44.1–2)[11]

In the next paragraph Augustine admonishes the Christian to protect his head, which is Christ, as the adder does (*Serm.* 44.3). That Augustine has

---

11. Cited in David L. Jeffrey, "Wise as Serpents," in *A Dictionary of Biblical Tradition in English Literature*, ed. David L. Jeffrey (Grand Rapids: Eerdmans, 1992), 839.

to labor to find a virtue in the serpent/adder imagery serves to confirm the prevailing negative connotation of the creature. Of course, in Christian exegesis this may be due as much to the role of the serpent in Adam's fall as to any physiognomic traditions concerning serpents.[12]

The physiognomic handbooks and other literary references to vipers provide a way to understand the culturally specific connotations of the saying. The "brood of vipers" in John's speech suggests that the people are "devoted to evil-doing," "wicked in spirit," "shameless," and "cruel." Given the advice to crush such venomous persons before they can strike (surely not idiosyncratic to Demosthenes), it is no wonder that John the Baptists queries, "Who warned you to flee from the wrath to come?"

Eyes and Seeing

We turn now to examples of the anatomical method, which Luke seems to use deliberately in his discussion of eyes and gazing.

The Lukan Eyes

In Luke 11:34–36 (and the parallel, Matt. 6:22–23), Jesus speaks of the relationship of the eye to the whole body: "Your eye is the lamp of your body. If your eye is healthy, your whole body is full of light; but if it is not healthy, your body is full of darkness. Therefore consider whether the light in you is not darkness. If then your whole body is full of light, with no part of it in darkness, it will be as full of light as when a lamp gives you light with its rays."

H. D. Betz, Dale Allison, and John Elliott have shed considerable light on this text by their appeal to Greek (Betz) and Jewish (Allison) theories of vision, and the evil-eye tradition in antiquity (Elliott).[13] None of them, however, appeals to the physiognomic tradition.

---

12. Nevertheless, we would do well to recall Foerster's caution against reading too much of Adam's fall into Luke 3:7 and Matt. 3:7: "In view of the plur., we are not to think of the serpent in Paradise, though of the many ideas associated with the poisonous snake, there may be some influence of the fact that it is repulsive and that it is to be radically opposed and destroyed" (*TDNT* 2:816).

13. See H. D. Betz, "Matthew vi.22f. and Ancient Greek Theories of Vision," in *Text and Interpretation: Studies in the New Testament Presented to Matthew Black*, ed. E. Best and R. McL. Wilson (Cambridge: Cambridge University Press, 1979), 43–56; Dale Allison, "The Eye Is the Lamp of the Body (Matthew 6.22–23 = Luke 11.34–36)," *New Testament Studies* 33 (1987): 61–83; John Elliott, "The Evil Eye and the Sermon on the Mount: Contours of a Pervasive Belief in Social Scientific Perspective," *Biblical Interpretation* 2 (1994): 51–84.

The eye, of course, is central in physiognomic thinking. According to pseudo-Aristotle, "The most favorable part for examination is the region around the eyes, forehead, head and face" (814b3–4). Pseudo-Aristotle follows his own advice, citing the eyes (ὄμματα) as a distinguishing mark of various character types no less than eighteen times in his treatise (cf. 807b1, 7, 19, 23, 29, 35; 808a1, 3, 8, 9, 12, 16, 28, 30, 34; 808b6; 812b8; 813a21). The anonymous author of the Latin treatise asserts: "now we discuss the eyes, where the sum total of all physiognomy is situated" (*De physiogn.*; ed. André, 66; cf. 142). Polemo agrees and devotes nearly one third of his work to the topic of eyes.[14]

Interest in the eyes was not confined to the physiognomic treatises. Cicero argued that the eyes were crucial for successful oratorical delivery:

> Everything depends upon the countenance, while the countenance itself is entirely dominated by the eyes . . . For a delivery is wholly the concern of the feelings, and these are mirrored by the face and expressed by the eyes . . . but it is the eyes that should be used to indicate the emotions, by now assuming an earnest look, now relaxing it, now a stare, and now a merry glance . . . and nature has given us eyes, as she has given the horse and the lion their mane and tail and ears, to indicate the feelings of the mind. (*De or.* 3.221–23)[15]

Furthermore, the connection of the eye to moral character is a common theme in the ancient world. Cicero elsewhere observes, "She [nature] has so formed his features as to portray therein the character that lies deep within him; for not only do the eyes declare with exceeding clearness the innermost feelings of our hearts, but also that which is called the countenance, which can be found in no living thing save man, reveals the character" (*Leg.* 1.26–27).[16] Once again we hear, "For every action derives from the soul, and the countenance is the image of the soul, the eyes its chief indicators" (*De or.* 3.221).

We see the connection between the eyes and the inner character also in Jewish literature. Persons with "good eyes" were morally sound: "[The person with] a good eye will be blessed, for he shared his bread with the poor" (Prov. 22:9, my translation), whereas Sirach claims: "He is hard who

14. See Polemo 1.20; ed. Foerster, 1:107 : "Scientiae physiognomoniae <summa> in oculi signis." His treatment of the eyes occupies pages 107–70 in Foerster's edition. Malina and Neyrey observe, "This perspective is further verified by the sheer space (that is, some 20 percent or more) that most physiognomists devote in their writings to the eyes" (*Portraits of Paul*, 127).

15. Cited by Malina and Neyrey, *Portraits of Paul*, 135.

16. Cited ibid., 126.

has an evil eye who turns his back on need and looks the other way. The evil eye is not satisfied with its share; greedy injustice shrivels the soul. Someone with an evil eye begrudges bread and keeps a bare table" (Sir. 14:8–10, my translation). In Christian literature, as with Cicero, we find this connection was expressed through a linking of "eyes" and "heart": Ephesians 1:18 speaks of "the eyes of your heart" (cf. *1 Clem.* 36.2).[17] Elliott's conclusion is apropos: "An integral eye, by contrast, betokens the moral integrity of its owner who seeks the welfare of others and is generous with all he or she possesses."[18]

The eye was not only the "chief indicator of the soul"; it was also the source out of which rays of light emitted, effecting upon those objects which they touched.[19] This theory of vision lay at the base of what was known as the "evil eye" tradition.[20] Envy was the emotion most associated with the one who possessed the evil eye, and this envy had a negative effect not only on the person with the evil eye but also on those upon whom the evil eye gazed. One of Plutarch's characters remarks:

> When those possessed by envy . . . let their glance fall upon a person, their eyes, which are close to the mind and draw from it the evil influence of the passion, then assail that person with poisoned arrows; hence, I conclude, it is not paradoxical or incredible that they should have an effect on the persons who encounter their gaze. (Plutarch, *Mor.* 681F–82)

In a fascinating passage that echoes aspects of both the racial and anatomical methods, Pliny the Elder asserts that among the African peoples there are

> families in the same part of Africa that wield the Evil Eye, whose praises cause meadows to dry up, trees to wither and infants to perish. . . . There are people of the same kind . . . who also injure by the evil eye and who kill those at whom they stare for a longer time, especially with furious eyes

17. It was common also in the ancient world to speak of the "eye of the soul." In describing Abraham's "awakening" and progression from self-knowledge to knowledge of God, Philo remarks, "In this creed Abraham had been reared, and for a long time remained a Chaldean. Then opening the soul's eye as though after a profound sleep and beginning to see the pure beam instead of the deep darkness, he followed the ray and discerned what he had not beheld before, a charioteer and pilot presiding over the world and directing in safety his own work" (*Abr.* 70, cf. *Sacr.* 36; Plato, *Resp.* 7.533D; *Soph.* 254A; Porphyry, *Vita Pyth.* 47; also *1 Clem.* 19.3, which speaks of "gazing at something with the eyes of the soul").

18. Elliott, "Evil Eye," 77.

19. On the ancient theories of ocular extramission, see Betz, "Matthew vi.22f.," 43–56.

20. See Elliott, "Evil Eye," 80–84, for bibliography related to the evil-eye tradition.

. . . their evil eye is most felt by adults; and . . . what is more remarkable is
that they have two pupils in each eye. (*Hist. nat.* 5.2.16–18)

The focus of Luke, however, is not on the effect of the eye's rays on
other objects but on the relationship of the eye to the inner body: "If your
eye is healthy, your whole body is full of light; but if it is not healthy, your
body is full of darkness" (Luke 11:34). Allison suggests that this verse
presents "a type of conditional sentence in which the causal condition is
found not in the protasis but in the apodosis, and in which the protasis
names the effect."[21] The effect of Allison's interpretation is something like,
"If the eye is sound, it will show that the body is full of light." Thus the
body's moral character is reflected in the eye, not the reverse. Otherwise,
Allison concludes, the verse would mean that "a good eye creates inner
light. This could only be the case if an intromission theory of vision were
being presupposed. But it is not. . . ."[22] While we agree that an intromission theory is not presupposed, it does not necessarily follow that this is
the only way that one could understand that the good eye creates inner
light and conversely that the evil eye creates darkness. Remember that
in physiognomic thought, "body and soul interact with each other" (ps.-
Aristotle 805a7–8). Thus the ancient reader, steeped in the physiognomic
consciousness, would not necessarily stop to think whether it was the eye
that produced the good light or vice versa.

What is important is the ethical admonition to focus on the inner character: "Therefore be careful lest the light in you be darkness" (Luke 11:35).
Allison is forced to conclusions not supported by his comparison:

> One first hears a (proverbial) statement which is taken to refer to the
> physical eye; but by the time the closing words ring out, one realizes that
> he has heard a statement about higher truths. Thus the listener is led to
> backtrack, to listen to the saying afresh, to rethink the whole of what he
> has heard. "The eye is the lamp of the body" now becomes a spiritual truth:
> one's moral disposition correlates with a religious state, with the darkness
> or the light within.[23]

But on the basis of physiognomy, one need not hear the proverbial
saying on two levels as Allison suggests; rather the physical *and* moral

21. Allison, "The Eye Is the Lamp of the Body," 74. Allison lists Luke 11:20 as an example among
others (75).
22. Ibid., 75.
23. Ibid., 76–77.

implications of "the eye is the lamp of the body" would have been front and center all the time.

Luke's understanding of the connection between the eyes and a person's inner light or moral character might illuminate two other texts in Acts. After his vision on the road to Damascus, Saul is left blind for three days, during which he took no food or drink (Acts 9:9). Paul's blindness during this period of penance symbolizes his former life of "breathing threats and murder against the disciples of the Lord" (9:1), and the obvious darkness of his soul. When he regains his sight, Luke reports that "something like scales fell from his eyes" (9:18a), and he was baptized and broke his fast (9:18b–19).

Later, Paul, the Christian missionary, confronts Elymas, a Jewish sorcerer. When Elymas tries to intervene in Sergius Paulus's conversion, the narrator reports that "Saul, also known as Paul, filled with the Holy Spirit, looked intently at him and said, 'You son of the devil, you enemy of all righteousness, full of all deceit and villainy, will you not stop making crooked the straight paths of the Lord? And now listen—the hand of the Lord is against you, and you will be blind for a while, unable to see the sun'" (Acts 13:9–11a). As a result, "immediately mist and darkness came over him, and he went about groping for someone to lead him by the hand" (13:11b). From a physiognomic view, it is only natural that Elymas's eyes be blinded to mirror the darkened condition of his soul. The inner light of his body is darkness, so his eyes are not sound.

The Lukan Gaze

The narrator mentions that Paul "looked intently" on Elymas (13:9). Several commentators have noted the frequency of ἀτενίζω ("stare, gaze intently") in the healing stories in Acts (Acts 3:4; 14:9; etc.), as well as this story of a punitive miracle. What light can physiognomy shed on this phenomenon? The eyes, of course, were among the most important features to physiognomists. One wonders how an audience shaped by this physiognomic consciousness would hear, for example, the reference to Peter staring at the lame man, followed by his command to the lame man to "Look at us!" before healing him. Furthermore, there is the predictive aspect of physiognomy. For example Ammianus Marcellinus writes about physiognomists: "Gazing long and earnestly on his (Julian's) eyes . . . they divine what manner of man he would be, as if they had perused those ancient books, the reading of which discloses from bodily signs the inward qualities of the soul" (*Res gest.* 25.8). This predictive element is found in the healing of the lame man at Lystra: "Paul, looking at him intently and seeing that he had faith to be healed . . ." (14:9). Paul, much like a professional physiognomist, is somehow able, through his stare, to look at the outer appearance of the lame man of Lystra and determine something vital about his inner moral being, namely that he had the "faith to be healed."

The foregoing examples might suggest that Luke accepts physiognomy and employs it uncritically. However, while there are aspects of physiognomy that Luke finds useful, we will see that he has grave reservations about using physiognomic methods as an entrance requirement into the community—in contrast to Pythagoras, the Qumraners, and apparently even Ambrose. It is noteworthy that nowhere does Luke provide any extended physical description of the main protagonists (Jesus, John the Baptist, and the disciples) or antagonists (religious and political leaders) in the story. This is especially striking in the case of John the Baptist. Both Mark (1:6) and Matthew (3:4) give a description of the Baptist's attire, but Luke omits even this; its inclusion might lead Luke's readers to draw moral inferences based on physical characteristics—the very kind of connection Luke is bent on breaking. Not only does Luke fail to use physiognomy as an "entrance test," he subtly but forcefully opposes the application of the conventions of physiognomy in this way. This is especially clear with regard to the Abrahamic covenant in Luke.

Physiognomy and the Abrahamic Covenant

The importance of the Abrahamic covenant for Luke's theology has often been noted.[24] Abraham can be an ancestor with whom persons share a genetic descent or an archetype who functions typologically. Abraham as archetype is certainly the focus of Luke.[25] John the Baptist makes this distinction: "Do not begin to say to yourselves, 'We have Abraham as our

24. See N. A. Dahl, "The Story of Abraham in Luke-Acts," in idem, *Jesus in the Memory of the Early Church* (Minneapolis: Augsburg, 1976), 66–86; Joel Green, "The Problem of a Beginning: Israel's Scriptures in Luke 1–2," *Bulletin for Biblical Research* 4 (1994): 61–85; Robert Brawley, "Abrahamic Covenant Traditions and the Characterization of God in Luke-Acts," in *The Unity of Luke Acts*, ed. J. Verheyden, BETL 142 (Leuven: Leuven University Press, 1999), 109–32; J. S. Siker, *Disinheriting the Jews: Abraham in Early Christian Controversy* (Louisville: Westminster John Knox, 1991). This is not to deny that other covenantal images are unimportant for Luke; see, for example, M. L. Strauss, *The Davidic Messiah in Luke-Acts: The Promise and Its Fulfillment in Lukan Christology*, JSNTSup 110 (Sheffield: Sheffield Academic Press, 1995).

25. On this, see Turid Karlsen Seim, "Abraham, Ancestor or Archetype? A Comparison of Abraham-Language in 4 Maccabees and Luke-Acts," in *Antiquity and Humanity: Essays on Ancient Religion and*

ancestor,' for I tell you, God is able from these stones to raise up children to Abraham" (Luke 3:8).

For Luke, being a son or daughter of Abraham is connected to God's promise that his progeny will number like the grains of sand; this promise is fulfilled in the eschatological community forming around the person of Jesus Christ. Moreover, Luke refuses to exclude anyone from the social body of this eschatological community on the basis of the shape of the physical body. In fact, as we shall see, the two characters to whom Luke assigns the titles of daughter and son of Abraham are, by physiognomic standards, inferior human beings. Yet they are children of Abraham. Despite their outward appearance, positive moral character is either revealed (in the case of the bent woman) or produced (in the case of Zacchaeus) through an encounter with Jesus. Zacchaeus is a son of Abraham by reflecting Abraham's virtue of hospitality; the bent woman reflects the Abrahamic virtue of courage. Of course, both Zacchaeus and the bent woman are also children of Abraham by genetic descent, but the focus is on Abraham as archetype; it sets the stage for an explication in Acts of the nature of the blessings that will accompany the family (so the healing of the lame man in Acts 3–4) and the inclusion of the Gentiles in the Abrahamic covenant (so the Ethiopian eunuch in Acts 8).[26] In each of these four cases, Luke introduces traditional understandings of physiognomy only to undermine them. No one is excluded from the eschatological community on the basis of his or her looks, and *this* is the message regarding physiognomy that Luke wishes to teach. We turn now to a consideration of these four stories.

Philosophy: Presented to Hans Dieter Betz on His 70th Birthday, ed. Adela Yarbro Collins and Margaret M. Mitchell (Tübingen: Mohr Siebeck, 2001), 27–42.

26. Further, see Dahl, "The Story of Abraham in Luke-Acts," 87–98, 69–70; Siker, *Disinheriting the Jews*.

4

OUGHT NOT THIS DAUGHTER OF ABRAHAM BE SET FREE?

Getting the Story of the Bent Woman Straight

Who belongs in this new family of God? Who qualifies as a child of Abraham? Luke begins his case for the inclusiveness of the Abrahamic covenant community with the story of the so-called bent woman.

The Bent Woman Ignored and Interpreted

Until recently, the story of the bent woman has largely been ignored in the scholarly literature. In fact, Dennis Hamm could write as late as 1987 that he could find only two articles devoted to Luke 13:10–17.[1] Those who did address the pericope often had little positive to say. Rudolf Bultmann claimed that when compared with other similar stories (Luke 14:1–6, Mark 3:1–6), Luke 13:10–17 exhibits the least skill in

1. M. Dennis Hamm, "The Freeing of the Bent Woman and the Restoration of Israel: Luke 13:10–17 as Narrative Theology," *Journal for the Study of the New Testament* 31 (1987): 23–44. Hamm (p. 39 n. 1) cites J. Wilkinson, "The Case of the Bent Woman in Luke 13:10–17," *Evangelical Quarterly* 49 (1977): 195–205, and L. Milot, "Guérison d'une femme infirme un jour de sabbat (Luc 13.10–17)," *Sémiotique et Bible* 39 (1985): 23–33.

composition.[2] This assessment no doubt rests in part on the fact that from a form-critical perspective this story seems to be a "hybrid form," drawing on elements of both a healing and a controversy story. Thus many who have studied the pericope have focused on the conflict story (vv. 14–16).[3]

When older studies did attend to the healing story, they often dealt with the diagnosis of the woman's ailment. The study by John Wilkinson (himself a medical missionary) would represent this approach taken to its logical conclusion.[4] In the chapter, "The Case of the Bent Woman," Wilkinson discusses various possible diagnoses to explain the woman's symptoms of being "bent double," finally concluding that ankylosing spondylitis is the "most probable diagnosis" in this case, although noting that this disease is more common in men.[5] However fascinating such a study may be for modern readers, Wilkinson's analysis is unlikely to shed much light on the function of the story in Luke's narrative.

Since Hamm's article appeared more attention has been paid to this passage. Contra Bultmann and others who failed to see any literary coherence in it, Robert O'Toole has argued that the story reveals "Luke's considerable literary skill."[6] He sees a diptych composed of two panels, with verses 11–13 paralleling 14–17:

First Panel (Luke 13:11–13)
1. Bent woman gets Jesus' attention (v. 11)
2. Jesus calls the woman and cures her (vv. 12–13a)
3. Twofold results of Jesus' actions (v. 13b)
   a. Immediately she is made straight
   b. She praises God
Second Panel (Luke 13:14–17)
1. Synagogue ruler objects (v. 14)
2. Jesus reacts to the ruler's words (vv. 15–16)
3. Twofold results of Jesus' words (v. 17)

2. Rudolf Bultmann, *The History of the Synoptic Tradition* (New York: Harper & Row, 1963), 12–13.

3. See, e.g., Paul Achtemeier, "The Lucan Perspective on the Miracles of Jesus: A Preliminary Sketch," *Journal of Biblical Literature* 94 (1975): 558; also, J. M. Creed, *The Gospel of Luke* (London: Macmillan, 1953), 181; W. Schmithals, *Das Evangelium nach Lukas* (Zurich: Theologischer Verlag, 1980), 152.

4. John Wilkinson, *Health and Healing: Studies in New Testament Principles and Practice* (Edinburgh: Handsel, 1980).

5. Ibid., 74.

6. Robert F. O'Toole, "Some Exegetical Reflections on Luke 13,10–17," *Biblica* 73 (1992): 84–107.

　　a. Jesus' adversaries are put to shame
　　b. All the people rejoice

O'Toole has also helpfully related this story to its immediate and larger context. Likewise, Joel Green has clarified the relationship between the healing story and the kingdom of God.[7] And of course, one must mention feminist studies that have also shed considerable light on this story. Pride of place here belongs to Elisabeth Schüssler Fiorenza, together with Turid Seim's enlightening discussion of the title, "Daughter of Abraham."[8] Still, questions remain. For example, what symbolic meaning is conveyed by details of the woman's illness in Luke's account?

Undermining Physiognomic Misogyny

Given the pervasive physiognomic consciousness of the Greco-Roman world, it would stand to reason that both Luke and his audience were familiar with these attempts to link physical features with inner moral characteristics. To the physical description of the woman as bent over and unable to stand up straight Luke appends the observation that she had "a spirit that had crippled her" (lit. "spirit of weakness," Luke 13:11), thereby connecting the physical and spiritual in physiognomic terms.

The physiognomic tractates address the phenomenon of being "bent" or "crooked." In pseudo-Aristotle we read:

> Those whose back is very large and strong are of strong character; witness the male. Those which have a narrow, weak back are feeble; witness the female. . . . (810b10–12)

> Those who have a large, fleshy and well-jointed back are strong in character; witness the male; those in whom it is weak, fleshless and badly jointed are weak in character; witness the female. Those in whom the back is very bent with the shoulders driven into the chest are of evil disposition; this is appropriate, because the parts in front which should be visible disappear. (810b25–32)

---

　　7. Joel B. Green, "Jesus and a Daughter of Abraham (Luke 13:10–17): Test Case for a Lucan Perspective on Jesus' Miracles," *Catholic Biblical Quarterly* 51 (1989): 643–54.

　　8. Turid Karlsen Seim, *The Double Message: Patterns of Gender in Luke and Acts* (Nashville: Abingdon, 1994), esp. 39–57. Elisabeth Schüssler Fiorenza, "Lk 13:10–17: Interpretation of Liberation and Transformation," *Theology Digest* (1989): 303–19.

Polemo writes:

> If you see that the back is broad, it is an indication of mighty and strong
> men, and it indicates great anger. If it is the opposite of that, it indicates
> weakness and the contrary of what the broad and strong back indicated.
> (11; ed. Foerster, 208)

According to physiognomic traditions, the bent woman's problem is
best understood as moral. Her bent back is the result of a feeble character,
even an evil disposition. This characterization sheds light on Luke's description of the woman as having a spirit of weakness, which, according to
the physiognomic handbooks, is a characteristically feminine problem.

In Luke/Acts, the term ἀσθενεία, in both its verbal and substantive
forms, typically refers to a physical infirmity and is often found in the
context of a healing story (cf. Luke 4:40; 5:15; 9:2; 10:9; Acts 4:9; 5:15,
16; 9:37; 19:12; 28:9). The term can, however, carry a moral or metaphorical sense, which Luke also knows. In Paul's Ephesian farewell address, he claims, "In all this I have given you an example that by such
work we must support the weak (ἀσθενούντων), remembering the words
of the Lord Jesus, for he himself said, 'It is more blessed to give than
to receive'" (Acts 20:35). Here the weak do not necessarily seem to be
limited to those with physical ailments but may include those who are
"weak" economically or socially.

Furthermore, the phrase "spirit of weakness" (13:10) is unique in Luke,
and even if the term generally carries the sense of a physical infirmity, the
fact that it is a *spirit* of weakness pushes the meaning in the direction of
the inner or moral.[9] Given the sequence of descriptors, we should not rule
out an understanding of the phrase in physiognomic terms as well.

In physiognomic thinking, women are weaker in moral character than
men and are therefore more prone to bent backs: no crooked man walking a crooked mile here, only bent women. In fact, the woman's crooked
stature was understood also to indicate, as pseudo-Aristotle suggests, an
"evil disposition," and it would have been apparent to the Lukan Jesus
that this was a physical manifestation of a satanic possession, the bonds
of which Jesus has decided to break. This explanation also clarifies Jesus'
comments: "you are set free . . ." (v. 12), and "whom Satan had bound"
(v. 16). Here Luke is giving a distinctively Jewish explanation for the
evil disposition: it was caused by Satan.

---

9. In this light, one might ponder the meaning of Luke 8:2: "Some women who had been cured of
evil spirits and infirmities . . ."

Luke does not let this misogynist characterization of women as "feeble" and of "evil disposition" go unchallenged. Rather, he introduces the traditional notion only to undermine it. At the end of the story, when challenged by the ruler of the synagogue, Jesus declares that the woman is a "daughter of Abraham," and here we may find another clue to Luke's strategy of introducing physiognomic concerns in order to subvert them.[10]

Strictly speaking, the phrase, "daughter of Abraham," is unique not only in the New Testament but also in all Jewish literature up to the time of Luke.[11] A similar, but not verbatim, phrase occurs in several passages in 4 Maccabees (14:20; 15:28; 17:6; 18:20), a Hellenistic Jewish document written sometime between the first century BCE and the first century CE, probably sometime before 70 CE, and echoed in the writings of Paul and Hebrews.[12] In each of these passages, Abrahamic categories are applied to the same woman, the courageous mother of the seven sons whom she encourages to accept martyrdom rather than violate food laws. After watching her seven sons die a cruel death, she herself is martyred.[13]

10. Most commentators simply note the presence of the phrase without delving into its possible meaning, e.g., W. Grundman, *Das Evangelium nach Lukas*, 3rd ed., THKNT 3 (Berlin: Evangelische Verlagsanstalt, 1964), 280; J. Schmid, *Das Evangelium nach Lukas*, RNT 3, 4th ed. (Regensburg: Friedrich Pustet, 1960), 21; E. E. Ellis, *The Gospel of Luke* (Greenwood, SC: Attic, 1966), 186. Given our comments that follow regarding the ox and the ass, G. Schneider, *Das Evangelium nach Lukas* (Gütersloh: Mohn, 1977), 300, is closer to the mark when he suggests the phrase means the woman is more valuable than house pets, but even he has underestimated its importance.

11. As Jacob Jervell, "The Daughters of Abraham: Women in Acts," in idem, *The Unknown Paul: Essay on Luke-Acts and Early Christian History* (Minneapolis: Augsburg, 1984), 148, notes: "Such a designation is unknown in the literature from this period, and attested to at a much later time than that of Luke. I suspect Luke himself coined the title, and by it intends to show the significance of women in the community."

12. Some of these references are discussed briefly in O'Toole, "Some Exegetical Reflections on Luke 13,10–17," 96–97, and more fully in Seim, *The Double Message*, 44–49. This section is indebted to Seim's analysis, although we reach slightly different conclusions in light of the physiognomic tradition. On the influence of the Maccabean martyrs on Hebrews, see David A. DeSilva, *Perseverance in Gratitude: A Socio-Rhetorical Commentary on the Epistle "to the Hebrews"* (Grand Rapids: Eerdmans, 2000). On its influence on Paul, see Stephen A. Cummins, *Paul and the Crucified Christ in Antioch: Maccabean Martyrdom and Galatians 1 and 2*, SNTSMS 114 (Cambridge: Cambridge University Press, 2001); David Seeley, *The Noble Death: Graeco-Roman Martyrology and Paul's Concept of Salvation*, JSNTSup 28 (Sheffield: JSOT Press, 1990).

13. On the Maccabean martyrs, see Jan Willem van Henten, *The Maccabean Martyrs as Saviours of the Jewish People: A Study of 2 and 4 Maccabees*, Supplements to the Journal for the Study of Judaism 57 (Leiden: Brill, 1997); Stephen D. Moore and Janice Capel Anderson, "Taking It Like a Man: Masculinity in 4 Maccabees," *Journal of Biblical Literature* 117 (1998): 249–73; R. D. Young, "The 'Woman with the Soul of Abraham': Traditions about the Mother of the Maccabean Martyrs," in *"Women Like This": New Perspectives on Jewish Women in the Greco-Roman World*, ed. A.-J. Levine (Atlanta: Scholars Press, 1991): 67–81, esp. 72.

In her willingness to sacrifice her sons and accept martyrdom for her faith, the woman of 4 Maccabees recalls the "strength" of Abraham. She is "the daughter of Abraham's strength" (4 Macc. 15:28). According to physiognomic tradition, the contrast between the apparent moral weakness of the bent woman and the moral strength of the Maccabean mother could not be starker. By having Jesus refer to the bent woman as a "daughter of Abraham," Luke is doing much more than making a bland reference to the fact that she is Jewish.[14] Rather, he echoes a tradition with which much of his audience would have been familiar, the tradition of the Jewish mother who courageously sacrificed both sons and self for her faith and thereby brought honor to the strength of Abraham, founder of her faith.[15] The bent woman, moreover, had always been a "daughter of Abraham" (Luke uses a present participle: "being a daughter of Abraham ..."). Thus Jesus acknowledges that the woman *is* a daughter of Abraham, not that she has now *become* one as a result of her healing. Her status as daughter of Abraham is "one of the premises of the healing, not a consequence of it."[16]

Our inquiry may also clarify other aspects of this story. When the ruler of the synagogue complains because Jesus has healed on the Sabbath (Luke 13:14), Jesus retorts, "You hypocrites! Does not each one of you on the Sabbath untie his ox or his donkey from the manger, and lead it away to give it water?" (13:15). Interpreters have long wondered about the choice of these specific animals to contrast with the bent woman. They are domestic animals, thus providing a way for Jesus to show that his opponents care more for livestock than for a fellow human, but is there any other point of contact? The zoological method of the physiognomic handbooks sheds some light here as well. Pseudo-Aristotle repeatedly identifies the character flaws of people with physical traits resembling those of cattle and asses: "Those that have thick extremities to the nostrils are lazy; witness cattle" (6.811a28–29; cf. 6.811b5–6, repeating the charge of laziness). In the next sentence we read, "Those with thin faces are careful, with fleshiness are cowardly, witness donkeys and deer" (6.811b6–7).

14. So Jervell, "Daughters of Abraham," 148.

15. While it is possible that Luke's audience knew 4 Maccabees, this assumption is not necessary to make the point that the audience (even Gentiles, whose Christian catechism would have included instruction about Jewish history, especially the Maccabean period) would have recognized an intertextual allusion to such an important story. On the connections between 4 Maccabees and Luke/Acts, especially with regard to the Abrahamic traditions, see Seim, "Abraham, Ancestor or Archetype?" 27–42.

16. Seim, *The Double Message*, 48.

Particularly interesting is a passage in which donkeys and cattle share a negative trait: "Those with large faces are sluggish: witness donkeys and cattle" (6.811b9–10). Elsewhere donkeys are depicted as stupid, because of their bulging eyes (6.811b25–26); insensitive, because of their round faces (6.811b31–32) or small heads (6.812a7–8); and insolent, because of their braying voices (6.813a31–32). Cattle are singled out as sluggish, because of their large eyes (6.811b21–22) or their large faces (6.811b30–31), and despondent, because their voices begin deep and end high-pitched (6.813a32–34).

To an audience familiar with these characterizations, the message of the Lukan Jesus would be clear. Not only are Jesus' opponents more willing to aid an animal than a woman, but they also are more than willing to aid those animals who symbolize such negative traits as cowardice, sluggishness, stupidity, laziness, or insolence than to help a daughter of Abraham whose status is masked, not reflected, by her physical condition.

Luke is able to critique the pervading physiognomic consciousness that would have presumed to know the woman's inner moral condition by her outward appearance. Though her physique might have prompted those around her to value cowardly, sluggish, or lazy animals above her, this woman, according to Jesus, was and always had been a daughter of Abraham, like the Maccabean mother. Jesus asks: "Ought not this woman, a daughter of Abraham whom Satan bound for eighteen long years, be set free from this bondage on the sabbath day?" (Luke 13:16). Her strong moral character had been hidden by her physical condition, and when Jesus unveiled her strength by loosing the satanic bonds he also exposed the limitations of physiognomic thinking. Upon release from the infirmity, "immediately she stood up straight and began praising God" (13:13).

Numerology and Physiognomy

Another unusual feature of our text lies in its use of the number eighteen. Numerology is not discussed in the physiognomic handbooks, but it should be noted that those interested in the hidden meaning of physical features were often interested in the hidden meaning of numbers. Pythagoras in particular, in addition to his well-known interest in mathematics (and numerical symbolism), was reputed to have "physiognomized" young men who applied for instruction under his tutelage; that is, he judged the candidates' intellectual aptitude on the basis of their physical appearance.[17] Moreover, numbers figure in several physiognomic texts, for example the nine-point scale in 4Q186, and may have some symbolic meaning (even if we are unable now to recover it). There is a special connection between predictive physiognomy and astrology, as Hippolytus disapprovingly notes (*Haer.* 4.15; this passage is quoted in full in chapter 2).

All three New Testament occurrences of the number eighteen are found in Luke 13, two of them in our pericope. Luke, of course, has a penchant for using numbers in various contexts, and some of the uses have apparent symbolic value. Think of the twelve apostles: Luke shares an interest in the symbolism of this number with the other evangelists and Paul, and is anxious to see it restored before the beginning of the apostles' public ministry at Pentecost (see Acts 1:15–26). Consider also the seven Hellenists: the symbolic value of this number (representing the Gentiles) is evidently distinctive to Luke (see Acts 6:1–6, and especially Acts 21:8, where "the Seven" is used as a title similar to "the Twelve").[18] However, Luke often cites numbers less precisely, with an approximating modifier: Jesus was "about thirty years old" when he began his public ministry (Luke 3:23); there were "about five thousand men" present at the feeding in the desert near Bethsaida (Luke 9:14); the number present at the election of Matthias to the circle of Twelve was "about one hundred twenty persons" (Acts 1:15); the number of converts baptized on the day of Pentecost was "about three thousand" (Acts 2:41); the number of John's disciples encountered by Paul in Acts "altogether . . . were about twelve" (Acts 19:7).[19]

Similarly, Luke rarely indicates the exact duration of an illness in a healing story. Often the length of illness is simply omitted. Consider, inter alia, from the Third Gospel and Acts: the man with the unclean spirit (Luke 4:31–37); Peter's mother-in-law (Luke 4:38–39); the man with leprosy (Luke 5:12–14); the paralytic (Luke 5:17–26); the man with the withered hand (Luke 6:6–11); the centurion's servant (Luke 7:1–10); the son of the widow of Nain (Luke 7:11–17); the boy with the convulsing

---

17. See the comments on this story in chapter 1.

18. The symbolic use of the number seven may be distinctive to Luke, especially in its titular use (see 21:8), but it was certainly not unique; see Mark 8:20; also Werner Kelber, *Mark's Story of Jesus* (Philadelphia: Fortress, 1979), 39.

19. I conclude that when approximate numbers are given, the burden of proof falls on those who would argue for a symbolic value to those numbers. However, given Luke's preference for approximations, precise numbers may be significant. For example, the specific number of those on the ship wrecked on the shoals of Malta, two-hundred and seventy-six, is striking and invites further consideration.

demon (Luke 9:37–42); the man with dropsy (Luke 14:1–6); Dorcas (Acts 9:36–41); the father of Publius (Acts 28:8). Occasionally the time is mentioned but left vague: the demon-possessed man of the Gadarenes was afflicted "for a long time" (Luke 8:27). The lame man of Acts 3–4, lame from birth, was "more than forty years old" (4:22).[20] The lame man from Lystra "had been crippled from birth" (Acts 14:8). The exception to the case, the woman with the flow of blood "for twelve years" (Luke 8:43), may prove the rule, since the length of her illness corresponds to the age of the daughter of the synagogue ruler (Luke 8:41–42, 49–56) and may have symbolic significance.[21]

Thus for Luke to mention the specific duration of the bent woman's illness is unusual, and to mention it twice is unprecedented. A variety of explanations have been offered. Some commentators suggest that the number eighteen is a conventional expression for "a long time."[22] Others conjecture that the length of time underscores the seriousness of her condition.[23] A few commentators suggest that the number of those killed by the collapsing tower of Siloam influenced the use of the number in our text, thus creating a kind of catchword to hold the otherwise disparate stories together.[24]

It seems, however, that the exegetical tradition has not fully explored the potential meaning of the reference. First, we note that commentators fail to observe that the wording for the number eighteen changes from δεκαοκτώ in Luke 13:4, 11 to δέκα καὶ ὀκτώ in 13:16. What is striking here is that the formula of 13:16, δέκα καὶ ὀκτώ, is reminiscent of a passage in

20. Actually, this text may contain symbolic reference to the forty years of Israel's wanderings; cf. chapter 6 and F. Scott Spencer, *Acts* (Sheffield: Sheffield Academic Press, 1997), 52.

21. The same may be true for Aeneas, "bedridden for eight years" (Acts 9:33). According to François Bovon, "Names and Numbers in Early Christianity," *New Testament Studies* 47 (2001): 283; citing the *Sibylline Oracles*, "the numeral 8 had been accepted by Christians as the number of Resurrection (the first day of the week being the eighth day)." Given that Aeneas is "raised up" from his bed, the length of his illness may certainly evoke a "resurrection/resuscitation" motif.

22. So John Nolland, *Luke 9:21–18:34*, WBC 35B (Dallas, TX: Word, 1993), 724; see also J. D. M. Derrett, "Positive Perspectives on Two Lucan Miracles," *Downside Review* 104 (1986): 274, 284 n. 14; O. Stein, "The Numeral 18," *Poona Orientalist* 1 (1936): 1–37; 2 (1937): 164–65; Frederick W. Danker, *Jesus and the New Age: A Commentary on St. Luke's Gospel*, completely revised and expanded (Philadelphia: Fortress, 1988), 261, cites the use of eighteen years in Judg. 3:14, 10:8, as evidence that the number refers to a long period of oppression, but also notes (ibid.) that "*Test. Judah* 9:1 applies the term to a period of peace."

23. See Darrell L. Bock, *Luke*, InterVarsity Press New Testament Commentary Series (Downer's Grove, IL: InterVarsity, 1994), 241.

24. See, e.g., Danker, *Jesus and the New Age*, 261. Danker cites the use of twelve in 8:42–43 as another example of a numerical narrative link, though he fails to mention that this link is found also in Mark 5:25, 42; here Luke has brought the two references much closer together.

Barnabas, a late first- or second-century Christian text, where the author explains that in Genesis 14:14 the number 318 has hidden meaning.

> Learn fully then, children of love, concerning all things, for Abraham, who first circumcised, did so looking forward in the spirit to Jesus, and had received the doctrine of three letters. For it says, "And Abraham circumcised from his household eighteen men and three hundred." What then was the knowledge that was given to him? Notice that he first mentions the eighteen, and after a pause the three hundred. The Eighteen is I (iota = ten) and H (eta = 8)—you have Jesus—and because the cross was destined to have grace in the T (tau) he says "and three hundred." So he indicates Jesus in the two letters and the cross in the other. He knows this who placed the gift of his teaching in our hearts. No one has heard a more excellent lesson from me, but I know that you are worthy. (*Barn.* 9.7–9)

In the version of Genesis used by *Barnabas*, the number is written "eighteen and three hundred" and was abbreviated ιητ, with the letters standing for numbers.[25] The ι and η have numerical values of ten and eight. (The archaic letter digamma stood for six.) [26]

α	=	1	ϝ	=	6
β	=	2	ζ	=	7
γ	=	3	η	=	8
δ	=	4	θ	=	9
ε	=	5	ι	=	10

Letters for Numerals

So the ι and η stand for eighteen, as *Barnabas* says, and the τ stands for three hundred.[27] *Barnabas* then elucidates the hidden meaning: eighteen is

25. For a discussion of this and related issues, see Reider Hvalvik, "Barnabas 9.7–9 and the Author's Supposed Use of *Gematria*," *New Testament Studies* 33 (1987): 276–82.

26. See Bruce Metzger, *Manuscripts of the Greek Bible: An Introduction to Palaeography* (Oxford: Oxford University Press, 1981), 9.

27. It is significant that Chester Beatty Papyrus 4 to Genesis (c. 300 CE) gives the number 318 as "three hundred and eighteen." Of course, this still differs from Barnabas's text, which he claims has "eighteen and three hundred." The Yale Genesis Fragment, Papyrus Yale 1 (c. 90 CE) has a lacuna at just this point in Genesis 14:14, and it has been conjectured that there is just enough space there for the abbreviation for 318; see Bovon, "Names and Numbers in Early Christianity," 282 n.95. Bovon (ibid.) cites additional literature on the Yale Genesis Fragment and its possible relationship to Barnabas: C. Bradford Welles, "The Yale Genesis Fragment," *The Yale University Library Gazette* 39:1 (1964): 1–8; C. H. Roberts, "P.Yale 1 and the Early Christian Book," in *Essays in Honor of C. Bradford Welles*, ed. Alan E. Samuel (New Haven: American Society of Papyrologists, 1966), 25–28.

ten (ι) and eight (η), and thus ten and eight (Luke's precise use in 13:16) represents the *nomen sacrum* of Jesus, ͞ιη.

This interpretation is not an idiosyncrasy of *Barnabas*, for Clement of Alexandria also knows of the christological use of the number eighteen and, interestingly, ties this numerology into astronomy, which we know was closely related to the predictive physiognomy:[28]

> As then in astronomy we have Abraham as an instance, so also in arithmetic we have the same Abraham. "For, hearing that Lot was taken captive, and having numbered his own servants, born in his house, 318 (τιη), he defeats a very great number of the enemy. They say, then, that the character representing 300 is, as to shape, the type of the Lord's sign, and that the Iota and the Eta indicate the Savior's name; that it was indicated, accordingly, that Abraham's domestics were in salvation, who having fled to the Sign and the Name became lords of the captives, and of the very many unbelieving nations that followed them. (*Strom.* 9)[29]

Clearly eighteen had christological value among some early Christian writers, but did it have this symbolism for Luke? Given the prominence of the number in Jesus' exclamation and the fact that other early Christians (including Luke) were finding symbolic meaning in numbers,[30] Luke may well be implying that Christ himself is hidden in the reference to eighteen. In other words, read properly, the number eighteen, evidently widely known to have christological symbolism, would have given the reader a rhetorical marker that the woman's time of illness has reached its "fullness," inasmuch as the number itself points to Christ. In this sense, eighteen functions for Luke in much the same way that fourteen (the value of David's name in Hebrew) does for Matthew in his infancy narrative, which features three periods of fourteen generations.[31] For the initiated audience, the 3 × 14 plan points to the fullness of time for the epiphany of the Messiah. For the initiated audience the very fact that the woman's illness had lasted eighteen years points to its cessation. As David is written over the salvation history of the Jews for Matthew, so Christ is written over the time limit of this woman's illness.

---

28. On this point, see Barton, *Power and Knowledge*.

29. Bovon ("Names and Numbers in Early Christianity," 283) also cites *Sibylline Oracles*, 1.342, as providing indirect evidence for reading eighteen as the numerical value of Jesus' name.

30. On the symbolic use of seven in Mark 8:1–9, see above.

31. On the symbolism of Matthew's 3 × 14 pattern in the infancy narrative, see Raymond E. Brown, *The Birth of the Messiah* (Garden City, NY: Doubleday, 1977), 74–81.

As already noted, although eighteen occurs twice in the passage, the number is not written in the same way (δεκαοκτώ being replaced by δέκα καὶ ὀκτώ), even though translations tend to render both forms simply as "eighteen." The use of the expanded form "ten and eight" in Luke 13:16 would aurally draw the attention of the hearer to the component parts of the number eighteen—ten *and* eight. The use of the exclamatory ἰδού in 13:16 is also an aural marker used to draw attention to the importance of what follows (see, e.g., 9:30, 24:4, and Acts 1:10, where what follows is also a number, in this case the "two men" who are witnesses to the transfiguration, resurrection, and ascension). Give the presumed propensity to equate the number eighteen (or "ten and eight") with Jesus, an audience hearing Luke 13:16 could have identified the "ten and eight" years with Jesus.

We find interesting corroborating evidence for this interpretation in $\mathfrak{P}^{45}$, one of the earliest (third century) witnesses to the Third Gospel. Although it has a lacuna at Luke 13:4, it is extant for the whole story of the bent woman. At both 13:11 and 13:16, eighteen is written as ιη̅, with an overstroke to indicate the letters are serving as a number. In 13:14 the name of Jesus is written in the same way, ιη̅, also with an overstroke, here to indicate the *nomen sacrum*. In the resultant visual phenomenon, the reader of $\mathfrak{P}^{45}$ would encounter the same abbreviation, ιη̅, for both "eighteen" and "Jesus," reinforcing the christological interpretation of the number eighteen in Jesus' response in 13:16.

An abbreviation like ιη̅, which uses the first two letters of the name, is called an abbreviation by suspension. Of the fifteen *nomina sacra* (sacred names abbreviated in early Christian writings: God, Holy Spirit, etc.), only the name Jesus uses the suspended form. Larry Hurtado plausibly argues that the suspended form of Jesus was actually the first of the *nomina sacra*. Thus the use of the overstroke to indicate a sacred name in Christian writings, which has long puzzled interpreters, is borrowed from the more widely practiced custom in secular Greek literature of using the overstroke on letters that stand for numbers (as here, with eighteen written ιη̅).[32]

Hurtado suggests that the association of eighteen with Jesus may extend back into the oral tradition when these stories were circulating in Hebrew and was originally intended to link Jesus with "life," since the numerical value of the Hebrew letters for life (חי) is eighteen:

---

32. See Larry W. Hurtado, "The Origin of the Nomina Sacra: A Proposal," *Journal of Biblical Literature* 117 (1998): 657, for a list of the fifteen *nomina sacra*.

I wonder if the repeated "18" in the two stories in Lk 13 explains in part why the two stories are connected by the Evangelist; and I wonder also whether the Evangelist or (perhaps more plausibly) earlier stages of the tradition saw the numbers as playing on/off the numerical significance of "life" and "Jesus" as life-giver. So, we have a group of "18" (a number connected with life) who undergo a tragic death; and we have a woman victimized for 18 years by Satan (again a number that is supposed to be associated with life, but here a period measured by captivity and torment), this woman was then released by "Jesus" the "life-giving Lord."[33]

It is tantalizing to suggest that the suspended form of Jesus' name in Greek began with Luke, but that is beyond verifiability. In any case, the use of the suspended *nomen sacrum* in $\mathfrak{P}^{45}$ stands in continuity with Luke in attaching symbolic value to the number eighteen.[34]

In his essay, "Names and Numbers in Early Christianity," François Bovon claims, "The early Christians used the categories of 'name' and 'number' as theological tools. Often they consciously interpreted names and numbers in a symbolic way."[35] The symbolic, specifically christological, function of the number "eighteen" in the story of the bent woman (Luke 13:10–17) corroborates Bovon's findings.[36]

The length of the bent woman's illness, "eighteen years," is the sacred name of Jesus himself. Despite the nature and length of her illness (or perhaps because of it), this woman is revealed by Jesus to be a daughter of Abraham, and one who, despite the nature of her illness, was a "woman of courage." Thus she takes her rightful place within the family of God.

---

33. In email correspondence dated November 12, 2002, quoted by permission of the author.

34. By about the fifth century the suspended form of Jesus' name fell out of use, though echoes of its significance may still be heard in the Lukan formula of δέκα καὶ ὀκτώ in Luke 13:16. According to Colin H. Roberts, *Manuscript, Society and Belief in Early Christian Egypt* (London: Oxford University Press, 1979), 36, forty-five occurrences of the suspended form of Jesus' name ($\overline{\text{ιη}}$) have been identified in seven Christian papyri.

35. Bovon, "Names and Numbers in Early Christianity," 267.

36. Despite Bovon's wide-ranging survey of the evidence, including evidence for the symbolic meaning of the number eighteen in early Christian circles, he does not explore Luke 13:10–17 in this light.

5

SHORT IN STATURE, SON OF ABRAHAM

The Height of Hospitality in the Story of Zacchaeus

The story of Zacchaeus is one of the best-known and best-loved biblical narratives. Many of us learned the story as children, and the little ditty that accompanied it: "Zacchaeus was a wee little man . . ." The children's song derives, of course, from Luke 19:3, where Zacchaeus is described as "small in stature" (ἡλικίᾳ μικρός).[1] This physical description is the third of three characteristics mentioned by the narrator: we are also told Zacchaeus's occupation (chief tax collector) and his socioeconomic status (he is rich). Both of these social locators, of course, are commonplace; we will return to them later in the chapter.

1. J. Rendel Harris, "On the Stature of Our Lord," *Bulletin of the John Rylands Library* 10 (1926): 112–26, explores the various traditions that Jesus himself was short in statue. He begins with an eighth-century anti-Nestorian manuscript, which refers to the "stature" of Christ as being smaller than that of the children of Jacob, and in turn takes up statements by Origen (*Cels.* 7.75), the *Acts of John*, the *Acts of Thomas*, and Ephrem the Syrian (*Hymni de ecclesia et virginibus*). In this light he considers whether the phrase "he was small in stature" might refer to Jesus rather than Zacchaeus, but concludes that this interpretation is "doubtful" (p. 123). Given that Zacchaeus is the subject of all the other verbs in this sentence and the fact that, if it were Jesus who was short, Zacchaeus would not be the only one having difficulty getting a glimpse of Jesus, it is best to understand the small stature to refer to Zacchaeus, not Jesus. Nonetheless, the noncanonical Christian texts discussed by Harris are fascinating.

Most commentators ignore or minimize the physical description of Zacchaeus. Joseph Fitzmyer, for example, argues that the reference is "a mere physical description of the man. We are not to conclude from the episode that Zacchaeus finds real 'stature' through the welcome extended him by Jesus. The Greek ἡλικία nowhere bears the connotation that the English word has in that understanding."[2] John Nolland, on the contrary, makes a passing reference to Zacchaeus's "'littleness' in the eyes of others" as "more than physical."[3]

Neither solution is particularly satisfying. As we shall see, contra Fitzmyer, it is μικρός and not ἡλικία that holds the potential clue to the phrase's meaning, while Nolland's intuition is, without some substantiation from Luke's larger literary environment, nothing more than a modern gloss.

"Short in Stature" and the Physiognomic Consciousness

So why mention that Zacchaeus is "short in stature"? The simplest explanation is that the reference to his physical stature is necessary to explain his subsequent action of running ahead of the crowd and climbing a tree to see Jesus. It is also true that in Luke the crowds often serve as an obstacle to be overcome by one seeking an audience with Jesus. One need only think of the story of the paralytic (Luke 5:17–26), or of the blind man (18:35–43), which immediately precedes this pericope. But there seems to be more involved here.

In the physiognomic way of thinking, shortness per se was not necessarily bad (provided the person were well proportioned), but neither was it a virtue. Short persons whom an author portrays positively are almost invariably also described as "well proportioned." Recall the description of Paul in *The Acts of Paul and Thecla*:

> [Paul] a man *small of stature*, with a bald head and crooked legs, *in a good state of body*; with eyebrows meeting and nose somewhat hooked, full of friendliness; for now he appeared like a man, and now he had the face of an angel. (*Acts Paul Thec.* 3; my emphasis)

Or consider Suetonius's description of Augustus:

2. Joseph A. Fitzmyer, *The Gospel according to Luke*, vol. 2, *Luke X–XXIV*, AB 28A (Garden City, NY: Doubleday, 1985), 1223.
3. John Nolland, *Luke 18:35–24:53*, WBC 35C (Dallas, TX: Word, 1993), 905.

His teeth were wide apart, small, and ill kept; his hair was slightly curly and inclined to golden; his eyebrows met. His ears were of moderate size, and his nose projected a little at the top and then bent slightly forward. His complexion was between dark and fair. *He was short of stature, but this was concealed by the fine proportion and symmetry of his figure, and was noticeable only by comparison with some taller person standing beside him.* (*Aug.* 79; emphasis added)

Unfortunately for Zacchaeus, there is no qualifier stating that Zacchaeus's well-proportioned physique compensated for his lack of height.

Smallness in physical stature was generally seen in physiognomic terms as reflecting "smallness in spirit" (μικροψυχία). Pseudo-Aristotle claimed, "These are the marks of a small-minded person. He is small-limbed, small and round, dry, with small eyes and a small face, like a Corinthian or Leucadian" (808a30). Conversely, "greatness of soul" was associated with great physical stature (cf. Aristotle, *Eth. Nic.* 4.3.1123b7; 4.8.1128a8–13).

But what does "smallness in spirit" suggest? The term has several possible nuances, each one suggestive in relation to Zacchaeus. According to Aristotle, "he that rates himself too high is vain but he that rates himself too low is small-spirited" (*Eth. Eud.* 1233a16–20). Others saw small mindedness as a form of greediness. For Chrysostom, "small-mindedness" was related to "pettiness" (*Comm. Gal.* 1.3; *Hom. Matt.* 10.1) or "greediness" (*Hom. Rom.* 18.7). Both low self-expectations and greediness can be seen in our story. In the profession of tax collector, Zacchaeus's low expectations could live happily with his greediness. In first-century Judea, tax collectors were puppets of the Roman government and were viewed as traitors by countrymen. They might or might not be snitches or moles, but this much did not change: they made their living by overcharging taxpayers and keeping the overage for themselves. Zacchaeus had done quite well. He had risen to middle management in the tax system, becoming a chief tax collector.

"Zacchaeus" may be a diminutive form of the name Zechariah (meaning "pure" or "innocent"), thus increasing the irony of the story.[4] Zacchaeus had been conditioned to have low expectations of himself, and Zacchaeus, the short man, "sells himself short" in terms of living up to his name. Zacchaeus grew up and took the only job open to someone like himself, an occupation that was far from pure and innocent.

4. See I. Howard Marshall, *The Gospel of Luke: A Commentary on the Greek Text* (Exeter: Paternoster, 1978), 696.

Even if these connotations are lost on the modern reader, the ancient audience, living in a world in which the physiognomic consciousness prevailed, would naturally interpret Zacchaeus's small stature as reflecting a small-spiritedness that accounts for both his occupation (he has "rated himself too low") and his greed. Cyril of Alexandria observes, "He [Zacchaeus] was little of stature, not merely in a bodily point of view, but also spiritually."[5]

"Short in Stature" and the Rhetoric of Ridicule

The citing of physical features in both encomia and invectives pervaded ancient rhetoric.[6] Small physique was a preferred target in the Greco-Roman world. Athenaeus reported that the poet Philetas of Cos was so small and thin that "he had to wear on his feet balls made of lead to keep him from being upset by the wind!" (Athenaeus, *Deipn.* 12.552b). The poet Lucillius wrote, "Short Hermogenes, whenever he drops anything on the ground, pulls it down with a spear" (i.e., he's so short that he can't even reach objects at ground level; *Anth. Gr.* 11.89). In a treatise attributed to Plutarch we read the following story about the Spartans:

> It is very proper also to bestow a word of praise on the Spartans for the noble spirit they showed in fining their king, Archidamus, because he had permitted himself to take to wife a woman short of stature, the reason they gave being that he proposed to supply them not with kings but with kinglets. (*Lib. ed.* 1D)

Cicero devotes an entire section in his rhetorical handbook on how the rhetor may use physical deformity to get a laugh from his audience. Sometimes the joke would backfire, as Cicero observed in the following story:

> A very small witness once came forward. "May I examine him?" said Philippus. The president of the Court, who was in a hurry, answered, "Only if you are short." "You will not complain," returned Philippus, "for I shall be just as short as that man is." Quite comical; but there on the tribunal sat Lucius Aurifex, and he was even tinier than the witness; all the laughter was directed against Lucius, and the joke seemed merely buffoonish. (Cicero, *De or.* 2.60.245)

5. Saint Cyril of Alexandria, *Commentary on the Gospel of Saint Luke*, trans. R. Payne Smith (n.p.: Studion Publishers, Inc., 1983), Homily 127 (pp. 505–6).
6. Barton, *Power and Knowledge*.

Note that Cicero did not discourage jesting based on physical appearance, but simply argued for a certain restraint: "In ugliness too and in physical blemishes there is good enough matter for jesting, but here as elsewhere the limits of license are the main question" (*De or.* 2.58.239). Rarely did such restraint deter the onslaught of "short jokes."

The widespread rhetorical practice of appealing to physical characteristics, including shortness, in invectives, along with physiognomy's negative assessment of shortness, suggest that the figure of Zacchaeus would have been viewed as laughable, even despicable. For Luke's audience the reference to Zacchaeus's shortness would have suggested, at the least, another tasteless joke deriding the deformed.

Zacchaeus and Pathological Dwarfism

At the end of his account of John the Baptist's birth, Luke tells us that John "grew and became strong in spirit" (Luke 1:80). Likewise at the end of the infancy account of Jesus, we hear that Jesus "increased in wisdom and in years [lit. "in stature"], and in divine and human favor" (2:52). But Zacchaeus did not grow in stature, did not become strong in spirit, and certainly did not increase in human favor.

The comment by the townspeople of Jericho that Jesus had "gone to be the guest of one who is a sinner" (Luke 19:7) may also reflect the ancients' understanding of congenital deformity as divine judgment. Zacchaeus is regarded as a sinner not only because he cheated people in his role as chief tax collector, as most commentators observe, but possibly also because of his physical imperfection, taken as a mark of divine displeasure. The association of congenital birth defects and even infant mortality with sinfulness is attested in the writings of Jews (2 Sam. 12:15b–23; *Ruth Rab.* 6.4), Christians (John 9:2), and Greeks (Hesiod, *Op.* 1.235; Herodotus 1.105; 4.67). Some illuminating imprecations have been found inscribed on Greek tomb monuments from the Roman Imperial period, which threaten potential tomb-robbers with the punishment that their wives will give birth "not in accordance with Nature."[7]

Luke's authorial audience would naturally have heard a double entendre in the crowd's pronouncement of Zacchaeus's sinfulness: he was born a sinner (as divine punishment) and he lived as a sinner (by cheating his fellow countryfolk out of their money). Unlike blindness or lameness,

---

7. *SEG* XVIII.561.7.

leprosy or dropsy, it appeared that shortness was an irreversible punishment. After all, the Lukan Jesus himself had mused, "Can any of you by worrying add a cubit to his stature?" (Luke 12:25, NRSV alternative reading).

Certain markers in the text, however, suggest an even more troubling reading of this story. Robert Garland describes the Roman Empire as a world obsessed with the "monstrous."[8] Physically deformed slaves would sometimes sell for three times what an able-bodied slave would bring. According to Pliny the Elder, human anomalies were put on display or paraded before the public (*Hist. nat.* 7.34). Emperors Nero and Domitian were reputed to have collected the physically malformed like trophies, and according to Pliny, Pompey the Great built the first theater to house such human anomalies. Suetonius reports that Augustus put on exhibition a young man named Lycius "because he was under two feet tall, weighed seventeen pounds, and possessed a very loud voice" (*Aug.* 43.3). Augustus also purchased a dwarf as a "pet" for his niece. In this world Luke lived and wrote. In this world was the story of Zacchaeus heard.

Of course, we cannot know exactly how short Zacchaeus is supposed to have been. We are told that he was unable to see over the crowd, which would lead the audience to suppose that he was well below the average height. Both lexical and contextual evidence suggest that at least some in Luke's audience would have viewed Zacchaeus's shortness as so extreme as to be pathological. Lexically, the Greeks had specific terms for extreme pathological dwarfism: πυγμή (first used in Homer, *Il.* 3.3), often used regarding ethnographic groups living at the edges of the known world, and νάνος (a form of which is first found in Aristophanes, *Pax* 790), often used to refer to dwarfism. The word used to describe Zacchaeus in Luke 19, μικρός, and its variant σμικρός, were also used of pathological dwarfism in texts from the fourth century BCE to the ninth century CE (Aristotle, *Hist. an.* 8.12.597; Photius, *Lex.* 72.46a, writing in the ninth century CE but quoting an earlier source). Since νάνος was the preferred term for pathological shortness in antiquity, at least in the extant sources, we cannot say with any certainty that the term μικρός in and of itself would have suggested that Zacchaeus was pathologically short. Nor can we eliminate this possibility on lexical grounds, since only here in

8. Garland, *Eye of the Beholder*, 48–49.

the New Testament does μικρός refer to a person's height.[9] Luke uses the term figuratively to refer to social standing "from the least to the greatest" in reference to the crowds in Acts 8:10 and 26:22 (cf. also Luke 7:28; 9:48). In general he avoids giving it the positive connotation found in Matthew, where it appears to refer to new Christians (Matt. 10:42; 18:6, 10, 14).[10]

When we turn to the contextual evidence, the case for reading μικρός as "pathologically short" gains momentum. Three details of the text take on added meaning. First, there is the reference to Zacchaeus "running" ahead of the crowd (Luke 19:3), a detail often interpreted as suggesting Zacchaeus's "shamelessness" in running, much like the father who runs out to meet the returning prodigal son (15:20).[11] Here the material remains of Greco-Roman civilization shed light on the way a first-century audience might have heard this text. Given that the Greeks idealized the symmetry and proportion of the human body (as did the Romans, despite their fascination with the grotesque), it is extraordinary to find a large number of Greek Archaic, Classical, and Hellenistic visual representations of pathological dwarfs. Even after eliminating vases in which a small figure could represent a child or may simply have been drawn small to fit available space, the image of the dwarf occurs so frequently as to constitute an iconographic convention. In Pompeii alone, hundreds of these figures were found on pottery, in painting, and as small sculptures.

A special favorite depiction in sculpture and on vases is the "dancing dwarf."[12] Literary evidence suggests that dwarfs were especially sought after as dancers at parties and symposia because their ungainly and awkward movements were regarded as comical. Lucian gives a vivid account of a clown named Satyrion, a "small, ugly fellow" who "danced by bending himself up double and twisting about so as to appear more ridiculous" (*Symp.* 18). Thus the literary image of Zacchaeus running ahead of the crowd, far from being a reference to oriental "shamelessness," suggests a cruel and ribald mockery.

9. So BDAG, p. 651, unless one reads James "the younger" (μικρός) as a reference to physical stature (ibid.).

10. The sole exception is Luke 17:2, which parallels Matt. 18:6.

11. Kenneth E. Bailey, *Poet and Peasant* (Grand Rapids: Eerdmans, 1976), 181–82; against this view, see Ronald Hock, "Romancing the Parables," *Perspectives in Religious Studies* 29 (2002): 17–25.

12. See plates 6, 8, and 9 in Garland, *Eye of the Beholder*, and also the images collected in Véronique Dasen, *Dwarfs in Ancient Egypt and Greece* (Oxford: Clarendon, 1993).

The crowd's reference to Zacchaeus as a "sinner" may also have been heard by Luke's audience as suggesting that Zacchaeus was not only socially alienated, but religiously ostracized as well. Leviticus states, "No one of your offspring throughout their generations who has a blemish may approach to offer the food of his God. For no one who has a blemish shall draw near, one who is blind or . . . a hunchback, or a dwarf, or a man with a blemish in his eyes or an itching disease or scabs or crushed testicles" (21:17, 20). The authorial audience would naturally have inferred that Zacchaeus was prohibited from full participation in the traditional temple cult because of his physical deformity. Admittedly the Hebrew text of Leviticus is very difficult at this point, but it is noteworthy that Codex Alexandrinus translates the very ambiguous Hebrew word *daq* ("thin") with the unambiguous νάνος ("dwarf").

Finally, our inquiry into the prejudice against pathological shortness in antiquity may also shed light on the note that Zacchaeus climbed a tree in order to see Jesus. A popular myth dating from Homer's time concerned two brothers, the Cercopes, who were highwaymen and thieves (see Diodorus Siculus, *Bibl. hist.* 4.31.7; Apollodorus, *Bibl.* 2.6.3; Ovid, *Metam.* 14.88; ps.-Nonnus, *Comm. Greg.* 4.39.7–21). They attempted to steal Heracles' weapons while he slept. He awakened, caught the thieves, and hung them on a stick like animals, upside down, facing one another. Their name, Cercopes, was synonymous with robbers and cheats (Aeschines, *Fals. leg.* 2.40; Plutarch, *Mor.* 60C). Ovid reports that Jupiter was so exasperated with the Cercopes that he transformed them into apes (*Metam.* 14.90–100; cf. Diodorus Siculus, *Bibl. hist.* 3.35.5).

A significant number of art works represent the Cercopes thus. The favorite scene depicts the two brothers naked and suspended upside down from either end of a stick carried by Heracles. In visual depictions from the Archaic to the Hellenistic periods and from Athens to South Italy, the brothers are very short and sometimes, anticipating or echoing Ovid, have apelike facial features. This story and its visual representations were widespread in the ancient world. An audience familiar with this story could well have associated the image of Zacchaeus—the short, tax-collecting, thief, scurrying apelike up and down a sycamore tree—with the Cercopes. Admittedly this myth may be only distantly related to Luke's story, but it adds to the cumulative effect of the evidence that Zacchaeus would have been seen as a pathological and ludicrous figure.

The Conversion of Zacchaeus

What was the rhetorical effect on the reader? First, Luke's audience would have heard the reference to Zacchaeus's small stature as something derogatory and demeaning. Consequently it is unnecessary to argue, as Joel Green does, that the reference here is to Zacchaeus's relative youth, youthfulness being (according to Green) the only way to account for the disdain of the crowd. In light of the pervasive physiognomic consciousness, one may retain the more natural reading of Zacchaeus being unable to see Jesus because of his diminutive physical stature and still recognize Green's point that the crowd was an obstacle to Zacchaeus "on account of their negative assessment" of him.[13]

This unflattering characterization joins with the other two descriptors of Zacchaeus—occupation and socioeconomic status—to paint a thoroughly negative picture. Zacchaeus holds the position of tax collector in Jericho, a much despised occupation in Judea (cf. *m. Tehar.* 7:6: "If tax-gatherers enter a house, the house becomes unclean"), and indeed throughout the Roman Empire (cf. Plutarch, *Mor.* 518E; Josephus, *Bell.* 7.218; see also Dio Cassius 65.7.2).

The internal evidence of Luke's Gospel confirms the negative characterization of the position of tax collector found in other first-century witnesses. Luke has shaped this characterization to serve his own purposes. In the story of Levi (Luke 5:27–32), the Pharisees ask of Jesus' disciples, "Why do you eat and drink with tax collectors and sinners?" (5:30; cf. 7:34; 15:1; 18:11).[14] Repeatedly Luke uses tax collectors, coupled with the generic category of "sinners," "as a religious metaphor for those who display the proper spirit of contrition and repentance."[15]

The epithet "rich" would also have been heard negatively, a point confirmed by the other occurrences of this term in Luke. Jesus includes the rich in the list of "woes" of the Sermon on the Plain: "Woe to you who are rich, for you have received your consolation" (6:24; cf. 12:16–21; 14:12; 16:1–13; 18:25; 21:1–4). Within the context of the Gospel, then, Zacchaeus's wealth

---

13. Joel B. Green, *The Gospel of Luke*, NICNT (Grand Rapids: Eerdmans, 1997), 670. Green is right to question whether the term here means "stature," since the other occurrences of the term in Luke are ambiguous and may refer either to age or physicality (Luke 2:52; 12:25).

14. See John R. Donahue, "Tax Collectors and Sinners: An Attempt at Identification," *Catholic Biblical Quarterly* 33 (1971): 39–61.

15. David A. Neale, *None but the Sinners: Religious Categories in the Gospel of Luke*, JSNTSup 58 (Sheffield: Sheffield Academic Press, 1991), 177. See Luke 5:30; 7:34; 15:1; 18:11.

would have been heard as a negative quality, one that he most likely gained at the expense of others and that served as an impediment to his salvation.[16]

This three-pronged negative characterization solves the ongoing debate as to whether the words of Zacchaeus are spoken as self-defense or as the consequence of a transforming experience: "Look, half of my possessions, Lord, I will give to the poor; and if I have defrauded anyone of anything, I will pay back four times as much" (Luke 19:8). Some take the verbs as customary present ("I always give to the poor"; "I always pay back") and argue that Zacchaeus is defending himself against the false accusations of the crowd ("He has gone to be the guest of one who is a sinner"). The traditional view takes the verb as iterative as does the NRSV: "I will give to the poor." Zacchaeus's statement is thus a resolve for the future and indicative of his moral transformation (i.e., "I will *begin* to give to the poor"). The rhetorical effect of Zacchaeus's negative characterization confirms the traditional view: Luke's audience would have heard the story of Zacchaeus as a conversion narrative.[17]

The Healing of Zacchaeus and the Townsfolk of Jericho

This is a healing story no less marvelous than any of the healings recorded in the Gospels. To be sure, when Zacchaeus walked out of his house the next day he was not a bit taller than he was when he entered it (cf. Luke 12:25), but the healing was no less real for being spiritual. In fact, one could easily imagine Zacchaeus's neighbors saying that, like the Grinch, his heart "grew three sizes" that day.

Drawing on the cultural context of the first century we can tease out another implication of this text. Jesus announces, "Today salvation has come to this house." "Salvation" has come to this house in the very person of Jesus. And that salvation has come for the "whole" house, everyone gathered in it (and around it), not just Zacchaeus. Though Luke does not tell us, when Jesus brought salvation to Zacchaeus's house one can envision that the walls of prejudice and bias of some of those living in

---

16. See Luke Timothy Johnson, *The Literary Function of Possessions in Luke-Acts*, SBLDS 39 (Missoula, MT: Scholars Press, 1977).

17. On this question see the recent exchange between Dennis Hamm and Alan Mitchell and the literature cited therein: Dennis Hamm, "Luke 19,8 Once Again: Does Zacchaeus Defend or Resolve?" *Journal of Biblical Literature* 107 (1988) 431–37; Alan Mitchell, "Zacchaeus Revisited: Luke 19, 8 as a Defense," *Biblica* 71 (1990) 153–76; Dennis Hamm, "Zacchaeus Revisited Once More: A Story of Vindication or Conversion?" *Biblica* 72 (1991) 249–52. See also, Fitzmyer, *The Gospel according to Luke*, 1220–21.

Jericho came tumbling down and that they recognized Zacchaeus for what he was, a true "child of Abraham"—and their conversion was no less real than that of Zacchaeus.

Conclusion

Luke has spared no insulting image to portray Zacchaeus as a pathetic, even despicable character. He paints a derisive and mocking picture of a traitorous, small-minded, greedy, physically deformed tax collector sprinting awkwardly ahead of the crowd and climbing a sycamore tree like an ape. But Luke exploits these conventional tropes only for the purpose of reversing them in the conclusion of the story. When Jesus announces that "today salvation has come to this house, because he too is a son of Abraham," the stranglehold of physiognomic determinacy is broken, and the ridicule is turned against itself. Just because Zacchaeus is small in stature does not mean he must be small in spirit. The fact that he is pathologically short does not mean that he is to be excluded from the family of God.

Luke's point is clear. Jesus did not dine with Zacchaeus to highlight his small stature. He ate with him to change his life and the lives of those around him. The virtue extolled here is not tolerance[18] but hospitality. In ancient hospitality the host extends certain benefits to the stranger, the ξένος. In an ironic twist it is Jesus, the guest, who extends hospitality to Zacchaeus, the stranger in his own town, in his own home.

Jesus comes along, spies Zacchaeus in the tree, and tells him that he is going to dine at his house. In so doing, the Lukan Jesus challenges the predominant prejudice of his day that predetermines one's place in the body politic by the shape of one's body. Jesus saw in Zacchaeus what others could not see: here was a son of Abraham. The Lukan Jesus would have found scriptural warrant to challenge these existing norms in his Jewish Bible: "The LORD does not see as mortals see; they look on the outward appearance, but the LORD looks on the heart" (1 Sam. 16:7). During the course of the meal, responding to the dignity and grace that Jesus has bestowed on him, Zacchaeus resolves, "Look, half of my possessions, Lord, I will give to the poor; and if I have defrauded anyone of anything, I will pay back four times as much" (Luke 19:8). Given the

18. See A. J. Conyers, *The Long Truce: How Toleration Made the World Safe for Power and Profit* (Dallas: Spence, 2001).

transformation Zacchaeus has just experienced, this is what the tax collector *must* do. Recall the tax collectors who came to John the Baptist for baptism and asked, "What should we do?" John the Baptist replied, "Do not extort money from anyone by threats or false accusation, and be satisfied with your wages" (Luke 3:13). Zacchaeus has resolved to do that and more.

In the Roman world of the first century, physical deformity was a fact of life, as was its public ridicule. Zacchaeus's occupation, his greed, and his physical stature combine to convince Luke's audience that this man is a sinner indeed. The story of Zacchaeus, read in light of Luke's critique of the physiognomic consciousness, the rhetoric of ridicule, and the plight of pathological dwarfs, serves to continue a familiar Lukan theme of concern for the outcast. The ancient audience would have presumed that Zacchaeus's physical deformity caused him to be socially marginalized in his society.

But not all accepted the conventions of the day: Luke turns the tables. This story, a cycle of salvation from ridicule to repentance, reminds the audience that "the Son of Man came to seek out and save the lost" (Luke 19:10). In the Third Gospel, God has taken two "stones," one badly misshapen and the other undersized, and raised from them a son and daughter of Abraham. The stage is set now to continue the story of the ingathering of this new Abrahamic family in the stories of the lame man and the Ethiopian eunuch in the Acts of the Apostles.

6

HIS FEET AND ANKLES
WERE MADE STRONG

Signs of Character
in the Man Lame from Birth

One important purpose of the healing of the lame man in Acts 3–4 is to show that the physical disability of being lame, however much it was despised in antiquity, does not disqualify one from membership in the eschatological community of the Way.[1] Whatever the historical value of the episode, as it now stands the story of the lame man joins the other examples from the Gospel of Luke (the bent woman and Zac-

1. The periodical literature, especially that focusing on the healing itself and not the accompanying speeches, is not nearly as dense as one might expect; see e.g., Paul Walaskay, "Acts 3:1–10," *Interpretation* 42 (1988): 171–75; Danielle Ellul, "Actes 3:1–11," *Etudes théologiques et religieuses* 64 (1989): 95–99. See also Gilberto Marconi, "History as a Hermeneutical Interpretation of the Difference between Acts 3:1–10 and 4:8–12," in *Luke and Acts*, ed. Gerald O'Collins and Gilberto Marconi (New York: Paulist, 1992), 167–80, 252–57. Nevertheless, I should mention the work of Dennis Hamm; although he does not explore physiognomy in any way, he argues for the symbolic and paradigmatic value of the lame man's story for Luke's theology. In that sense, his work stands close to what I am attempting to do: M. Dennis Hamm, S. J., "This Sign of Healing: Acts 3:1–10: A Study in Lucan Theology," (Ph.D. dissertation, St. Louis University, 1975); idem., "Acts 3:12–26: Peter's Speech and the Healing of the Man Born Lame," *Perspectives in Religious Studies* 11 (1984): 199–217; idem., "Acts 3:1–10: The Healing of the Temple Beggar as Lucan Theology," *Biblica* 67 (1986): 305–19.

chaeus) to undermine the assumption that physical appearance reflects moral character.[2]

Ankles, Feet, and Ancient Physiognomy

Note the structure of Acts 3:1–4:31 and its placement in the narrative of Acts. This is a well-defined narrative segment: Narrative summaries on either side of our text (2:41–47 and 4:32–35) make the section "readily isolated from what precedes and what follows."[3] Furthermore this narrative segment is comprised of four scenes (3:1–10, 3:11–4:4, 4:5–22, 4:23–31) demarcated by temporal and spatial shifts.[4] The temporal shift from day 1 to day 2, effected by a "nocturnal pause" between 4:4 and 5, links scenes 1–2 and 3–4 closely to each other. The theme of healing is found in every scene, either with specific reference to the lame man (3:2, 16; 4:9–10, 22) or to healing in general (4:30).[5] The healing of a lame man also has parallels in the ministries of Jesus (Luke 5:17–26) and Paul (Acts 14:8–18).

With this description of the literary contours of our narrative, we begin our physiognomic analysis. In many ways, the key text is Acts 3:7b, where the narrator, in recounting the healing, notes that "immediately his feet and ankles were made strong." This verse was a favorite among those who advanced the thesis that Luke's so-called medical vocabulary proved that the author was a physician. W. K. Hobart was probably not the first to comment on this verse, but he surely made more of it than most. About βάσις ("feet") he commented that the word was employed to "show that the writer was acquainted with medical phraseology, and

2. On questions of historicity of this story, see Gerd Luedemann, whose skepticism toward miracles still dominates modern New Testament scholarship: "There is no historical nucleus to the tradition of the miracle story in vv. 1–10. Those who are lame from their childhood are (unfortunately) not made whole again" (*Early Christianity according to the Tradition in Acts: A Commentary* [Minneapolis: Fortress, 1989], 54). For a defense of the historicity of miracles in Acts generally, see Colin Hemer, *The Book of Acts in the Setting of Hellenistic History* (Tübingen: Mohr Siebeck, 1989), 439–43. On the question of miracles in Acts, see the balanced presentation by Charles Talbert in *Reading Acts: A Literary and Theological Commentary on the Acts of the Apostles* (New York: Crossroad, 1997), 251–53.

3. Robert W. Funk, *The Poetics of Biblical Narrative* (Sonoma, CA: Polebridge, 1988), 83. See also Mikeal Parsons, "Acts," in *Acts and Pauline Writings*, ed. Watson Mills, et al., Mercer Commentary on the Bible 7 (Macon, GA: Mercer University Press, 1997), 9.

4. For a slightly different proposal of the structure of Acts 3–4, see Talbert, *Reading Acts*, 51–52. It is unusual to have such a long connected segment, since New Testament narratives are noted for their episodic nature; see Stephen Moore, "Are the Gospels Unified Narratives?" in *Society of Biblical Literature Seminar Papers* 26, ed. Kent Harold Richards (Chico, CA: Scholars Press, 1987), 443–58.

5. Parsons, "Acts," 9.

had investigated the nature of the disease under which the man suffered." In typical fashion, he cites Galen and others in support of this claim. Furthermore he claims that σφυδρά ("ankles") is "the technical term for the ankles, thus defined by Galen."[6] Adolf Harnack, in his attempt to refine Hobart's thesis by eliminating the less convincing examples, omits reference to feet but claims that "σφυδρόν is a very rare word . . . ; it is the Term. Tech. for the condyles of the leg-bones," again citing Galen.[7]

By showing the widespread use of vocabulary in Hellenistic writings that were labeled as uniquely or distinctly medical terminology by Hobart and Harnack, Henry Cadbury, in his Harvard dissertation, dismantled the thesis that such terminology proves that the author of Luke/Acts was a physician.[8] Cadbury's graduate students used to jest that Cadbury had earned his doctorate by taking Luke's away from him.

Cadbury notes that the term βάσις occurs in Plato, Aristotle, Josephus, Philostratus, Aelius, the Septuagint, and Apollodorus.[9] A search of the Thesaurus Linguae Graecae database for this term produced more than 1,600(!) references, thus confirming Cadbury's point.[10]

The case of σφυδρόν, Cadbury recognized, was a bit more complicated, since he was able to find it only here and in the writings of Hesychius. Cadbury notes that, given the infrequency of σφυδρόν, Harnack emends

6. W. K. Hobart, *The Medical Language of St. Luke* (Dublin: Hodges, Figgis, 1882; repr., Grand Rapids: Baker, 1954), 35. Hobart built on the work of practicing physician and medical historian John Friend, who devoted one chapter of his 1750 *Historia medicinae* to the presence of medical knowledge in early Christian writings (see *Historia medicinae a Galeni tempore usque ad initium saeculi decimi sexti: In qua ea praecipue notantur quae ad praxim pertinent* [Leiden, 1750]). More recently, Annette Weissenrieder, *Images of Illness in the Gospel of Luke: Insights of Ancient Medical Texts*, WUNT 164 (Tübingen: Mohr Siebeck, 2003), has examined the way Luke constructs illness in his gospel and concludes, "[T]he author of Luke-Acts had a particular interest in images of illness and healing, which were plausible within the ancient medical context, and far exceed word analogies" (p. 365). On the issue of whether this knowledge can be traced to Luke's professional occupation, Weissenrieder compares Luke's interest and knowledge with that of Philo, and concludes "whether or not they [Luke and Philo] may therefore be considered ancient physicians remains uncertain" (p. 366).

7. Adolf Harnack, *Luke the Physician: The Author of the Third Gospel and the Acts of the Apostles*, trans. J. R. Wilkinson (New York: G. P. Putnam's Sons, 1907), 191.

8. Henry J. Cadbury, *The Style and Literary Method of Luke*, HTS 6 (Cambridge, MA: Harvard University Press, 1920). Unfortunately, subsequent Lukan scholarship has often gone beyond the cautious Cadbury to claim that Cadbury's work proved the corollary that Luke was not a physician. Cadbury resolutely refused to draw that conclusion on the grounds that it exceeded the evidence.

9. Cadbury, *Style and Literary Method*, 13.

10. Thanks to my graduate assistants, Chad Hartsock and Jason Whitlark, who performed these searches of the Thesaurus Linguae Graecae and other helpful tasks in preparing this manuscript for publication.

to the alternative spelling σφυρόν, which is also the reading of the Textus Receptus at Acts 3:7 and is "found also in LXX, Josephus, Plutarch, Lucian, and other non-medical writers."[11] In fact the term is hardly rare; a search of the Thesaurus Linguae Graecae yielded well more than one hundred references to σφυρόν.

In the wake of Cadbury's work commentators often fail to comment on these words[12] or limit themselves to the observation that "feet" and "ankles" are not medical terms.[13] Feet and ankles were, however, of considerable interest to the compilers of the physiognomic handbooks. About ankles, pseudo-Aristotle writes:

> Those who have strong and well-jointed ankles are brave in character; witness the male sex. Those that have fleshy and ill-jointed ankles are weak in character; witness the female sex. (810a25–29)

Adamantius, likewise, comments on the importance of ankles:

> Perfect, solid ankles belong to a noble man, those which are soft and smooth to a more unmanly man and those which are very thin to a cowardly and intemperate man. All those who have thick ankles, thick heels, fleshy feet, stubby toes and thick calves are for the most part stupid or mad. (7)[14]

The comments about feet (here the more familiar πόδες) are similar:

> Those who have well-made, large feet, well-jointed and sinewy, are strong in character; witness the male sex. Those who have small, narrow, poorly-jointed feet, are rather attractive to look at than strong, being weak in character; witness the female sex. Those whose toes of the feet are curved are shameless, just like creatures which have curved talons; witness birds with curved talons. (ps.-Aristotle 810a15–22)

In Polemo, we find another description:

11. Cadbury, *Style and Literary Method*, 56 n. 36.

12. So Joseph A. Fitzmyer, *The Acts of the Apostles*, AB 31 (New York: Doubleday, 1998).

13. See Ernst Haenchen, *The Acts of the Apostles*, trans. Bernard Noble and Gerald Shinn (Oxford: Blackwell's, 1971), 200. John Wilkinson, a medical missionary, suggests that the most probable diagnosis for the lame man in Acts 3–4 "is a severe degree of clubfoot or what is known medically as congenital talipes equino-varus"; *Health and Healing: Studies in New Testament Principles and Practice* (Edinburgh: Handsel, 1980), 88.

14. The translation is from Swain, *Seeing the Face*. Similarly, see also *Epitom. Matr.* 18; Polemo 51; ed. Foerster, 1:357.

If you see contracted, strong feet, and their tendons are straight and strong, and their joints are evenly proportioned, these are the signs of powerful and mighty men. If the feet are very fleshy and soft, they indicate weakness, softness, and laxity. (5.15–19)[15]

In a culture where the physiognomic consciousness pervaded, "well-made" ankles and feet are a sign of a "robust character";[16] conversely, the lame man's weak ankles would have been viewed as an outward physical sign of his inner weak moral character, his μαλακός, his "soft," "timid," "cowardly," or "effeminate" nature.[17] This weakness is confirmed by his passivity in the narrative: he "is carried"; he is "laid daily at the gate"; "Peter took him by the right hand" and "raised him up."[18]

The man's moral weakness is reinforced by Peter's reference in 4:9 to the lame man as an ἀνθρώπου ἀσθενοῦς (4:9), not the same lexeme as in pseudo-Aristotle, but certainly in the same semantic range. While ἀνθρώπου ἀσθενοῦς is usually translated "cripple" or "sick," it literally means "weak man."[19] Although the various forms of the ἀσθεν- stem often refer to a physical infirmity (cf. Luke 4:40; 5:15; 9:2; 10:9; Acts 5:15, 16; 9:37; 19:12; 28:9), the term can carry a moral or metaphorical sense, which Luke also knows.[20] In Paul's Ephesian farewell address, he claims, "In all this I have given you an example that by such work we must support the weak (ἀσθενούντων), remembering the words of the Lord Jesus, for he himself said, 'It is more blessed to give than to receive'" (Acts 20:35; cf. Luke 13:11). Here the weak do not necessarily seem to be limited to those with physical ailments. Thus Peter's description of the man here as "weak" may refer both to his former physical and moral state.

15. This translation of the Arabic version of Polemo found in the Leiden manuscript is from Swain, *Seeing the Face*. G. Hoffman's reconstructed Latin text (found in Foerster, *Scriptores*, 1.200) reads: "Si pedes adstrictos robustos et eorum nervos aequales et robustos atque articulos moderatos vides, ii virorum heroum strenuorum signa sunt. Si pedes valde carnosi molles sunt, infirmitatem mollitiem et languorem produnt."

16. On feet and ankles as a sign of strong moral character, see Sabine Vogt, *Physiognomonica*, Aristoteles Werke in deutscher Übersetzung 18.6 (Berlin: Akademie, 1999), 155–56.

17. See BDAG, 613, for definitions of and references to μαλακός.

18. As Funk notes (*Poetics of Biblical Narrative*, 64): "The lame man is the 'subject' of the mini-narrative. This does not mean that he is the agent of the principal action, but that the narrative is 'about' him."

19. RSV, NIV, "cripple"; NASB, "sick man"; NRSV, "someone who was sick."

20. See L&N, 88.117. Forms of the ἀσθεν- stem occur in ps.-Aristotle 807b8–9 in a description of the signs of a coward (δειλοῦ σημεῖα), "weak eyes" and a "weak thigh" (cf. also 810.b11, 27), but these references appear to refer to physical, not moral, weakness (though of course they are signs of the morally weak or cowardly).

The Lame Man and Ancient Perceptions of Disability

That the audience would have viewed the lame man negatively is further confirmed by the attitude of the ancient world,[21] which treated the disabled and especially the lame as objects of ridicule and derision.[22] Robert Garland comments at length on the popularity of crippled dancers at symposia:

> *Crippled dancers* feature prominently on Corinthian pots, as, for instance, on an alabastron which depicts a padded dancer with clubbed feet who is about to have his leg pulled away by another dancer—to the side-splitting laughter no doubt of the drinkers witnessing this prank. Whether scenes like these were acted out by genuine cripples or by actors taking their parts makes no difference. Evidently the joke was deemed sufficiently amusing to bear frequent repetition in the artistic repertoire, which presumably reflects its popularity at symposia.[23]

In a similar vein, Plutarch "informs us that the typical kinds of commands that an insensitive symposiarch or master of drinking might give to test the guests' ability to hold their liquor included ordering a stammerer to sing, a bald man to comb his hair, or *a lame man to dance on a greased wineskin* (emphasis mine, *Mor.* 621E).[24]

Such derisive ridicule was not limited to the pagan world. This point is underscored in an exhortation to good works in the late first-century Jewish document *4 Ezra*, which commands, "Do not ridicule a lame man" (*4 Ezra* 2.21). The *Apocryphon of Ezekiel* (first century BCE or first century CE)

---

21. The physiognomic handbooks do not themselves specifically mention the term "lameness" (χωλός) in conjunction with physiognomic signs (though some of their descriptions naturally lead to the conclusion that someone suffering from such symptoms would necessarily be unable to walk; see above). Foerster, *Scriptores*, 2:270, however, does list two passages from *Problemata*, a text falsely attributed to Aristotle that mention the lame as evidence of physiognomic interest outside the treatises: "Both birds and lame men are lustful for the same reason; for in both the nourishment below is small owing to the deficiencies of their legs, so it passes into the upper region and forms secretions of semen" (*Probl.* 880b5–8; cf. a similar passage in *Probl.* 893b13–17).

22. Two cripples feature prominently in this derision of the disabled in Homer's writings. See Hephaistos (*Il.* 1.600 and *Od.* 8); Thersites (*Il.* 2.217–19).

23. Garland, *Eye of the Beholder*, 84.

24. Another popular and degrading "gag" was to have a cripple serve the wine at the symposium. In fact, in one of the more familiar scenes on Greek pottery, the divine ironsmith, crippled Hephaistos, pours the wine for the Olympiad symposium, which causes "unquenchable laughter" to break out (*Il.* 1.600). "The incident involving Hephaistos as wine-pourer is made all the more comical by the fact that in real life, just as in myth, the role of wine-pourer was usually reserved for a young man of outstanding beauty . . . by prompting comparison with that graceful and perfect-limbed youth, the ungainly Hephaistos becomes a natural vehicle for parody" (Garland, *Eye of the Beholder*, 84).

assumes, in its handling of the reuniting of body and soul in the resurrection, that a lame man and a blind man are each only "half a man."[25]

Whether the lame were formally and ritually excluded from the first-century temple is hotly debated and probably irresolvable. In any case, the location of the lame man at "the gate of the temple" raises a question: would the authorial audience have inferred that the man was socially ostracized, lying, as it were, "outside" the boundaries of institutional religion?

F. Scott Spencer suggests that Lev. 21:16–24 laid the foundation "for stereotyping crippled persons throughout Israelite society, not just in priestly circles, as 'dead dogs'; that is pathetic, impotent, despicable creatures (2 Sam. 9:8)."[26] Joachim Jeremias, citing *m. Shabbat* 6.8, argues that those who were ambulatory (with assistance) were allowed into the temple, while "for those who were altogether lame or legless and had to be carried around on a padded seat, this was forbidden. The impotent man in Acts 3:2 is probably an example of this."[27] Beverly Gaventa is right to point out that the restrictions found in Leviticus 21:16–18 "apply only to priests who are offering sacrifices."[28]

In the larger Greco-Roman world, pagan priests were often excluded from temple service because of physical blemishes. Plato claimed that a priest must "be whole in body and legitimate" (*Resp.* 6.759c). Pausanias reports that in archaic Achaia "the boy who won the beauty contest" was appointed priest of Zeus (*Descr.* 7.24.4). Admission to the priesthood of Apollo fell to the young man "who was himself good-looking and strong" (*Descr.* 9.10.4). On the Roman side, Dionysius of Halicarnassus reports that Romulus required priests to be without bodily defect (*Ant. Rom.* 2.21.3); likewise, vestal virgins could have no speech or hearing impediment "nor any other bodily defect" (Aulus Gellius, *Noct. Att.* 1.12.3). Garland suggests these physical requirements might have extended beyond priests to pagan worshipers:

25. For a translation of the surviving fragments of the text, see J. R. Mueller and S. E. Robinson, "Apocryphon of Ezekiel," in *The Old Testament Pseudepigrapha*, vol. 1, *Apocalyptic Literature and Testaments*, ed. James H. Charlesworth (Garden City, NY: Doubleday, 1983), 492–95. For discussions of the text, see J. R. Mueller, *The Five Fragments of the Apocryphon of Ezekiel: A Critical Study*, JSPSup 5 (Sheffield: Sheffield Academic Press, 1994); Marc Bregman, "The Parable of the Lame and the Blind: Epiphanius' Quotation from an Apocryphon of Ezekiel," *Journal of Theological Studies* 42 (1991): 125–38; Richard Bauckham, "The Parable of the Royal Wedding Feast (Matthew 22:1–14) and the Parable of the Lame Man and the Blind Man (*Apocryphon of Ezekiel*)," *Journal of Biblical Literature* 115 (1996): 471–88.

26. Spencer, *Acts*, 45.

27. Joachim Jeremias, *Jerusalem in the Time of Jesus* (Philadelphia: Fortress, 1969), 117.

28. Beverly Gaventa, *Acts*, ANTC (Nashville: Abingdon, 2003), 84. On 2 Sam. 5:8, see above, p. 42.

We do not know to what extent the deformed and disabled were denied access to Greek or Roman sanctuaries . . . but it would hardly be surprising if the more distressing cases were excluded from participation in the processions and festivals which were such a prominent feature in the civic life of ancient communities in order not to offend the gods.[29]

In any case, the healing of the lame man of Acts 3–4 would have been a healing of the body and a transformation of the soul, underscored in part by the movement from outside to inside the temple precinct.[30] The physiognomic understanding of weak ankles and feet combined with the reality of the derision of the disabled in Greco-Roman society and the possible social exclusion hinted at by his location outside the gate would have caused Luke's audience to view the lame man as a thoroughly negative character, a morally weak and passive man who is unable to stand on his own two feet.[31]

Transformation of Character

The strengthening of the lower extremities would be an outward sign of his newly found inner moral strength of character; what pseudo-Aristotle calls εὔρωστος ("stout," "strong," or "robust").[32] A few examples from ancient pagan, Jewish, and Christian sources will help delineate the meaning of the term. In his novel, Achilles Tatius uses the term to describe a "robust" or "muscular" sailor (*Leuc. Clit.* 2.17.3; 3.4.1). Josephus uses the term to describe a Jewish archer named Mosollamus who was intelligent and "robust" (εὔρωστος; *C. Ap.* 1.201.4). The *Sibylline Oracles* uses the word to refer to a "bracing" (εὔρωστος) storm (3.369). Eusebius, in a quotation attributed to Clement, describes the moral corruption of a young man whose rush away from God was like an "unbroken and powerful (εὔρωστος) horse" (*Hist. eccl.* 3.23.10). In an interesting passage, Plutarch claims (in relation to the character of Aemilius) that the spirit (ψυχή) that is "vigorous and strong" (εὐρωστία καὶ ἰσχύς) "is neither spoiled nor elated by the insolence which prosperity brings, nor humbled by adversity" (*Tim.* 2.5). Though Luke does not use the term εὔρωστος, he shows the restored "vigor" and "robustness" of the lame man's

---

29. Garland, *Eye of the Beholder*, 64.

30. A similar symbolic use of space may be seen in Luke 16:20 where Lazarus lies at the gate (πυλών) of the rich man.

31. Furthermore, the note that the man was "lame from birth" might have been understood to suggest some kind of divine retribution for transgression (cf. John 9:1–2).

32. LSJ, 731.

character through the physical manifestations of standing and walking (Acts 3:8–9). The outer physical healing thus provides empirical proof for the inner moral and spiritual transformation, a point underscored by the double sense of σῴζω in Acts 4:9 as both "heal" in a physical sense and "save" in a moral or spiritual sense, a double entendre that conforms nicely to physiognomic expectations.

We see this point borne out in the narrative as well. The lame man moves from inactivity to walking, from paralysis to praise. He also moves from sitting to clinging (Acts 3:11), to standing unassisted alongside Peter and John. As such he shares in the "boldness" (παρρησία) of the apostles (4:13),[33] a point noted long ago by John Chrysostom: "Great was the boldness of the man; that even in the judgement-hall he has not left him. For had they said that the fact was not so, there was he to refute them."[34] Building on the use of the word θεωρέω in Acts 4:13, where the religious authorities "saw" the apostles' boldness, Chrysostom also claims that this boldness was not confined to words, but rather was "seen" in the apostles' "body language": "[Not only by their words,] but by their gesture also, and their look and voice, and, in short, by everything about them, they manifested the boldness with which they confronted the people."[35] Even though he does not speak, the lame man's boldness is seen also in his "body language," as he boldly takes his stand in solidarity with the persecuted apostles, and his transformation is complete.

Subverting the Physiognomic Conventions

If this were the whole story, then it would appear that Luke had followed the conventions of physiognomy precisely. The lame, morally weak man becomes a whole, morally bold man. But that is not all there is to it. We must yet decide what to make of the lame man's actions recorded in Acts 3:8: "Jumping up, he stood and began to walk, and he entered

33. The term παρρησία was particularly associated with the "frank speech" of the Cynic philosophers. See Dio Chrysostom, Or. 32.11; 77/8.37, 45; esp. Lucian, Piscatores, cited by Luke Timothy Johnson, The Acts of the Apostles, SP 5 (Collegeville, MN: Liturgical Press, 1992), 78; S. B. Marrow, "Parrhēsia and the New Testament," Catholic Biblical Quarterly 44 (1982): 431–46.

34. John Chrysostom, "Homily X," in The Homilies on the Acts of the Apostles (Oxford: John Henry Parker, 1851), 143; cf. PG 60:87.33–36.

35. Chrysostom, "Homily X," 147; cf. PG 60:89.50–52. For other occurrences of θεωρέω in Luke/Acts, see Luke 10:18; 14:29; 21:6; 23:35, 48; 24:37, 39; Acts 3:16; 4:13; 8:13; 9:7; 10:11; 17:16, 22; 19:26; 20:38; 21:20; 25:24; 27:10. All these uses have the sense of physical seeing or beholding, thus supporting Chrysostom's interpretation of this verse.

the temple with them, walking and leaping and praising God."[36] Form-critically this action is typically labeled a "demonstration of healing," but it certainly goes beyond the typical demonstration (cf. Luke 5:25; Acts 14:10). The references to leaping and praising God should, in the first instance, be taken as a spontaneous response of exhilarating joy at having his body restored and being able, for the first time, to become ambulatory.[37] The leaping is also symbolic of the restoration of Israel (see below), and finally, by moving from total inactivity to excessive activity, in his joy the lame man breaks physiognomic convention. He does not simply "walk like a man," but rather leaps in grateful response to this benefaction of God.

More than one commentator has focused on the intertextual echoes with Isaiah 35:6: "Then the eyes of the blind shall be opened, and the ears of the deaf unstopped; then the lame shall leap like a deer" (ἁλεῖται ὡς ἔλαφος ὁ χωλός; cf. ἁλλόμενος in Acts 3:8). The image is of the restoration of Israel as part of the vision of God as cosmic king.[38] As in Isaiah, the lame man in Acts symbolizes the potential restoration of Israel (cf. Acts 1:6) as part of the establishment of God's cosmic reign, inaugurated by Jesus and continued through the ministry of the apostles and Paul. In this light it is difficult to resist seeing the more than forty years of the lame man's illness as symbolic of the exiled and restored Israel.

Nevertheless, Johnson warns against such symbolic reading: "There is an obvious temptation to see a symbolic resonance here except that Luke

36. I see the emphases in this text as part of Luke's intentional rhetoric, contrary to C. K. Barrett (*A Critical and Exegetical Commentary on the Acts of the Apostles*, 2 vols., ICC [Edinburgh: T & T Clark, 1994], 1:184), who claims, "How Luke came to write such a clumsy sentence is another question to which no answer seems satisfactory; it is perhaps best to leave the sentence as one of a number of indications that Acts did not receive a final stylistic revision."

37. It is difficult, if not impossible, for an able-bodied person to comprehend the excessive joy and display for its own sake in this kind of hearing, and the response at the most fundamental level must be taken as a sign of this inexpressible joy. I am grateful to Dr. Rebecca Raphael, chair of the SBL consultation on the Bible and Disability Studies, for this insight. Nonetheless, the fact remains that of all the other healing stories, especially those related to the lame walking, the exuberant reaction of the lame man of Acts 3–4 remains unique in Luke's writings and invites further reflection (see in particular, Luke 5:17–26, esp. v. 25, and Acts 14:8–13, esp. v. 10).

38. On the messianic role of the Israelite community in God's cosmic kingship, see Edgar W. Conrad, *Reading Isaiah*, OBT (Minneapolis: Fortress, 1991). Regarding Israel's destiny in Isaiah, Conrad writes, "The vocation of the Davidic kingship, once the function of individuals such as Ahaz and Hezekiah, has become the vocation of the community" (p. 145). I am indebted to my colleague Jim Kennedy for this reference.

uses the specific number forty (well hallowed by the biblical tradition) so frequently."[39] Consider also Spencer's remarks:

> Apart from providing a symbol of hope for the poor and disadvantaged in Israelite society, the healed lame man also represents an image of restoration for the entire nation. We have already noted the connection to Isa. 35.6 where the leaping lame typify Israel's glorious deliverance from exile through the desert (cf. 35.1–10). . . . The lame man's restoration after forty years of paralysis establishes a key temporal link to this same national tradition. As God's saving purpose for ancient Israel was finally realized after forty years of stumbling and meandering through the wilderness, so the moment of fresh renewal—signalled by the dance of a forty-year cripple—has dawned upon the present Israel. To join this joyous dance, however, Israel must now follow the lead not only of Moses, but also of the promised "prophet like Moses," the crucified and risen Jesus of Nazareth, in whose name alone God brings full salvation to his people.[40]

Spencer's comments echo the words of the Venerable Bede, written well over a millennium earlier:

> According to the historical sense, this [age] shows that the man's mature age [made him] invincible to detractors. Allegorically, however, [the passage signifies that] the people of Israel . . . in the land of promise continued always to limp along [*claudicabat*] with the rites of idols together with those of the Lord.[41]

But there is yet more to the story, and here the physiognomy texts shed further light. Maud Gleason claims that deportment—the way one carries oneself—was also a telltale sign of a person's character. The walk of the lion "in the zoological shorthand of physiognomy" represented the ideal male.[42] Pseudo-Aristotle echoes this sentiment in his description of the lion as "the most perfect share of the male type" (809a15–16). After describing the fine features of the lion's head and back, the author has this to say about the lion's lower body:

39. Johnson, *Acts*, 79. The references Johnson cites against giving forty a symbolic value could just as easily be used in its favor.

40. Spencer, *Acts*, 52

41. Venerable Bede, *Commentary on the Acts of the Apostles*, trans. Lawrence T. Martin (Kalamazoo: Cistercian Publications, 1989), 51. Bede's use of the verb *claudicabat* recalls the description of the lame man as *claudus*; see translator's note, 54–55.

42. Gleason, *Making Men*, 61–62.

His legs are strong and muscular, his walk is vigorous, and his whole body is well-jointed and muscular. . . . He moves slowly with a long stride and swings his shoulders as he moves. These then are his bodily characteristics; in character he is generous and liberal, magnanimous and with a will to win; he is gentle, just, and affectionate towards his associates. (809b30–36)

By contrast, Polemo describes the effeminate or cowardly: "You may recognize him by his provocatively melting glance and by the rapid movement of his intensely staring eyes . . . his loins do not hold still, and his slack limbs never stay in one position. He minces along with little jumping steps."[43]

Interest in the implications of one's gait was not limited to the physiognomic handbooks. Aristotle speaks of the "great-souled man" whose step is slow, whose voice is low, and whose speech is measured and deliberate (*Eth. Nic.* 1125a34). Dio Chrysostom observes, "Walking is a universal and uncomplicated activity, but while one man's gait reveals his composure and the attention he gives to his conduct, another's reveals his inner disorder and lack of self-restraint" (*Or.* 35.24).[44] Gleason concludes:

The physiognomists, astrologers, and popular moralists of antiquity thought in terms of degrees of gender-conformity and gender-deviance. They shared a notion of gender identity built upon polarized distinctions . . . that purported to characterize the gulf between men and women but actually divided the male sex into legitimate and illegitimate members.[45]

Concern about the "hasty gait" is also seen in later Christian texts. Clement of Alexandria said, "A noble man should bear no sign of effeminacy upon his face or any other portion of his body. Nor should the disgrace of unmanliness ever be found in his movements or his posture" (*Paed.* 3.11.73–74). Ambrose observes, "Modesty must be guarded in our very movements and gestures and gaits. For the condition of the mind is often to be seen in the attitude of the body. . . . Thus, the movement of the body is a sort of voice of the soul" (*Off.* 1.18.67, 70–71).[46]

43. This translation is a composite of Polemo 61 (Foerster, 1:276) and *De physiogn.* 98 (Foerster, 2:123–24; André, *Anon.* 124) made by Gleason, *Making Men*, 63. On gait specifically, see *De physiogn.* 76 (Foerster, 2:100; André, 108–9).

44. See also Demosthenes, who "concedes the unattractiveness of a hasty gait" (*Or.* 37.52; 45.77). Likewise, Cicero condemns a hasty gait as an impediment to masculine *dignitas* (*Off.* 1.131).

45. Gleason, *Making Men*, 80.

46. Cf. also Tertullian, *Cult. fem.* 2.1, 8, 13; *An.* 5, 20, 25, 32; Basil, *Ep.* 1.2, 20–21, 132–35.

The lame man, once healed of his former "inadequacies," does not immediately adopt a slow, dignified gait, the sort of deportment that would show him to be a man of courage and vigorous character—in other words, a "manly man." Rather, by depicting the formerly lame man as leaping and praising God, Luke shows that he is an enthusiastic and grateful member of the eschatological community of God.[47] It is more important, in Luke's opinion, to respond appropriately to God's benefaction than to conform one's deportment to cultural conventions of masculine behavior. The authorial audience experiences both continuity with and discontinuity from physiognomic conventions as Luke subverts them in the name of Jewish eschatological expectation.[48]

Conclusion

If we call to mind the paradigmatic and symbolic function of the man born blind (John 9) in the Fourth Gospel, where believing is portrayed as a kind of seeing, then we should not be surprised to find that in Acts, where the Christian enterprise is called the Way (which of course implies walking), the healing of the man born lame functions analogously.[49] Luke has used and ultimately subverted Greco-Roman physiognomic conventions to lure his audience into his story. By employing allusions to the Old Testament (especially Isa. 35), he encourages them to accept his conclusion that the lame man's healing is paradigmatic for the

47. On praising God as a Lukan equivalent to faith, see Luke 17:11–19 esp. vv. 18–19 (so Talbert, *Reading Acts*, 53). It is interesting to note here that in the physiognomic handbooks, the deer is the symbol of timidity (although the handbooks nowhere link leaping per se with the timidity of deer): "For the deer, the hare and sheep are the most timid of all animals" (ps.-Aristotle 806b8; cf. 807a20; 811a16; 811b3; 811b7). The lion, as we have seen, is uniformly the symbol of courage and traditional masculinity (see ps.-Aristotle 809b30–36). In fact, when the writer wants to highlight the necessity of using peculiar characteristics of animals, rather than common ones, he contrasts lions and deer: "So that, when a man resembles an animal not in a peculiar but in a common characteristic, why should he be more like a lion than a deer?" (805b18). The Lukan authorial audience, shaped by the physiognomic consciousness, would expect the lame man to prowl like a lion, not leap like a deer. But Luke seems to be calling this very expectation into question.

48. Hamm, "Acts 3:1–10," 313, also suggests a possible allusion in Luke's use of ἐξαλλόμενος in Acts 3:9 to the remnant of Israel in Mic 2:13–14 (LXX): "I will surely receive the remnant of Israel; I will cause them to return together as sheep in trouble (ὡς πρόβατα ἐν θλίψει), as a flock in the midst of their fold. They shall rush forth (ἐξαλοῦνται) among men through the breach made before them; they have broken through and passed the gate and gone out of it, and their king has gone out before them and the Lord shall lead them."

49. Hamm, "Acts 3:1–10," 305. Contra S. John Roth, *The Blind, the Lame, and the Poor: Character Types in Luke-Acts*, JSNTSup 144 (Sheffield: Sheffield Academic Press, 1997), 220–21, who denies any paradigmatic use of these healing stories in Acts.

potential restoration of Israel within the establishment of the cosmic reign of God.

The lame man's healing is also a fulfillment of the Abrahamic blessing that Peter mentions in his speech to the religious leaders: "You are the descendants of the prophets and of the covenant that God gave to your ancestors, saying to Abraham, 'And in your descendants all the families of the earth shall be blessed'" (Acts 3:25).[50]

Finally, but no less importantly, Luke invokes the categories of physiognomy and cultural biases against the disabled only to overturn them. The lame man (along with the bent woman, Zacchaeus, and, as we shall see, the Ethiopian eunuch) would have been viewed by Luke's auditors as morally weak, corrupt, or even evil, yet Luke claims that the eschatological community is comprised of such as these, for "God shows no partiality" (Acts 10:34). If the lame man's body language in standing with the bold apostles fulfills physiognomic conventions, his actions of leaping and praising defy them. In other words, the literary characterization of the lame man is unfolded in the story of the transformation of the lame man's moral character—and this without a single word of his recorded in the story. In a curious and perhaps unintended way, Ambrose was right: "The movement of the body is a sort of voice of the soul."[51]

---

50. Brawley, "Abrahamic Covenant," 126, claims that the healing of the lame man should be taken as "a concrete case of the blessing available to all the people."

51. See p. 59 above.

7

WHAT IS TO PREVENT ME?

*Ambiguity, Acceptance,
and the Ethiopian Eunuch*

In the previous three chapters the Abrahamic covenant was front and center. The bent woman and Zacchaeus were a daughter and a son of Abraham, respectively. In the course of explaining the significance of the lame man's healing, Peter quotes the Abrahamic blessing (Acts 3:25; cf. Gen. 12:2–3, 22:18, 26:4). Although explicit reference to Abraham is missing in Acts 8:26–40, the story of Philip and the Ethiopian eunuch is the logical conclusion to Luke's interest in physiognomy and the Abrahamic covenant: a Gentile who is both an Ethiopian and a eunuch is converted to Christianity. The promise that Abraham's "seed" would be a blessing to all the nations (or Gentiles) is now fulfilled.

Thus the conversion of the Ethiopian eunuch in Acts is not so much the beginning of the Gentile mission per se as it is the culmination of Luke's argument that those who are physically "defective" by the prevailing cultural standards are in no way excluded from the body of the new Abrahamic community. This explains why the story of the Ethiopian eunuch is not cited subsequently in Acts. The Gentile mission per se commences with the story of Cornelius (Acts 10–11), and to that event the narrative returns when the question of the Gentiles emerges with full

123

force in Acts 15. Luke's interest in the Ethiopian eunuch has less to do with a proleptic fulfillment of Jesus' command to take the gospel "to the ends of the earth" (though this is not entirely missing) than with the inclusion into the eschatological community of those who might otherwise be excluded because of their physical characteristics. Both the eunuch's place of origin and his physical condition take on added meaning when seen through the lens of physiognomy.

In all four of these scenes (bent woman, Zaccheus, lame man, and Ethiopian eunuch), physiognomic conventions are introduced only to be overturned. Luke does not allow these assumptions to stand unchallenged. In challenging them, he seeks to shape his audience with regard not only to their assessment of these specific stories but also to their moral character and identity. How did Luke learn to write this way and what kind of character was he seeking to form in his audience?

According to Raffaella Cribiore, education in the ancient world, not unlike today in many quarters, "was based on the transmission of an established body of knowledge, about which there was wide consensus."[1] The transmission of traditional values included also the formation of the moral character of students (or audience).[2] Theon of Alexandria confirms this point several times: "Surely the exercise in the form of the *khreia* (or anecdote) not only creates a certain faculty of speech but also good character [*ethos*], while we are being exercised in the moral sayings of the wise" (60.18; Kennedy, 4; see also 71.6; 78.9). Thus, beyond acquiring facility in grammar and rhetoric, a fortunate byproduct of the rhetorical exercises from the teacher's point of view was the shaping of moral habits that reflected the prevailing cultural values of the day. This cultural repertoire or literacy included the physiognomic consciousness. Through his rhetorical education Luke presumably learned *ethos* argumentation (e.g., how to shape the moral character of his audience). One aspect of moral formation, whether of the teacher's students or the writer's audience, was the use of physiognomic categories to describe, praise, condemn, or otherwise evaluate the moral character of a literary or historical figure or event, and thus to inculcate those values in the moral vision of the student or audience.

1. Raffaella Cribiore, *Gymnastics of the Mind* (Princeton, NJ: Princeton University Press, 2001), 8.

2. On this, see Todd Penner, "Reconfiguring the Rhetorical Study of Acts: Reflections on the Method in and Learning of a Progymnastic Poetics," *Perspectives in Religious Studies* 30 (2003): 425–39; esp. 438: "A progymnastic poetics thus causes us to think much more seriously about *ethos* argumentation than we are wont to do."

Physiognomic Methods Explained in the Handbooks

In this text Luke employs aspects of all three methods of physiognomic analysis—what have been called the anatomical method, the zoological method, and the ethnographical method—found in pseudo-Aristotle's *Physiognomica* and discussed earlier in this book.[3] A brief rehearsal of those methods is in order.

In the anatomical method the physiognomist looks at a given facial feature (the scowl or the furrowed brow) and identifies its corresponding emotion.[4] Whenever the expression is subsequently observed on a different person, the corresponding character trait can be inferred. As pseudo-Aristotle notes, physiognomists "have made a collection of superficial (physical) characteristics, and the dispositions which follow each—the passionate man, the fearful, the sexual, and each of the other affections" (805a30–32).

The zoological method seeks to determine a person's character by observing similarities in appearance between the person and certain features of various kinds of animals.[5] To cite pseudo-Aristotle again, "they have supposed one type of body for the animal and then have concluded that the man who has a body similar to this will have a similar soul" (805a22–23). Thus all deer and hares are timid, all lions are courageous, all foxes are wily and cunning. The physiognomist identifies the physical characteristics peculiar to specific animals (deer, lion, fox, etc.) and then looks for those characteristics in the human subject. Any human sharing these features can usually be assumed to share the inner nature of that animal.

In the ethnographical method, "they have based their conclusions on the genus, man itself, dividing him into races, in so far as they differ in appearance and character . . . and have made a corresponding selection of characteristics" (ps.-Aristotle 805a26–29). However much we may find such ideas repugnant, the ethnographical method seeks to identify behaviors and moral characteristics distinctive to particular races or nationalities and links them to distinctive physical features.

Pseudo-Aristotle considers each of these methods critically: he makes least use of the racial method (citing only Corinthians and Ethiopians in his physiognomic analysis) and most use of the anatomical method (rightly understood).

3. See André, *Anon.*, 12,
4. Armstrong, "The Methods of the Greek Physiognomists," 53.
5. Ibid., 53–54.

Physiognomic Methods Reflected in the Progymnasmata

The progymnasmata were "handbooks that outlined 'preliminary exercises' designed to introduce students who had completed basic grammar and literary studies to the fundamentals of rhetoric that they would then put to use in composing speeches and prose."[6] As such, these graded series of exercises were probably intended to facilitate the transition from grammar school to the more advanced study of rhetoric.[7] If Luke's rhetorical training taught him how to present his characters in such a way as to shape the moral character of his audience, what if anything do the progymnasmata tell us about the role of physiognomy in such training?

While the progymnasmata do not show any sustained interest in the theories of physiognomy, there are some passages that are further illuminated by the physiognomic consciousness. In fact, careful reading suggests that allusions are made to each of the three kinds of physiognomic methods. Although the exercises sometimes differ, their intent remains basically the same: to praise or blame or otherwise describe the moral character of a literary or historical character. Physical characteristics and place of origin are important to these descriptions.

> Since good things especially are praised and some good things relate to the mind and character, others to the body, and some are external to us, clearly these would be the three large classes of things from which we shall get an abundance of arguments for an encomium. External goods are, first, good birth, and that in twofold, either from the goodness of (a man's) city and tribe and constitution, or from ancestors and other relatives. Then there is education, friendship, reputation, official position, wealth, good children, a good death. Goods of the body are health, strength, beauty, and acuteness of sense. Important ethical virtues are goods of the mind and the actions resulting from these; for example, that a person is prudent, temperate, courageous, just, pious, generous, magnanimous, and the like. (Theon 109–10; Kennedy, 50)

6. Willi Braun, *Feasting and Social Rhetoric in Luke 14*, SNTSMS 85 (Cambridge: Cambridge University Press, 1995), 146. On Luke and the progymnasmata, see Mikeal C. Parsons, "Luke and the Progymnasmata: A Preliminary Investigation into the Preliminary Exercises," in *Contextualizing Acts: Lukan Narrative and Greco-Roman Discourse*, ed. Todd Penner and Caroline Vander Stichele (Atlanta: Scholars Press, 2004), 43–63.

7. Quintilian refers to the preliminary exercises as part of the educational curriculum of young boys (*Inst.* 1.9). On the role of rhetoric in the educational curricula of antiquity, the standard works remain S. F. Bonner, *Education in Ancient Rome* (Berkeley: University of California Press, 1977); D. L. Clark, *Rhetoric in Graeco-Roman Education* (New York: Columbia University Press, 1957); H. Marrou, *A History of Education in Antiquity* (London: Sheed & Ward, 1956).

Theon also writes:

> Immediately after the prooemion we shall speak of good birth and other
> external and bodily goods, not arranging the account simply and in any
> random order but in each case showing that the subject used the advan-
> tage prudently and as he ought, not mindlessly—for goods that resulted
> from chance rather than moral choice are the least source of praise—; for
> example, that in good fortune he was moderate and humane and that he
> was just toward friends and exercised self-control in his bodily endow-
> ments. (Theon 111; Kennedy, 51–52)

Similarly, Hermogenes argues that "the best method in encomia as are
concerned with activities is to consider those participating in them, in
terms of what are their states of mind and body; for example, hunters are
manly, daring, quick-witted, vigorous in body" (Hermogenes 17; Kennedy,
83). Aphthonius the Sophist, discussing encomia, states that mind, body
and fortune are divisions of "deed": "mind, as courage or prudence; body,
as beauty or swiftness or strength; and fortune, as power and wealth and
friends (Aphthonius 22R; Kennedy, 108).

Given this interest in the connection between the "goods of the body"
and a person's "moral character," so reminiscent of physiognomic concerns,
we should not be surprised to find allusions in the progymnasmata to
each of the different physiognomic methods of character examination.
It is important to note that in each case, the physiognomic tenets are
assumed, not argued.

Anatomical Method

"Ecphrasis (*ekphrasis*) is descriptive speech, as they say, vivid and bringing what is being shown before the eyes" (Theon 118.7; Kennedy, 86).
There is ecphrasis of persons and events and places and periods of time.
In some of the progymnasmata, the goal of the rhetorical exercise called
ecphrasis is similar to the exercise called ethopoeia (speech-in-character).
John of Sardis claims that "ethopoeia . . . moves the hearer to share the
emotion of the speaker by presenting his character" and later in the
same paragraph, "The same thing can be said in the case of ecphrasis. . . .
Ethopoeia has been put first, and ecphrasis follows, as requiring greater
skill; for it is more difficult than ethopoeia."[8]

8. John of Sardis 194, 195 (Kennedy, 213, 214).

An instance of ecphrasis of persons is, for example, found in the Homeric line that Theon quotes about Thersites: "He was bandy-legged, lame in one foot, and his two shoulders / Stooped over his chest,' and so on."[9] The physical description of Thersites in Homer couples with his actions to portray him as a negative character in a way that resembles later physiognomic theory.[10] The physiognomic handbooks reflect conventions that have evolved over several centuries. It is not surprising to see evidence of physiognomy in practice well before the time of the appearance of the handbooks themselves, as we observe here in Homer. The earlier usage helped create the conventions, and the conventions helped shape and interpret the usage.[11]

The description of Thersites fits well into the physiognomic conventions later recorded in pseudo-Aristotle.[12] Homer describes Thersites as the "most shameful man" (αἴσχιστος ἀνήρ) ever to come to Ilios and then offers the physical description cited as an ecphrasis by Theon as evidence of that judgment: "he was bandy-legged and lame in the one foot, and his two shoulders were rounded, stooping together over his chest [and in a passage not quoted by Theon] and above them his head was pointed, and a scant stubble grew thereon" (Il. 2.216–19).

As we saw in an earlier chapter, the later physiognomic handbooks confirm Homer's negative assessment. According to pseudo-Aristotle, those whose "shoulders are driven into the chest are of evil disposition" (κακοήθεις; 810b). "Pointed" heads (φοξοί) are a sign of the "shameless"

9. Theon 118.13–15 (Kennedy, 45). In the notes to his edition of Theon, Michel Patillon attributes the slight change in text from Homer to Theon to the probability that Theon is citing Homer from memory (p. 67 n. 326). Thersites is also cited under ecphrasis by Hermogenes (22; Kennedy, 86) and mentioned by Nicolaus (68l; Kennedy, 167), and Eurybates by Aphthonius (37R; Kennedy, 117). Theon also cites Homer's description of Eurybates as an example of ecphrasis: "Round-shouldered, swarthy-skinned, woolly-haired" (Od. 19.246). The pervasive use of Homer in rhetorical education in antiquity is well documented. See especially Raffaella Cribiore, Writing, Teachers, and Students in Graeco-Roman Egypt (Atlanta: Scholars Press, 1996); Ronald F. Hock, "Homer in Greco-Roman Education," in Mimesis and Intertextuality in Antiquity and Christianity, ed. Dennis R. MacDonald (Harrisburg, PA: Trinity Press International, 2001), 56–77.

10. Evan N. Postlethwaite, in his attempt to rehabilitate Thersites, recognizes that Homer implies "failings of character through his ugliness." See idem, "Thersites in the Iliad," in Homer, ed. Ian McAuslan and Peter Walcot (Oxford: Oxford University Press, 1998), 83–95, esp. 85.

11. On this, see DeLacy, review of Physiognomics in the Ancient World, by Elizabeth C. Evans, 508–10.

12. Dio Chrysostom praised Homer for his economy of portraiture (see Or. 21.16–17). While it is true to say that in general Homer, the author of the "Greek Bible," "refrained from detailed portraiture of his characters," such literary depictions are not altogether missing from Homer's work (Evans, Physiognomics, 58.) See especially on this passage, Geneva Misener, "Iconistic Portraits," Classical Philology 19 (1924): 103–4.

or "impudent" (ἀναιδεῖς; 812a).[13] According to Adamantius, those who are "rounded" (κυρτοί) are thought to be "stupidly wicked" (μωροπόνηρος; 1.425.4). Finally, pseudo-Aristotle comments, "Those who have small, narrow, poorly-jointed feet, are . . . weak in character" (μαλακοὶ τὰ περὶ τὴν ψυχήν; 810a). From head to foot, Thersites is characterized by Homer as an evil, shameless, and weak man, indeed the "most shameful man" ever to come to Ilios, a negative characterization fulfilled in the immediate episode, where Thersites chides Achilles, Odysseus, and Agamemnon only to be upbraided by Odysseus. The negative assessment is seconded by later physiognomic canons.[14]

In the progymnasmata Thersites is mentioned once by Theon (112) and once by Libanius (see §1 of the appendix). Theon understands that Thersites is hardly a noble or laudatory character, a point made clear later in his discussion of *synkrisis* (comparison), where he makes the following observation: "Let it be specified that synkriseis are not comparisons of things having a great difference between them; for someone wondering whether Achilles or Thersites was braver would be laughable" (Theon, 112; Kennedy, 53). It is reasonable to conclude that at least part of Theon's negative judgment about Thersites is due to his (im)moral character implied by his physical appearance and borne out in the subsequent narrative. Thus Theon accepts the basic physiognomic premise that outward physical appearance is a clue to inward moral character and, by choice of example, encourages his reader to accept it, too. Even Libanius's encomium on Thersites is, in a sense, to display Libanius's rhetorical prowess, not necessarily to extol the "virtues" of Thersites. In other words, he has chosen the "extreme case" to try to praise one about whom "Homer has spoken badly." Thus the encomium may say less about divided opinion in antiquity about how to view Thersites and more about Libanius's abilities.

Zoological Method

Pseudo-Aristotle observed, "It is also evident that the forms of the body are similar to the functions of the soul, so that all the similarities

---

13. LSJ glosses "sugar loaf head."

14. Andrea Kouklanakis comes to a similar conclusion without appeal to physiognomy: "the character of Thersites represents dissent and rebellion on a social level, and this dissent is magnified into a caricature of both his verbal style and his physical appearance"; see "Thersites, Odysseus, and the Social Order," in *Nine Essays on Homer*, ed. Miriam Carlisle and Olga Levaniouk (Lanham, MD: Rowman & Littlefield, 1999), 35–54, esp. 45.

in animals are evidence of some identity" (808b27–30). While humans might seek to mask their inner moral character, animals have no such pretensions. Rather, the character traits of certain animals are fixed and transparent for all to observe. Hence, when the physical feature in question is peculiar to a particular animal and that animal is characterized by certain character traits, the physiognomist may infer that the person and animal share certain moral qualities.

Although pseudo-Aristotle is somewhat reserved in his use of the zoological method,[15] he approvingly cites the lion when discussing the ideal male type (809b15). He discusses the lion's bodily characteristics in some detail, then asserts that "in character he [the lion] is generous and liberal, magnanimous and with a will to win; he is gentle, just, and affectionate toward his associates" (809b34–36).

In the exercise on encomium in Hermogenes we find this text: "in the case of Achilles, [that] he was nurtured on lions' marrow. . . . You will say about his body that it was beautiful, large, swift, strong; about his mind that it was just, wise, brave" (16; Kennedy, 82).[16] From a physiognomic point of view it is no accident that Achilles, who was nurtured on lions' marrow, should exhibit characteristics typical of the lion: he was just, wise, and brave. Once again, the specific example encourages the students and audience to conclude that Achilles is just, wise, and brave like a lion in part because he has ingested these virtues from the marrow of the animal of which they are most characteristic. In Libanius, Achilles' diet is presented positively (in an encomium that terms his diet "far superior"), and negatively in an invective and a comparison. The physiognomic connection is maintained between the lion's marrow and Achilles' behavior even in negative examples (acting like "wild animals"; see §§2–4 of the appendix).

Ethnographic Method

As we noted in chapter 1, Polemo provides the preeminent example of the ethnographic method of physiognomy.[17]

It follows from the indices and signs of this discipline that as often as you judge any race or a people of the world on the basis of these indices,

15. On this reluctance, see ps.-Aristotle 805b10–27.

16. Interestingly, Nicolaus destroys this comparison by arguing that Achilles was fed on the marrow of deer (52; Kennedy, 157).

17. See Malina and Neyrey, *Portraits of Paul*, 119. On the geocentrism often associated with the ethnographic method of physiognomy, also see chapter 1 above.

you will judge them correctly. However you will find that some signs typical of a people are negative and lead them to deviance, while others are positive, correcting the deviance. For example you will scarcely find keen insight and excellence in letters among the Egyptians; on the other hand keen insight is widespread among the Macedonians; and you will find among Phoenicians and Cilicians the pursuit of peace and pleasure; and finally you will be offended by Scythians, a treacherous and devious people. (31.236)

We also find evidence in the progymnasmata of the ethnographic method. John of Sardis suggests that a speaker's place of origin may influence the way the writer shapes ethopoeia, since certain places produce certain kinds of speakers: "the words of a Laconian will be 'few and clear' and those of a man of Attica garrulous." In an invective against Philip, Aphthonius criticizes the homeland and ancestors of Philip: "Macedonians are the worst of the barbarians, and Pella is the most undistinguished city in the land of the Macedonians ... and coming from such a place, he [Philip] had the worst ancestors in the land."[18]

Conclusion

Mostly unchallenged as they are, these "physiognomic echoes" in the progymnasmata inculcate certain cultural values in the students; they form a small but important part of the *ethos* argumentation of the exercises. Luke shares with the rhetoricians this concern to shape the moral character of his audience through the literary presentation of his characters' morality. One rhetorical strategy Luke employs in this regard is the use (and sometimes strategic subversion) of physiognomic conventions. We now turn our attention to the story of the Ethiopian eunuch.

The Physiognomic Methods Subverted in Acts 8

In the story of Philip and the Ethiopian eunuch in Acts 8 Luke deploys, develops, and subverts all three physiognomic methods: ethnographic, anatomical, and zoological.[19]

18. John of Sardis, 196 (Kennedy, 214); Aphthonius 29R (Kennedy, 112).

19. I do not mean to imply that these comments exhaust any kind exegetical treatment; I suggest only that an awareness of the physiognomic consciousness and its contribution to *ethos* argumentation (as found in the progymnasmata) sheds considerable additional light on this text. For more on Acts

Ethiopia and the Ethnographic Method

The treasurer of the Candace in Acts 8 is an Ethiopian. This fact gives the audience clues as to the geographic and ethnographic significance of this conversion. Ethiopia was viewed by people of antiquity as lying at the southernmost end or limit of the earth.[20] It is also well documented that the ancients viewed skin color as one of an Ethiopian's most distinctive features.[21] These ethnographic feature's reinforce the significance of the Ethiopian's conversion for Luke: "the story of a black African . . . from what would be perceived as a distant nation to the south of the empire is consistent with the Lukan emphasis on 'universalism,' a recurrent motif in both Luke and Acts, and one that is well known."[22] This theme is related to Luke's understanding of the Gentile mission as underpinned by the Abrahamic covenant that God's chosen people would be a "blessing to all the nations" (Gen. 12:1–3).

Early references to the Ethiopians were very positive. Homer referred to the "blameless Ethiopians" whose homeland provided a kind of retreat center for the Olympian gods (*Il.* 1.423–24).[23] Later, though, the assessment was not always so flattering. Herodotus attests to the belief that those who dwell farthest from the center of the inhabited world (specifically citing the Persians) are held in the least honor (*Hist.* 1.134).[24] The physiognomic handbooks also reflect a negative ethnocentric bias toward the Ethiopians. Pseudo-Aristotle says, "Those who are too swarthy [dark-skinned] are cowardly; this applies to Egyptians and Ethiopians."[25] If this negative view of Ethiopians is in the cultural repertoire of Luke's audience, Luke encourages the setting aside of those prejudices, since nothing precludes the inclusion of this Ethiopian in Luke's eschatological community.

8, see Mikeal C. Parsons, "Isaiah 53 in Acts 8: A Reply to Morna Hooker," in *Isaiah 53 and Christian Origins*, ed. William Bellinger, Bruce Corley, and William Farmer (Sheffield: Sheffield Academic Press, 1998), 104–19.

20. See, e.g., Homer, *Il.* 23.205–97; Herodotus 3.114–15; Strabo 1.2.27–28; 2.2.2; Esther 8:9.

21. See Homer, *Od.* 19.244–48; Herodotus 2.29–32; 3.17–24; 4.183, 197; Seneca, *Nat.* 4a218; and Jer. 13:23. The word αἰθίοψ means "burnt-face" (LSJ).

22. Clarice Martin, "A Chamberlain's Journey and the Challenge of Interpretation for Liberation," *Semeia* 47 (1989): 114.

23. On this see James S. Romm, *The Edges of the Earth in Ancient Thought: Geography, Exploration, and Fiction* (Princeton, NJ: Princeton University Press, 1992), esp. chap. 2.

24. The view was presumably not that of Herodotus himself; see Romm, *Edges of the Earth*, 54–60.

25. Ps.-Aristotle 812a12–13. Consider also the negative connotations of identifying Ethiopians as descendants of Ham (cf. Gen. 10:6; Cush = Ethiopia).

The Eunuch and the Anatomical Method

The opening unit is given over to a description of the man whom Philip meets: "an Ethiopian eunuch, a court official of the Candace, queen of the Ethiopians, in charge of her entire treasury" (Acts 8:27). Of these descriptors, the most import is that the man is a eunuch.

But what did the term "eunuch" mean in late antiquity?[26] There is some evidence that the word functioned simply as an official title. Genesis 39:1 reports that "Joseph was brought down to Egypt; and Potiphar an officer (LXX, εὐνοῦχός) of Pharaoh." Since Potiphar was married, "eunuch" here probably refers to his standing in Pharaoh's court. Some early Christian writings developed the notion of eunuch as a reference to those who remain celibate. Athenagoras wrote in *A Plea for the Christians*: "If to remain a virgin and *abstain from sexual intercourse* (εὐνουχία) brings us closer to God . . ." (33.3; cf. Clement of Alexandria, *Strom.* 3.1; Matt. 19:12). Nonetheless the overwhelming majority of instances of "eunuch" from the classical period to late antiquity refer to one who was sexually mutilated (see Philostratus, *Vit. Apoll.* 6.42; Lucian, *Sat.*, 12) or, much more rarely, born with a congenital defect (see Aristotle, *Gen. an.* 2.7.25).

How is the reader to understand the word in Acts 8? Clearly the nuance of celibacy is not at work here, and no interpreter has ever argued such. There is some debate about whether "eunuch" here should be taken literally to refer to a castrated or mutilated person or whether it simply refers to the title of a court official. The advantage to the latter view is that the Ethiopian may be viewed as a Jewish proselyte returning home from temple worship and dutifully reading Isaiah. Even more important for some is the fact that if the Ethiopian eunuch is a Jewish proselyte, then Cornelius is the first Gentile admitted for baptism.

Several factors militate against this view and in favor of understanding "eunuch" in its physical sense. First, the status of the Ethiopian as a high-ranking official is established in Acts 8:27 quite apart from the use of this term. He was "a court official of the Candace, queen of the Ethiopians, in charge of her entire treasury." The use of the term "official" (δυνάστης) is interesting here. The only other occurrence in Luke and Acts is in the Magnificat where Mary pronounces that God has "brought down the mighty ones (δυνάστας) from their thrones and exalted those of low degree" (Luke 1:52). Furthermore, this man is sufficiently wealthy to be

---

26. Some of the following material is taken from my essay, "Isaiah 53 in Acts 8."

driven in a chariot (see Acts 8:27, 38) and to possess an expensive Greek scroll of Isaiah. To reduce the term "eunuch" to mean nothing more in this context than a "high-ranking official" is to render it redundant.

It is more likely that the Ethiopian eunuch here is a physically muti-lated man. His service as a close adviser to a queen, the Candace, makes it likely that he was castrated, since male attendants for female royalty often were (see Herodotus 8.105; Esther 2:3, 14; 4:4–5). Further, for the remainder of the story the official is referred to not as an Ethiopian (an exotic dark-skinned fellow) or as a minister or official (signifying power and wealth) but simply as the "eunuch" (Acts 8:34, 36, 38, 39). If this is his dominant, defining characteristic, then two questions emerge: What was the status of eunuchs in the Mediterranean world of late antiquity? How would Luke's readers have understood this text in light of the larger cultural script for eunuchs?

Eunuchs in antiquity "belonged to the most despised and derided group of men."[27] One of Herodotus's characters, Hermotimus, a eunuch, took revenge on the man who had castrated him and sold him as a slave into the court of Xerxes, calling the activity "the wickedest trade on earth" (8.104–6). Elsewhere, Lucian of Samosata tells of a supposed eunuch vying for a chair of philosophy in Athens. His assumed status as a eunuch (he claimed to be a eunuch to avoid charges of adultery) led to an invective by one of his opponents who claimed that it was "an ill-omened, ill-met sight if on first leaving home in the morning, one should set eyes on any such person [a eunuch]." Eunuchs, he claimed, "ought to be excluded ... not simply from all that [philosophy] but even from temples and holy-water bowls and all the places of public assembly" (*Eunuch.* 6–11).

This attitude was also prevalent among Greek-speaking Jews of the first century. Josephus wrote,

> Shun eunuchs and flee all dealings with those who have deprived them-selves of their virility and of those fruits of generation, which God has given to men for the increase of our race; expel them even as infanticides who withal have destroyed the means of procreation. (*Ant.* 4.290–91)

Why were eunuchs thus demonized and ostracized in antiquity? In part, the answer lies in their ambiguous sexual identity. To quote Lucian again, a eunuch "was an ambiguous sort of creature like a crow, which cannot be reckoned either with doves or with ravens"; he was "neither

---

27. See Scott Spencer, "The Ethiopian Eunuch and His Bible: A Social-Science Analysis," *Biblical Theology Bulletin* 22 (1992): 156.

man nor woman but something composite, hybrid and monstrous, alien to human nature" (*Eunuch.* 6–11). Josephus comments similarly: "For plainly it is by reason of the effeminacy of their soul that they changed the sex of their body also. And so with all that would be deemed a monstrosity by the beholders" (*Ant.* 4.291). Likewise, Philo of Alexandria claims that eunuchs were "men who belie their sex and are affected with effemination, who debase the currency of nature and violate it by assuming the passions and the outward form of licentious women" (*Spec.* 1.324–25). In a culture where honor was gender-based, to be sexually ambiguous was to blur clear-cut gender roles and expectations and thus to bring shame upon oneself and one's community.[28]

Jews reasoned that eunuchs, by belonging neither to the cultural expectations of male nor female, had violated purity codes.[29] Like amphibians, which live in two worlds but belong to neither, eunuchs were considered unclean (see Lev. 11:9–12; 21:19–20). In addition, the physical body and the corporate social body were thought to mirror each other, so a physical body that was damaged or mutilated had the potential of defiling the social body.[30]

This was especially true in Judaism where the physically defective, like eunuchs, were presumably forbidden from entering into the temple and interacting with the larger social body: "No one whose testicles are crushed or whose penis is cut off shall be admitted to the assembly of the LORD" (Deut. 23:1). The Ethiopian eunuch, as Scott Spencer has noted, "embodied impurity as much as he exhibited shame. His ambiguous sexual identity ('neither male nor female') denied him a distinctive place on the purity map of the social body, even as his defective genital anatomy depicted his polluted map of the physical body."[31] This is the kind of person whom Philip is directed by the Spirit to approach (Acts 8:29)—a man excluded, because of his physical condition, from participation in Jewish worship at the temple in Jerusalem, a man understood by Luke's readers to be a social outcast, liminal in terms of his sexual identity, his religious identification, and his socioeconomic status.

---

28. See Bruce J. Malina and Jerome H. Neyrey, "Honor and Shame in Luke-Acts: Pivotal Values of the Mediterranean World," in *The Social World of Luke-Acts: Models for Interpretation*, ed. Jerome H. Neyrey (Peabody, MA: Hendrickson, 1991), 41–44.

29. See Spencer, "The Ethiopian Eunuch and His Bible," 158–59. See also by the same author, *The Portrait of Philip in Acts: A Study of Roles and Relations*, JSNTSup 67 (Sheffield: JSOT Press, 1992), 168–72.

30. See Jerome H. Neyrey, "The Symbolic Universe of Luke-Acts: 'They Turn the World Upside Down,'" in idem., ed., *Social World*, 278–85.

31. Spencer, "The Ethiopian Eunuch and His Bible," 159.

The physiognomic handbooks reinforce this negative view of eunuchs.[32] Much of the discussion about eunuchs is found in Polemo's invective against the sophist Favorinus, who was, according to Polemo, "born without testicles" (1.160; ed. Foerster).[33] Polemo generalizes against eunuchs as a way of criticizing Favorinus, usually without mentioning him by name:

> Therefore I have known eunuchs to be an evil tribe: they are greedy and replete with tendencies to dissipation. You should be aware, moreover, that castrated eunuchs undergo a change in the general appearance: complexion, and physique that they had before castration. In contrast, those who are born without testicles exhibit altered characteristics that are different from those shown by the castrated. Hence no one is more perfectly evil than he who is born without testicles. Therefore, when you see the eyes I described at the outset of this discussion, you will find that their owner resembles the class of eunuchs. (1.162–64, ed. Foerster)[34]

For Luke, however, this physical "deformity" does not indicate a social or sexual flaw so severe that it disqualifies him from entrance into the eschatological community.[35]

The "Sheep Led to Slaughter" and the Zoological Method

The passage that the Ethiopian eunuch is reading at the time of his encounter with Philip is from Isaiah: "Like a sheep he was led to the slaughter, and like a lamb silent before its shearer, so he does not open his mouth. In his humiliation justice was denied him. Who can describe his generation? For his life is taken away from the earth" (Acts 8:32–33; cf. Isa. 53:7–8).[36]

32. It is conceivable that Luke knew about the characterization of eunuchs from actual classroom exercises. For example, Libanius (in *Prog.* 11.26) poses the question, "What words would a eunuch say when he falls in love?"

33. For more on the dispute between Polemo and Favorinus, see Gleason, *Making Men*, 131–58.

34. The translation is taken from Gleason, *Making Men*, 47. That Polemo's description of "one born without testicles" refers to Favorinus is clear from his earlier remark where Favorinus is clearly in view: "I don't think that I have ever seen but a single example of that type of man (born without testicles); he came from the land of the Celts" (1.160, ed. Foerster). I am also grateful to Simon Swain for providing prepublication access to an alternative translation of the Arabic destined for publication in *Seeing the Face*: "I do not know if I have seen any of this description [congenital eunuch] except for one man. He was from a land called Celtas."

35. Whereas it may have disqualified him from entrance into the temple; cf. Acts 8:27; Lev. 21:20; 22:24; Josephus, *Ant.* 4.290–91; Philo, *Spec.* 1.324–25.

36. The passage quoted here takes up just after the reference to the servant's vicarious suffering ("and the Lord has laid on him the iniquity of us all," Isa. 53:6) and ends just before a similar note in Isa. 53:8:

The passage as it stands in Acts tends rather to emphasize the humiliation of the unnamed sufferer, and perhaps also his vindication.

The key word here is "humiliation" (ταπείνωσις), found in the middle of the citation. The reference to ταπείνωσις here is to a "social position within Mediterranean society" that "was severely reprobative."[37] A passage from Lucian's *Somnium* is illustrative of the social ostracism conveyed by ταπείνωσις (see also Pollux, *Onom.* 5.162–64). In this dream, Lucian is warned to choose a career in education and not sculpture. If he refuses, his lot will surely be that of an outcast:

> On the other hand, if you turn your back upon these men so great and noble, upon glorious deeds and sublime words, upon a dignified appearance, upon honor, esteem, praise, precedence, power and offices, upon fame for eloquence and felicitations for wit, then you will put on a filthy tunic, assume a servile appearance . . . with your back bent over your work; you will be a groundling, with groundling ambitions, *lowly in every manner* [πάντα τρόπον ταπεινός] . . . you will make yourself a thing of less value than a block of stone. (*Somn.* 13; emphasis added)

The connection between sheep and timidity/lowliness is another important connection. Once more pseudo-Aristotle's comments are illuminating: "Soft hair shows timidity and stiff hair courage. This is based on observation of all the animal kingdom. For the deer, the hare and the sheep are the most timid of all animals and have the softest hair" (806b8).

Again these comments are not limited to the physiognomic handbooks. The defenselessness of lambs against wolves is well known and forms part of their "lowliness."[38] Certainly the metaphor is common in Jewish literature: "What has a wolf in common with a lamb, or a sinner with someone who fears God" (Sir. 13:17).[39] Libanius records a parable of wolves and sheep, indicating their gullible nature:

("by a perversion of justice he was taken away"), as has been frequently noted; see esp. Morna Hooker, *Jesus and the Servant: The Influence of the Servant Concept of Deutero-Isaiah in the New Testament* (London: SPCK, 1959). Rather than enter a debate at this point on Luke's understanding (or lack thereof) of the atoning dimensions of Jesus' death, I note simply that the passage as it stands in Acts focuses on humiliation and possibly also vindication; see Parsons, "Isaiah 53 in Acts 8."

37. See Braun, *Feasting and Social Rhetoric*, 50.

38. Homer, *Il.* 22.263; *Epig. Gr.* 1038.38 (in *Anth. Gr.* 1050); Dio Chrysostom, *Or.* 64 [14] 2; Philostratus, *Vit. Apoll.* 8.22; Didymus, *In Gen.* 86.18.

39. "The devout of God are like innocent lambs among them" (*Pss. Sol.* 8.23; cf. *4 Ezra* 5.18). "Hadrian said to Rabbi Jehoshua: 'There is something great about the sheep [Israel] that can persist among the seventy wolves [the nations]'" (*Tanh. Tol.* 5; cited by Str-B 1.574). Cf. also Isa. 11:6; 40:11; Ezek. 34:11–31; Philo, *Praem.* 86.

The wolves were seeking peaceful relations with the sheep, and so they said, "This day will be the beginning of great and wonderful things for you and for us; for when we have rid ourselves of war and other evils, we will be able to roam around without fear. So let us pour libations to commemorate our agreement. But if this treaty is to be effective at all, and if we do not intend to break it as soon as it is ratified, you must chase away those wicked, hostile dogs. Even now they are raising a commotion, and they always hold us wolves in suspicion; for oftentimes, when we are simply passing by the flocks, some of them jump out and bark at us, while others, though reluctantly, become provoked and harass us. So why do you need dogs when you have a treaty with us wolves?" The sheep were persuaded; for their species is very gullible. And so the dogs were sent packing, the wolves came into power, and the sheep, now deserted, were gobbled up. (Libanius, *Prog.* 1.1.1–2)[40]

It is not surprising that the eunuch, whose access to wealth is tenuous at best and ironically dependent upon his socially debased position, should be drawn to this figure in Isaiah who, like the eunuch, is described as being in a state of humiliation "like a sheep . . . led to the slaughter" or "a lamb silent before its shearer" and to whom, like the eunuch, "justice was denied" (Acts 8:32–33). He, too, is like a lamb before its "cutter," reduced to silence in humiliation.

This figure in Isaiah is not only socially marginalized, but also depicted as unclean or polluted. The Isaianic figure is identified as a slaughtered lamb and a shorn sheep (Acts 8:32). On the Jewish map of purity, both similes evoke images of pollution. Corpses, whether animal or human, were unclean and taboo to the touch (see Lev. 11:24–40; 21:1–4). Likewise, priests were required to follow certain regulations regarding shaving their bodies: "They shall not make bald spots upon their heads, or shave off the edges of their beards . . ." (Lev. 21:5; cf. also Num. 6:1–21; see Acts 21:23–26). The eunuch in Luke's narrative would have closely identified with the Isaianic figure since both are depicted as ritually unclean.

To be sure, within Judaism there existed the eschatological vision of Isaiah that eunuchs and foreigners and other outcasts would be reincorporated in the end days: "To the eunuchs who keep my sabbaths, who choose the things that please me and hold fast my covenant, I will give,

---

40. Appreciation is expressed to Dr. Craig Gibson for permission to quote his translation of this fable. Other versions may be found in Babrius 93; Aesop, *Fab.* 158; ps.-Nicolaus (Walz 1.267.13–20). The theme is noted in Nicolaus 8.

in my house and within my walls, a monument and a name better than sons and daughters; I will give them an everlasting name that shall not be cut off" (Isa. 56:4–6). But rather than provide hope for the eunuch, it stood as a reminder of the gulf between this vision of future inclusion in the temple cult and the present reality of exclusion from temple worship, which the eunuch may have just experienced (Acts 8:27).

When Luke shows that nothing hinders the eunuch from being baptized, ritually cleansed, and incorporated into the body of Christ, he perhaps intends a thinly veiled antitemple polemic. What is held out as a promise for the future but is denied by the current practices of the temple cult is offered freely by the representative of the Way, whose founder and community were now radically redrawing the Jewish purity map of places and persons. The status of the socially despised and ritually polluted eunuch is ritually transformed by the act of Christian baptism.

But the passage from Isaiah, as understood by Luke, does not limit its vision to a description only of the servant's debased status. Rather, there are allusions, albeit ambiguous, to a radical reversal of social status. The first hint of reversal may come in the phrase in Acts 8:33 often translated "justice was denied him." Some prefer the translation "judgment was removed from him" (on Luke's use of "judgment," see Luke 10:14; 11:31–32). The next phrase is likewise ambiguous: "Who can describe his generation?" Is this a lament over the fact that the servant is cut off from his descendants or a note rejoicing the coming "indescribable generation" too large to count? The last phrase in the citation, "for his life is taken away from the earth" (Acts 8:33), is ambiguous as well. The reference may be either to the figure's death or his "lifting up" in exaltation, symbolized in Jesus' ascension in Acts 1:9.[41]

Luke understands the death and exaltation of Jesus as inextricably tied up into one event. Although he narrates the death, crucifixion, and ascension separately, they are not separate, unrelated episodes for Luke, but rather three aspects of one event. Two key texts justify this conclusion. In the Lukan transfiguration scene, Jesus is depicted as conversing with Moses and Elijah about "his departure, which he was about to accomplish in Jerusalem" (Luke 9:31). Now either this singular "departure" (lit. "exodus") refers to the entire death-exaltation transit, or it refers to only one of those events. If what must be accomplished "in Jerusalem" is limited to the final departure in Luke 24:50–53, this

---

41. Or as Johnson puts it: "the LXX can be read by the Messianist who confesses a resurrected prophet as 'life is lifted from the earth'" (*Acts of the Apostles*, 156).

stands in tension with the passion predictions, which clearly speak of his "death" as the event which must be "fulfilled in Jerusalem" (see Luke 18:31–33).

If the "exodus" refers only to his death, however, then the final departure scene in 24:50–53 is superfluous, and there is tension between this passage and 9:51, where we are told that "the days drew near for him to be taken up." I have argued elsewhere that the word "taken up" (ἀνάλημψις, Luke 9:51) carries a double entendre in the semantic currency of late antiquity and is best seen as a reference to the entire death/resurrection/exaltation of Jesus.[42] Thus it is not difficult to imagine that a writer who has already closely aligned the death and exaltation of Jesus (see Luke 9:31, 51; Acts 1:2) and for whom the larger theological pattern of reversal is well known in Luke and Acts (cf. Luke 1:48; 3:5–6; 14:11; 18:9–14; Acts 2:32–33) would see a double entendre in the Greek of Isaiah 53 and end his quotation by reversing the despised status of the servant with reference to his exaltation through death, his "being lifted up from the earth."

The eunuch is attracted to this figure described in Isaiah 53:7–8. These verses allow Luke to recapitulate the suffering/vindication of Jesus the servant very economically. To have gone beyond the reference, "For his life is taken away [i.e., up] from the earth," would have destroyed the death/exaltation schema.

The allusion to vindication, to be sure, is implicit, and so the ambiguous nature of the scripture requires a Christian interpreter. The eunuch asks, "About whom, may I ask you, does the prophet say this, about himself or about someone else?" So Philip "began to speak, and starting with this scripture, he proclaimed to him the good news about Jesus" (Acts 8:35). This good news, no doubt, included the vindication as well as the suffering of Jesus (cf. Acts 2:23–24; 3:13–15) and what may have been ambiguous in the scripture is now made clear in its Christian exposition. And while Philip certainly offers a christological interpretation, the passage offers hope for the reversal of status for the humiliated, rejected eunuch as well.[43]

---

42. See Mikeal C. Parsons, *The Departure of Jesus in Luke-Acts: The Ascension Narratives in Context*, JSNTSup 21 (Sheffield: Sheffield Academic Press, 1987), 128–33. In these pages I also argue for a similar understanding of ἀνελήμφθη in Acts 1:2. For a reference to ἀνάλημψις meaning "death," see *Pss. Sol.* 4:18. For other examples from late antiquity on the meaning of ἀνάλημψις as "passing away" and "taken up," see P. A. van Stempvoort, "The Interpretation of the Ascension in Luke and Acts," *New Testament Studies* 5 (1959): 32–33.

43. See especially Spencer, *Portrait of Philip*, 176–83.

Conclusion

Like the progymnasmata, Luke uses rhetorical conventions of characterization, including appeal to certain physiognomic principles, to present the moral character of certain figures.[44] And like the progymnasmata, Luke hopes also to form the moral character of his audience. However, in Acts 8 Luke invokes the methods and categories of physiognomy against the disfigured only to overturn them, a rhetorical move of *ethos* argumentation that he no doubt learned from the very teachers of grammar and rhetoric whose moral vision he so severely challenges. Luke's own moral vision was formed, not by the dominant cultural values espoused by his teachers of rhetoric, but rather by the teaching of Israel's scriptures—"The LORD does not see as mortals see; they look on the outward appearance, but the LORD looks on the heart" (1 Sam. 16:7)—and the teachings of Jesus himself (e.g., the Good Samaritan in Luke 10).

The Ethiopian eunuch would have been viewed by Luke's auditors as sexually ambiguous, socially ostracized, and morally evil (greedy and cowardly). Yet when the eunuch asks, "What is to prevent me from being baptized?" Luke's response is surely that neither the eunuch's physical condition, nor his place of origin, nor his likeness to a sheared sheep prevents his entrance into the eschatological community in fulfillment of the Abrahamic promise of a blessing to "all the families of the earth" (Acts 3:25; cf. Gen. 22:18). In that community "God shows no partiality" (Acts 10:34).

44. Evans, *Physiognomics*, 5, 12.

Epilogue

When my father, John Quincy Parsons, was twelve years old, he lost his right arm in a hunting accident. In his adult years he ran a sawmill, prompting casual acquaintances to assume he lost his arm in an industrial accident. In public he always wore a prosthesis with a hook—covered by a long-sleeved shirt (even in the middle of a hot North Carolina summer), which served no functional purpose. In the privacy of our home, he would occasionally don a T-shirt, leaving exposed the stub of his arm, amputated just above the elbow.

It never occurred to any of us in the immediate family that this physical impairment should cause my father to be viewed as disabled or handicapped in any way.[1] He did most everything a two-armed man could do; he even drove a manual transmission truck to work—though first-time passengers were sometimes taken aback to see him steer with his knees while he reached over his body to shift gears with his left hand! That others viewed him as "different," however, was made clear every day by passing comments or inquiries. Even within our family the arrival of grandchildren prompted new questions. At some point, each of the eight grandchildren became aware of the hook that dangled from their grandfather's right arm, and the responses were always the same: curiosity mingled with varying amounts of fear. The moment when a grandchild

---

1. On the distinctions between impairment as "an abnormality or loss of physiological form or function," disability as "the consequences of the impairment, that is an inability to perform some task or activity considered necessary," and handicap as "a social disadvantage that results from an impairment or disability," see Nancy L. Eiesland, *The Disabled God: Toward a Liberatory Theology of Disability* (Nashville: Abingdon, 1994), 27.

143

draws up enough courage to ask "Pa-paw" how he lost his arm has become a rite of passage in our family. As one generation is now yielding to the next, the story has become part of the Parsons' family lore.

This book has not been about perceptions of physical disability in the ancient world per se, nor consequently has it drawn very deeply on the burgeoning field of disability studies.[2] Nonetheless, my father's story has remained persistently in the background as I, an able-bodied male, have explored the ancients' views concerning the relationship between physique and moral character.

Furthermore, we read and hear these ancient texts in a contemporary cultural context that knows the "emancipation proclamation" embodied in the Americans with Disabilities Act of 1990,[3] on the one hand, and the reality of racial profiling in a post–9/11 world, on the other. In these contexts, Luke's stories of the bent woman, short Zacchaeus, the lame man, and the eunuch have remarkable relevance for contemporary theological reflection and homiletical exposition. I hope the preceding chapters have laid a foundation that invites such illuminating reflection and exposition beyond what I have done, whether in relation to disability studies, theological reflection, or homiletical exposition.

We may never know whether Luke was the "beloved physician" referred to in the Pauline corpus (Col. 4:14),[4] but Luke the physiognomist (or rather, antiphysiognomist) has made clear that the lowly who are exalted in this Gospel (cf. 1:52) include those whose physical traits and limitations might lead others to label them as outcasts according to conventional physiognomic canons. Luke uses physiognomic conventions to subvert them. For the Lukan Jesus, one's moral character is not determined by the color, shape, size, or limitations of one's body. This fact explains why

2. See Eiesland, *The Disabled God*; Nancy L. Eiesland and Don E. Saliers, eds., *Human Disability and the Service of God: Reassessing Religious Practice* (Nashville: Abingdon, 1998); David T. Mitchell and Sharon L. Snyder, eds., *The Body and Physical Difference: Discourses of Disability* (Ann Arbor: University of Michigan Press, 1997); Hector Avalos, *Health Care and the Rise of Christianity* (Peabody, MA: Hendrickson, 1999); idem, *Illness and Health Care in the Ancient Near East* (Atlanta: Scholars Press, 1995). On disability and biblical studies, see Rebecca Raphael, "What Has Biblical Literature to Do with Disability Studies?" *SBL Forum*, April 2004, http://www.sbl-site.org/Article.aspx?ArticleId=250.

3. So called by Eiesland, *The Disabled God*, 19. The Act reads in part: "The Nation's proper goals regarding individuals with disabilities are to assure equality of opportunity, full participation, independent living, and economic self-sufficiency."

4. When I first began this study, I was hopeful that I might explain previous attempts to attribute Luke and Acts to the "beloved physician" on the basis of so-called medical terminology in terms of Luke's use and critique of physiognomic concepts and canons in ways similar to, say, Galen the physician (see chapter 1). I quickly abandoned this quest, however, in favor of the connection between our four stories and Luke's understanding of them in light of the Abrahamic covenant.

Luke does not give physical descriptions of other characters in his works (Jesus, the disciples, John the Baptist, the Pharisees, etc.), since to do so would reinforce the same connection between outer appearance and inner character that he elsewhere struggles to break.

Luke has radically redrawn the map of who is in and who is out. He has done so under scriptural warrant, based on his understanding of the implications of the Abrahamic covenant for those so often excluded, whether because of physical condition or gender or ethnic and racial identity. For Luke, God's covenant people can be a blessing to the nations only by including Gentiles in the community itself. Luke's vision of this Abrahamic community is based also on his understanding of the teachings of Jesus, who held up the positive example of an otherwise despised Samaritan (Luke 10). Luke is adamant: "God shows no partiality" (Acts 10:34). Consequently, the covenant messianic community, the "whole" body of Christ, includes even—perhaps especially—those who do not themselves have, in the eyes of the larger culture, a "whole" body. The kingdom of God belongs to these, and they to God's covenant community.

Appendix

Illustrations from the *Progymnasmata* of Libanius

L ibanius of Antioch was the leading pagan rhetorician of the second half of the fourth century. Born in 314 to a prominent Antiochene family and trained at Athens, he taught rhetoric in the imperial capitals Constantinople and Nicomedia before returning to Antioch for the remainder of his career. He was a friend and consultant to emperors, notably Constantius II and Julian ("the Apostate"), and teacher to numerous leading orators of his day, pagan and Christian alike (most likely including John Chrysostom, Theodore of Mopsuestia, Basil of Caesarea, and Gregory of Nazianzus). The surviving corpus of his orations includes a set of progymnasmata. While of course dating from the fourth century, these exercises for rhetoric students are deeply rooted in traditions that extend back to the days of the author of Luke and Acts and beyond. The four examples given here show how to turn the tables on convention by praising the despised Homeric character Thersites and by praising or blaming, as need might dictate, the Homeric hero Achilles. See pages 129 and 130 above for discussion. Dr. Craig Gibson has generously provided these translations and the accompanying footnotes from a complete translation of the *Progymnasmata* of Libanius that he is preparing for publication in the Society of Biblical Literature's Writings from the Greco-Roman World series. They are included here by permission of the Society of Biblical Literature. The Greek texts are in *Libanii opera*, vol. 8, edited by Richard Foerster (Leipzig: Teubner, 1915).

1. *Encomium of Thersites* (*Prog.* 8.4.1–19)

1 Begging Homer's pardon, I myself will attempt to praise this man of whom the poet wished to speak badly—by whom I mean Thersites. I will try to discuss him a little, offering Homer himself as witness to certain points.

2 First of all, therefore, he was not descended from lowly or anonymous parents, unless anyone regards Agrius and his father and grandfather as lowly,[1] but no one sensible would do so. So that if Thersites wanted to exalt himself among the Greeks because of his ancestry, as did his relative Diomedes,[2] he would not have been at a loss for words, but would also have been able to say of himself: "For three blameless sons were born to Portheus."[3] But in fact, not even when he was being wronged by Odysseus did he mention his ancestors as one might do, thinking that he deserved good repute among the others because of his family. 3 Having been raised, therefore, as seems reasonable for someone descended from such ancestors, and being able to participate in deeds befitting heroes, he went against the boar, when Meleager brought together all the other best men against that bane of the land,[4] but after leaving from there he became sick and the disease injured his body. 4 This did not, however, make his soul worse or drive out of it either his courage or his desire for glory. There is evidence for this: for when the Atreidae were assembling the fleet against the barbarians, although, if he wanted to live a carefree life, he had the misfortune to his body as an attractive pretext for doing so, he could not bear hearing about the action as he waited at home, but rather, although he was free of the necessity imposed by the oath, which had forced the rest to board the ships,[5] he set sail just as though he had sworn all the oaths, and his anger against the wrongdoers spurred him

---

1. His father was Agrius (Apollodorus, *Bibl.* 1.8.6), grandfather Porthaon, and great-grandfather Hippodamas (1.7.10).

2. Thersites' father Agrius (schol. in Homer, *Il.* 2.212) had a brother Oeneus (ibid. and Homer, *Il.* 14.115–17), who was Diomedes' paternal grandfather (Homer, *Il.* 14.118).

3. Homer, *Il.* 14.115. The sons' names were Agrius, Melas, and Oeneus (lines 116–17).

4. Schol. in Homer, *Il.* 2.212, with citations of Pherecydes (*FGrH* 3 F123) and Euphorion (frag. 106, Powell). For the story of the Calydonian boar, see Apollodorus, *Bibl.* 1.8.2–3.

5. Apollodorus, *Bibl.* 3.10.8–9.

on, and though he was bandy-legged,[6] he believed that the war needed a soul that knew how to be daring, so that it seems to me that the man who contributed such a body to the Trojan War also made the rest more eager to put out to sea. 5 For which of the others would not be ashamed to seek exemption from military service, when Thersites was so in love with spears and wounds? But hearing, as seems reasonable, that both Odysseus and the noble son of Peleus[7] were disgracefully trying to hide themselves from the struggles, and that one had taken on the guise of a girl and the other a reputation for insanity,[8] he both mocked them and spoke words suitable for such wickedness, not because he envied the one his intelligence or the other his courage, since he would thus have envied Ajax, son of Telamon, and he would thus have envied Nestor, who was sweeter than honey.[9] 6 But rather, as I believe, he could not resist vilifying their evil actions. Therefore he did not speak against Achilles when he was convening the assembly during the plague,[10] nor did he delight in Achilles' being robbed of his honor, but rather he—quite the contrary— grieved along with him. Nor, therefore, did he slander the man who had robbed him of it, not even when Odysseus was leading out the embassy.[11] But rather, he was moved to words and accusations against the wrongdo- ers by the mishandling of the situation, and he did not fear the fortunes of some, and he did not flatter those in power while being harsh to men of the people, foully abusing and persecuting those who were weaker. 7 For he knew that not living a life of luxury would be enough to make the latter behave with self-control, but for those in power and with full tables and riches, there was need of someone with wisdom and a bene- ficial frankness of speech, who would understand the wrongs being done and would rebuke and shout down and prevent some of them, but correct others, and who would fear nothing at all—neither a sceptre, nor a man's rhetorical ability, nor a host of friends, nor those who were shielding them. 8 Just such a man would later happen to be born among the Athe- nians: Demosthenes,[12] who judged the common benefit more important than what would profit himself, and by saying what he knew would heal the people he chose to anger rather than wickedly gratify them. 9 To this

6. Homer, *Il.* 2.216–19, esp. 217.

7. I.e., Achilles. These were the two heroes who hated Thersites the most (Homer, *Il.*, 2.220).

8. Apollodorus, *Bibl.* 3.13.8; *Epit.* 3.7.

9. Homer, *Il.* 1.249.

10. Ibid. 1.53–67.

11. The embassy to Chryses is meant (Homer, *Il.* 1.430–31).

12. Athenian statesman and orator, 384–322 BCE, frequently praised in Libanius's collection.

post Thersites also assigned himself. And, as seems likely, many assemblies received many noble public speeches from this orator, not speaking briefly about important matters, but rather amplifying his words to fit the need, and it is very worthy to admire this man, who was also found worthy to be remembered by Homer. **10** For when Thersites saw the man who deigned to rule the rest being a slave to captive women, and at one time being responsible for the plague on the army, at another cutting Achilles out of his forces, now because of the daughter of Chryses, now because of the daughter of Briseus, and looking only to how he might enjoy the beauty of their bodies,[13] but not caring whether the affairs of the Greeks would become any worse because of it, and openly mentioning retreat, but secretly preparing to stay,[14] and saying some things himself, but doing others through flatterers, and doing a deed uncharacteristic even of a private soldier, let alone a king—when he came forward to speak, Thersites used words very worthy of his lineage, immediately bringing up Agamemnon's love of money,[15] for which Achilles had also criticized him earlier.[16] And yet how is it not terrible that whenever Achilles speaks, his speech is not foolish, but when the other speaks, —? **11** Therefore, the fact that he made truthful accusations <demonstrates> the righteousness of Thersites, while his anger over Achilles' withdrawal from the alliance demonstrates his concern for the commonwealth, and his bold criticism of the one in power and his declaration that the one who was being abused was better than he demonstrates his courage. **12** And from what he says about him, Homer makes it clear that he both attacked cities and took captives.[17] For he would not have been so shameless as to brag falsely in front of those who knew otherwise, but rather having his actions as his witness he naturally used reverent words in the assembly—unless someone would claim that he had gone mad. But Homer did not say this; rather, he stated that Thersites was pointy-headed and bald with thinning hair, and that he talked too much, and things like that,[18] but he did not add "mad." Therefore the man of sound mind would never suffer the symptoms of a madman. And so Thersites was one of those feared by the enemy, if he was in fact leading their sons off in chains. **13** But if this was not the case, but rather he was absolutely useless, he would not have come

13. Homer, *Il.* 2.232–33.
14. Ibid., 2.73–74, 110–41.
15. Ibid., 2.225–31.
16. Ibid., 1.122.
17. Ibid., 2.229–31.
18. Ibid., 2.212–19.

at all, because Diomedes would not have allowed it;[19] but even if Diomedes had overlooked that, he would not have allowed him to make a nuisance of himself in the assemblies or praise himself in an unbecoming manner, knowing that he himself would also share in the disgrace. 14 Come now, how was he worse than Nestor in what he said?[20] But more to the point, how was he not better? For Nestor tried to placate both men, both the one who made the threat and the one who was grossly abused, and he understood everything well but clearly did not dare to say what he was thinking. 15 But Thersites held nothing back and put virtue before fortune. And he said this not because he was jealous about Briseis, but rather because he saw what would happen if Achilles did not fight alongside them, which Homer himself also narrates. And so Thersites' frankness of speech seems greater than Nestor's, who was now serving as king for a third generation.[21] 16 Therefore, he did not especially hate Achilles, but rather, as seems reasonable, he criticized him for his self-importance, but collided with the rest on his behalf whenever circumstances called for it, not allowing anyone to be wronged by anyone else, so far as he could prevent it. 17 And the Greeks testified to his reputation as a good speaker, neither saying that he should be thrown out in the midst of his speech, nor demanding punishment for what he said, because, as I believe, it would have been spoken truthfully. But there was someone who was behaving with gross violence, who wanted to be a speaker, who was being stung by the flow of words from Thersites and slandered his skill with a speech.[22] 18 Therefore, Thersites took these two men as witnesses to the fact that he had used his words justly—both the one who struck him and Agamemnon, the latter by his silence, the former by the fact that he struck him.[23] For this was an acknowledgment that he could not refute him at all; this is to the discredit not of the one who suffered the blows, but rather of the one who dealt them. 19 And one might naturally blame fortune for his body and the man who violated the laws of hubris for his rudeness. And Thersites might also be admired for this: that although he suffered terribly, he knew how to bear it and did not desert to the enemy, whom he could have raised up and emboldened by telling them all the secrets of the Greeks.

19. Presumably because of their kinship.
20. Homer, *Il.* 1.275–77.
21. Ibid., 1.252.
22. I.e., Odysseus (Homer, *Il.* 2.244–64).
23. Odysseus strikes Thersites (Ibid., 2.265–69).

2. Excerpt from *Encomium of Achilles* (*Prog.* 8.3.2)

As to the fact that his ancestor was the chief of the gods and the family of the Aeacidae was mightier than the other demigods, why must I dwell on these points, too?[24] So many can be found who share this in common with him. But his mother was a goddess and his food was the marrow of lions rather than milk.[25] In both of these ways he was very different.[26] For no nurse took up the child and nursed him at her breast, but rather Cheiron[27] devised for him whatever <food> he knew would contribute to his courage, rejecting the common food of men.

3. Excerpt from *Invective against Achilles* (*Prog.* 9.1.3)

Therefore, I will show clearly that Achilles was just such a man, stating by way of introduction that those who revere him say that under his guardian Cheiron[28] his food was the marrow of lions rather than milk.[29] Therefore, let it be granted that the Centaur was divine; and yet who could believe that the form of his body was composed of a man and a horse? And while not disputing the claim about the food, I would say that the proper food for men is milk, and that this conforms to the law of nature. Whoever has had the misfortune to have been raised in this way, this clearly works to his detriment. The one food is proper for civilized men, but the other would make them like wild animals.

4. Excerpt from *Comparison of Ajax and Achilles* (*Prog.* 10.2.3)

Someone considers it strange that Achilles was raised on the marrow of lions.[30] To this person I will say that Ajax's food was more customary. And so any man who has been raised as befits a man is better in this very respect than one raised outside of human customs.

24. Achilles was the son of Peleus, grandson of Aeacus, and great-grandson of Zeus (Apollodorus, *Bibl.* 3.12.6).
25. Apollodorus, *Bibl.* 3.13.6.
26. Or "far superior"?
27. Apollodorus, *Bibl.* 3.13.6.
28. Centaur who taught many Greek heroes (see Xenophon, *Cyn.* for a list; cf. Apollodorus).
29. Apollodorus, *Bibl.* 3.13.6.
30. Ibid.

Abbreviations

General

AB	Anchor Bible
ANF	Alexander Roberts and James Donaldson. *The Ante-Nicene Fathers.* 10 vols. 1885–1887. Repr. Peabody, MA: Hendrickson, 1994.
ANTC	Abingdon New Testament Commentaries
BDAG	F. W. Danker. *A Greek-English Lexicon of the New Testament and Other Early Christian Literature.* 3rd ed. Chicago: University of Chicago Press, 1999.
BETL	Bibliotheca Ephemeridum Theologicarum Lovaniensium
FGrH	*Die Fragmente der griechischen Historiker.* Edited by Felix Jacoby. Leiden: Brill, 1954–1964.
HTS	Harvard Theological Studies
ICC	International Critical Commentary
JSNTSup	Journal for the Study of the New Testament: Supplement Series
JSPSup	Journal for the Study of Pseudepigrapha: Supplement Series
JSOTSup	Journal for the Study of the Old Testament: Supplement Series
L&N	J. P. Louw and E. A. Nida. *Greek-English Lexicon of the New Testament: Based on Semantic Domains.* 2nd ed. New York: United Bible Societies, 1989.
LCL	Loeb Classical Library. Cambridge, MA: Harvard University Press.
LSJ	H. G. Liddell, R. Scott, H. S. Jones. *A Greek-English Lexicon.* 9th ed. with revised supplement. Oxford: Oxford University Press, 1996.
LXX	Septuagint
NASB	New American Standard Bible
NICNT	New International Commentary on the New Testament
NIV	New International Version

NPNF	Philip Schaff. *Nicene and Post-Nicene Fathers*. 28 vols. 1886–1889. Repr. Peabody, MA: Hendrickson, 1994.
NRSV	New Revised Standard Version
OBT	Overtures in Biblical Theology
P.Oxy.	*Oxyrhynchus Papyri*. London: Egypt Exploration Fund, 1898–.
RE	J. J. Herzog. *Realencyklopädie für protestantische Theologie und Kirche*. Leipzig: Hinrichs, 1896–1913.
RNT	Regensburger Neues Testament
RSV	Revised Standard Version
SBL	Society of Biblical Literature
SBLDS	Society of Biblical Literature Dissertation Series
schol.	scholiast
SEG	*Supplementum epigraphicum graecum*. 1923–.
SNTSMS	Study for New Testament Studies Monograph Series
SP	Sacra Pagina
Str-B	H. L. Strack and P. Billerbeck. *Kommentar zum Neuen Testament aus Talmud und Midrasch*. 6 vols. Munich: Beck, 1922–1961.
TDNT	G. Kittel and G. Friedrich. eds. *Theological Dictionary of the New Testament*. Translated by G. W. Bromiley. 10 vols. Grand Rapids: Eerdmans, 1964–1976.
THKNT	Theologischer Handkommentar zun Neuen Testament
WBC	Word Biblical Commentary
WUNT	Wissenschaftliche Untersuchungen zum Neuen Testament
ZNW	*Zeitschrift für die neutestamentliche Wissenschaft und die Kunde der älteren Kirche*

Old Testament

Gen.	Genesis	Job	Job
Exod.	Exodus	Ps. (Pss.)	Psalms
Lev.	Leviticus	Prov.	Proverbs
Num.	Numbers	Eccles.	Ecclesiastes
Deut.	Deuteronomy	Song	Song of Songs
Josh.	Joshua	Isa.	Isaiah
Judg.	Judges	Jer.	Jeremiah
Ruth	Ruth	Lam.	Lamentations
1–2 Sam.	1–2 Samuel	Ezek.	Ezekiel
1–2 Kings	1–2 Kings	Dan.	Daniel
1–2 Chron.	1–2 Chronicles	Hosea	Hosea
Ezra	Ezra	Joel	Joel
Neh.	Nehemiah	Amos	Amos
Esther	Esther	Obad.	Obadiah

Jon.	Jonah	Zeph.	Zephaniah
Mic.	Micah	Hag.	Haggai
Nah.	Nahum	Zech.	Zechariah
Hab.	Habakkuk	Mal.	Malachi

New Testament

Matt.	Matthew	1–2 Thess.	1–2 Thessalonians
Mark	Mark	1–2 Tim.	1–2 Timothy
Luke	Luke	Titus	Titus
John	John	Philem.	Philemon
Acts	Acts	Heb.	Hebrews
Rom.	Romans	James	James
1–2 Cor.	1–2 Corinthians	1–2 Pet.	1–2 Peter
Gal.	Galatians	1–3 John	1–3 John
Eph.	Ephesians	Jude	Jude
Phil.	Philippians	Rev.	Revelation
Col.	Colossians		

Deuterocanonical Books

| Sir. | Sirach |
| 4 Macc. | 4 Maccabees |

Pseudepigrapha

1–2 En.	*1–2 Enoch*	*T. Gad*	*Testament of Gad*
Gk. Apoc.		*T. Jos.*	*Testament of Joseph*
Ezra	*Greek Apocalypse of Ezra*	*T. Naph.*	*Testament of Naphtali*
Jub.	*Jubilees*	*T. Sim.*	*Testament of Simeon*
Pss. Sol.	*Psalms of Solomon*	*T. Zeb.*	*Testament of Zebulun*

Dead Sea Scrolls

| 1QSa | Community Rule |
| 4QD | Damascus Document |

Rabbinic Literature

b.	Babylonian Talmud	*Num. Rab.*	*Numbers Rabbah*
m.	Mishnah	*Ruth Rab.*	*Ruth Rabbah*
Ber.	*Berakot*	*Sanh.*	*Sanhedrin*
Eccles. Rab.	*Ecclesiastes Rabbah*	*Tanh. Qed.*	*Tanhuma Qedoshim*
Gen. Rab.	*Genesis Rabbah*	*Tanh. Tol.*	*Tanhuma Toledot*
Lev. Rab.	*Leviticus Rabbah*	*Tehar.*	*Teharot*

Miscellaneous Early Christian Writings

Acts Paul Thec.	*Acts of Paul and Thecla*
Barn.	*Barnabas*
1 Clem.	*1 Clement*
2 Clem.	*2 Clement*

Other Ancient Writings

Author	Abbreviation	Title
Achilles Tatius	*Leuc. Clit.*	*Leucippe et Cleitophon*
Adamantius		*Physiognomonica*
Aeschines	*Fals. leg.*	*De falsa legatione*
Aeschylus	*Cho.*	*Choephori*
Aesop	*Fab.*	*Fabulae*
Ambrose	*Off.*	*De officiis ministrorum*
Ammianus Marcellinus	*Res gest.*	*Res gestae*
Anth. Gr.		*Anthologia Graeca*
Aphthonius the Sophist	(without title abbrev.)	*Progymnasmata*
Apollodorus	*Bibl.*	*Bibliotheca*
Apuleius	*Metam.*	*Metamorphoses*
Aristophanes	*Pax*	*Pax*
Aristotle	*Eth. Eud.*	*Ethica Eudemia*
Aristotle	*Eth. Nic.*	*Ethica Nichomachea*
Aristotle	*Gen. an.*	*De generatione animalium*
Aristotle	*Hist. an.*	*Historia animalium*
Aristotle	*Part. an.*	*De partibus animalium*
Ps.-Aristotle	(without title abbrev.)	*Physiognomica*
Ps.-Aristotle	*Probl.*	*Problemata*
Athenaeus	*Deipn.*	*Deipnosophistae*
Augustine	*Serm.*	*Sermones*
Aulus Gellius	*Noct. Att.*	*Noctes Atticae*
Babrius	(without title abbrev.)	*Mythiambi Aesopici*
Basil	*Ep.*	*Epistulae*
Cicero	*De or.*	*De oratore*
Cicero	*Fat.*	*De fato*
Cicero	*Leg.*	*De legibus*
Cicero	*Off.*	*De officiis*
Cicero	*Pis.*	*In Pisonem*
Cicero	*Tusc.*	*Tusculanae disputationes*
Clement of Alexandria	*Paed.*	*Paedagogus*
Clement of Alexandria	*Strom.*	*Stromata*
De physiogn.		*De physiognomia*
Demosthenes	*1 Aristog.*	*In Aristogitonem*
Demosthenes	*Or.*	*Orationes*

Author	Abbreviation	Title
Didymus	In Gen.	In Genesim
Dio Cassius	(without title abbrev.)	Historiae Romanae
Dio Chrysostom	Or.	Orationes
Diodorus Siculus	Bibl. hist.	Bibliotheca historica
Diogenes Laertius	Vit.	Vitae philosophorum
Dionysius of Halicarnassos	Ant. Rom.	Antiquitates Romanae
Epictetus	Diatr.	Diatribai
Epig. Gr.		Epigrammata Graeca
Epitom. Matr.		Epitomis Matritensi
Eusebius	Hist. eccl.	Historia ecclesiastica
Galen	Anim. mor.	Quod animi mores corporis temperamenta sequantur
Galen	Mixt.	Mixtura
Gregory Nazianzen	Or.	Orationes
Hermogenes	(without title abbrev.)	Progymnasmata
Herodotus	Hist.	Historiae
Hesiod	Op.	Opera et dies
Hesiod	Theog.	Theogonia
Hippocrates	Aër.	De aëre, aquis, et locis
Hippocrates	Epid.	Epidemiae
Hippocrates	Lex	Lex
Hippolytus	Haer.	Refutatio omnium haeresium
Homer	Il.	Ilias
Homer	Od.	Odyssea
Iamblichus	Vit. Pyth.	De vita Pythagorica
Irenaeus	Haer.	Adversus haereses
John Chrysostom	Comm. Gal.	In epistulam ad Galatas commentarius
John Chrysostom	Hom. Matt.	Homiliae in Matthaeum
John Chrysostom	Hom. Rom.	Homiliae in epistulam ad Romanos
John of Sardis	(without title abbrev.)	Progymnasmata
Josephus	C. Ap.	Contra Apionem
Josephus	Ant.	Antiquitates Judaicae
Josephus	Bell.	De bello Judaico
Justin	1 Apol.	Apologia
Libanius	Or.	Orationes
Libanius	Prog.	Progymnasmata
Lucian	Eunuch.	Eunuchus
Lucian	Sat.	Saturnalia
Lucian	Somn.	Somnium
Lucian	Symp.	Symposium
Marcus Aurelius	Med.	Meditationes
Nicolaus	(without title abbrev.)	Progymnasmata
Ps.-Nonnus	Comm. Greg.	In iv orationes Gregorii Nazianzeni commentarii
Origen	Cels.	Contra Celsum

Author	*Abbreviation*	*Title*
Ovid	*Metam.*	*Metamorphoses*
Pausanias	*Descr.*	*Graeciae descriptio*
Philo of Alexandria	*Abr.*	*De Abrahamo*
Philo of Alexandria	*Legat.*	*Legatio ad Gaium*
Philo of Alexandria	*Praem.*	*De praemiis et poenis*
Philo of Alexandria	*Prob.*	*Quod omnis probus liber sit*
Philo of Alexandria	*Sacr.*	*De sacrificiis Abelis et Caini*
Philo of Alexandria	*Spec.*	*De specialibus legibus*
Philostratus	*Vit. Apoll.*	*Vita Apollonii*
Philostratus	*Vit. soph.*	*Vitae sophistarum*
Photius	*Lex.*	*Lexicon*
Pindar	*Pyth.*	*Pythionikai*
Plato	*Resp.*	*Respublica*
Plato	*Soph.*	*Sophista*
Pliny the Elder	*Hist. nat.*	*Historia naturalis*
Plutarch	*Cat. maj.*	*Cato major (Marcus Cato)*
Plutarch	*Mor.*	*Moralia*
Plutarch	*Tim.*	*Timoleon*
[Ps.-]Plutarch	*Lib. ed.*	*De liberis educandis*
[Ps.-]Polemo	(without title abbrev.)	*Physiognomonica*
Pollux	*Onom.*	*Onomasticon*
Polybius	*Hist.*	*Historiae*
Porphyry	*Vita Pyth.*	*Vita Pythagorae*
Quintilian	*Inst.*	*Institutio oratoria*
Seneca the Younger	*Ep.*	*Epistulae morales*
Seneca the Younger	*Nat.*	*Naturales quaestiones*
Strabo	*Geogr.*	*Geographia*
Suetonius	*Aug.*	*Divus Augustus*
Suetonius	*Cal.*	*Gaius Caligula*
Suetonius	*Tib.*	*Tiberius*
Tertullian	*An.*	*De anima*
Tertullian	*Bapt.*	*De baptismo*
Tertullian	*Cult. fem.*	*De cultu feminarum*
Theon of Alexandria	(without title abbrev.)	*Progymnasmata*
Xenophon	*Cyn.*	*Cynegeticus*

BIBLIOGRAPHY

Achtemeier, Paul. "The Lucan Perspective on the Miracles of Jesus: A Preliminary Sketch." *Journal of Biblical Literature* 94 (1975): 547–62.

Alexander, Philip S. "Physiognomy, Initiation, and Rank in the Qumran Community." In *Geschichte—Tradition—Reflexion: Festschrift für Martin Hengel zum 70. Geburtstag; Band I. Judentum,* edited by Hubert Cancik, Hermann Lichtenberger, and Peter Schäfer, 385–94. Tübingen: J. C. B. Mohr, 1996.

Allison, Dale. "The Eye Is the Lamp of the Body (Matthew 6.22–23 = Luke 11.34–36)." *New Testament Studies* 33 (1987): 61–83.

Ambrose. *Les Devoirs: Introduction.* Edited and translated by Maurice Testard. Paris: Belles Lettres, 1984.

André, Jacques, ed. and trans. *Anonyme Latin: Traité de Physiognomonie.* Paris: Belles Lettres, 1981.

Armstrong, A. MacC. "The Methods of the Greek Physiognomists." *Greece and Rome* 5 (1958): 52–56.

Atkins, Margaret. "Early Christians and Animals." *Journal of Eccleiastical History* 51 (2000): 774–75.

Avalos, Hector. *Health Care and the Rise of Christianity.* Peabody, MA: Hendrickson, 1999.

———. *Illness and Health Care in the Ancient Near East.* Atlanta: Scholars Press, 1995.

Bailey, Kenneth E. *Poet and Peasant.* Grand Rapids: Eerdmans, 1976.

Balentine, Samuel E. *Leviticus.* Interpretation: A Commentary for Preaching and Teaching. Louisville: Westminster John Knox, 2002.

Ballók, János. "The Description of Paul in the Acta Pauli." In *The Apocryphal Acts of Paul and Thecla,* edited by Jan N. Bremmer, 1–15. Kampen: Pharos, 1996.

Baltzer, Klaus. *Deutero-Isaiah: A Commentary on Isaiah 40–55.* Translated by Margaret Kohl. Hermeneia. Minneapolis: Fortress, 2001.

Barrett, C. K. *A Critical and Exegetical Commentary on the Acts of the Apostles.* 2 vols. International Critical Commentary. Edinburgh: T&T Clark, 1994.

Barton, Tamsyn S. *Power and Knowledge: Astrology, Physiognomics, and Medicine under the Roman Empire.* Ann Arbor: University of Michigan Press, 1994.

Bauckham, Richard. "The Parable of the Royal Wedding Feast (Matthew 22:1–14) and the Parable of the Lame Man and the Blind Man (*Apocryphon of Ezekiel*)." *Journal of Biblical Literature* (1996): 471–88.

Bede. *Commentary on the Acts of the Apostles.* Translated by Lawrence T. Martin. Kalamazoo, MI: Cistercian Publications, 1989.

Best, Ernest. *Second Corinthians.* Louisville: John Knox Press, 1987.

Betcher, Sharon V. "Rehabilitating Religious Discourse: Bringing Disability Studies to the Theological Venue." *Religious Studies Review* 27 (2001): 341–48.

Betz, H. D. "Matthew vi.22f. and Ancient Greek Theories of Vision." In *Text and Interpretation: Studies in the New Testament Presented to Matthew Black,* edited by E. Best and R. McL. Wilson, 43–56. Cambridge: Cambridge University Press, 1979.

Blenkinsopp, Joseph. *Isaiah 40–55.* Anchor Bible 19. New York: Doubleday, 2002.

Bock, Darrell L. *Luke.* InterVarsity Press New Testament Commentary Series. Downer's Grove, IL: InterVarsity, 1994.

Bonner, S. F. *Education in Ancient Rome.* Berkeley: University of California Press, 1977.

Boorstin, Daniel J. *The Discoverers.* New York: Random House, 1983.

Bousset, W. *The Antichrist Legend: A Chapter in Christian and Jewish Folklore.* Translated by A. H. Keene, introduced by D. Frankfurter. Text and Translation Series 24. Atlanta: Scholars Press, 1999.

Bovon, François. "Names and Numbers in Early Christianity." *New Testament Studies* 47 (2001): 267–88.

Bowersock, G. W. *Augustus and the Greek World.* Oxford: Clarendon, 1965.

Boys-Stones, George. "Physiognomy and Ancient Psychological Theory." In *Seeing the Face, Seeing the Soul: Polemon's Physiognomy from Classical Antiquity to Medieval Islam,* edited by Simon Swain. Oxford: Oxford University Press, 2006.

Braun, Willi. "Physiotherapy of Femininity in the *Acts of Thecla.*" In *Text and Artifact in the Religions of Mediterranean Antiquity: Essays in Honour of Peter Richardson,* edited by Stephen G. Wilson and Michel Desjardins, 209–30. Waterloo, Ont.: Wilfrid Laurier University Press, 2000.

———. *Feasting and Social Rhetoric in Luke 14.* Society for New Testament Studies Monograph Series 85. Cambridge: Cambridge University Press, 1995.

Brawley, Robert. "Abrahamic Covenant Traditions and the Characterization of God in Luke-Acts." In *The Unity of Luke Acts,* edited by J. Verheyden, 109–32. Bibliotheca Ephemeridum Theologicarum Lovaniensium 142. Leuven: Leuven University Press, 1999.

Bregman, Marc. "The Parable of the Lame and the Blind: Epiphanius' Quotation from an Apocryphon of Ezekiel." *Journal of Theological Studies* 42 (1991): 125–38.

Brown, Raymond E. *The Birth of the Messiah.* Garden City, NY: Doubleday, 1977.

Brueggemann, Walter. *Isaiah 40–66*. Louisville: Westminster John Knox, 1998.

Bultmann, Rudolf. *The History of the Synoptic Tradition*. New York: Harper & Row, 1963.

Buth, R. "That Small-Fry Herod Antipas, or When a Fox Is Not a Fox." *Jerusalem Perspective* 40 (1993): 7–14.

Cadbury, Henry J. *The Style and Literary Method of Luke*. Harvard Theological Studies 6. Cambridge, MA: Harvard University Press, 1920.

Clark, D. L. *Rhetoric in Graeco-Roman Education*. New York: Columbia University Press, 1957.

Cohen, Kenneth. "King Saul: A Bungler from the Beginning." *Bible Review* 10 (1994): 34–39, 56–57.

Conrad, Edgar W. *Reading Isaiah*. Overtures in Biblical Theology. Minneapolis: Fortress, 1991.

Conyers, A. J. *The Long Truce: How Toleration Made the World Safe for Power and Profit*. Dallas: Spence, 2001.

Cooper, Howard. "'Too Tall by Half'—King Saul and Tragedy in the Hebrew Bible." *Journal of Progressive Judaism* 9 (November 1997): 5–22.

Coussin, J. "Suétone physiognomiste dans les vies des XII Césars." *Revue d'études latines* 31 (1953): 234–56.

Creed, J. M. *The Gospel of Luke*. London: Macmillan, 1953.

Cribiore, Raffaella. *Gymnastics of the Mind*. Princeton, NJ: Princeton University Press, 2001.

———. *Writing, Teachers, and Students in Graeco-Roman Egypt*. Atlanta: Scholars Press, 1996.

Cross, Frank, and Emmanuel Tov. "The Composition of 1 Samuel 16–18 in the Light of the Septuagint Version." In *Empirical Models for Biblical Criticism*, edited by Jeffrey H. Tigay, 97–130. Philadelphia: University of Pennsylvania Press, 1985.

Cummins, Stephen A. *Paul and the Crucified Christ in Antioch: Maccabean Martyrdom and Galatians 1 and 2*. Society for New Testament Studies Monograph Series 114. Cambridge: Cambridge University Press, 2001.

Cyril of Alexandria. *Commentary on the Gospel of Saint Luke*. Translated by R. Payne Smith. [n.p.]: Studion, 1983.

Dahl, N. A. "The Story of Abraham in Luke-Acts." In *Jesus in the Memory of the Early Church*, 66–86. Minneapolis: Fortress, 1976.

Daley, L. W., trans. *Aesop without Morals*. New York: Thomas Yoseloff, 1961.

Danker, Frederick W. *Jesus and the New Age: A Commentary on St. Luke's Gospel*. Rev. ed. Philadelphia: Fortress, 1988.

Darr, John. *Herod the Fox: Audience Criticism and Lukan Characterization*. Journal for the Study of the New Testament: Supplement Series 163. Sheffield: Sheffield Academic Press, 1998.

Dasen, Véronique. *Dwarfs in Ancient Egypt and Greece*. Oxford: Clarendon, 1993.

DeLacy, Philip. Review of *Physiognomics in the Ancient World*, by Elizabeth C. Evans. *American Journal of Philology* 92 (1971): 508–10.

Derrett, J. D. M. "Positive Perspectives on Two Lucan Miracles." *Downside Review* 104 (1986): 274–84.

DeSilva, David A. *Perseverance in Gratitude: A Socio-Rhetorical Commentary on the Epistle "to the Hebrews."* Grand Rapids: Eerdmans, 2000.

"Digital Physiognomy Software—Match a Person's Face to His or Her Character." http://www.uniphiz.com/physiognomy.htm (accessed October 2005).

Donahue, John R. "Tax Collectors and Sinners: An Attempt at Identification." *Catholic Biblical Quarterly* 33 (1971): 39–61.

Eiesland, Nancy L. *The Disabled God: Toward a Liberatory Theology of Disability.* Nashville: Abingdon, 1994.

Eiesland, Nancy L., and Don E. Saliers, eds. *Human Disability and the Service of God: Reassessing Religious Practice.* Nashville: Abingdon, 1998.

Elliott, John. "The Evil Eye and the Sermon on the Mount: Contours of a Pervasive Belief in Social Scientific Perspective." *Biblical Interpretation* 2 (1994): 51–84.

Ellis, E. E. *The Gospel of Luke.* Greenwood, SC: Attic, 1966.

Ellul, Danielle. "Actes 3:1–11." *Etudes théologiques et religieuses* 64 (1989): 95–99.

Eslinger, Lyle. "'A Change of Heart': 1 Samuel 16." In *Ascribe to the Lord: Biblical and Other Studies in Memory of Peter C. Craigie,* edited by Lyle Eslinger and Glen Taylor, 341–61. Journal for the Study of the Old Testament: Supplement Series 67. Sheffield: JSOT Press, 1988.

Evans, Elizabeth C. "Descriptions of Personal Appearance in Roman History and Biography." *Harvard Studies in Classical Philology* 46 (1935): 43–84.

———. "Galen the Physician as Physiognomist." *Transactions and Proceedings of the American Philosophical Association* 76 (1945): 287–98.

———. *Physiognomics in the Ancient World.* Transactions of the American Philosophical Society 59, part 5. Philadelphia: American Philosophical Society, 1969.

Fitzmyer, Joseph A. *The Acts of the Apostles.* Anchor Bible 31. New York: Doubleday, 1998.

———. *The Gospel according to Luke.* 2 vols. Anchor Bible 28–28A. Garden City, NY: Doubleday, 1981–1985.

Foerster, Richard, ed. *Scriptores Physiognomonici Graeci et Latini.* 2 vols. Leipzig: Teubner, 1893.

Ford, J. Massyngbaerde. "The Physical Features of the Antichrist." *Journal for the Study of the Pseudepigrapha* 14 (1996): 23–41.

Ford, Jeffery. *The Physiognomy.* New York: Avon Books, 1997.

Friend, John. *Historia medicinae a Galeni tempore usque ad initium saeculi decimi sexti: In qua ea praecipue notantur quae ad praxim pertinent.* Leiden, 1750.

Funk, Robert W. *The Poetics of Biblical Narrative.* Sonoma, CA: Polebridge, 1988.

García Martínez, Florentino. *The Dead Sea Scrolls Translated: The Qumran Texts in English.* Translated by Wilfred G. E. Watson. Leiden: E. J. Brill, 1992.

García Martínez, Florentino, and Eibert J. C. Tigchelaar, eds. *The Dead Sea Scrolls Study Edition.* Vol. 1, *1Q1–4Q273.* Leiden: Brill, 1997.

Garland, Robert. *The Eye of the Beholder: Deformity and Disability in the Greco-Roman World.* Ithaca, NY: Cornell University Press, 1995.

Garnsey, Peter. *Ideas of Slavery from Aristotle to Augustine.* Cambridge: Cambridge University Press, 1996.

Gaventa, Beverly. *Acts.* Abingdon New Testament Commentaries. Nashville: Abingdon, 2003.

Geffcken, J. *Christliche Apokryphen.* Tübingen: Mohr, 1908.

Gleason, Maud W. *Making Men: Sophists and Self-Presentation in Ancient Rome.* Princeton, NJ: Princeton University Press, 1995.

Gow, A. S. T. *Theocritus.* 2nd ed. Cambridge: Cambridge University Press, 1952.

Graham, John. "Lavater's Physiognomy in England." *Journal of the History of Ideas* 22 (1961): 561–72.

Grant, Robert M. "The Description of Paul in the *Acts of Paul and Thecla.*" *Vigiliae Christianae* 36 (1982): 1–4.

———. *Early Christians and Animals.* London: Routledge, 1999.

Green, Joel B. *The Gospel of Luke.* New International Commentary on the New Testament. Grand Rapids: Eerdmans, 1997.

———. "Jesus and a Daughter of Abraham (Luke 13:10–17): Test Case for a Lucan Perspective on Jesus' Miracles." *Catholic Biblical Quarterly* 51 (1989): 643–54.

———. "The Problem of a Beginning: Israel's Scriptures in Luke 1–2." *Bulletin for Biblical Research* 4 (1994): 61–85.

Grimm, W. "Eschatologischer Saul wider eschatologischen David: Eine Deutung von Lc. Xiii 31ff." *Novum Testamentum* 15 (1973): 114–33.

Gruenwald, I. "Further Jewish Physiognomic and Chiromantic Fragments." *Tarbiz* 40 (1971): 301–19.

Grundman, W. *Das Evangelium nach Lukas.* Theologischer Handkommentar zum Neuen Testament 3. Berlin: Evangelische Verlagsanstalt, 1964.

Gunn, David. *The Fate of King Saul.* Sheffield: JSOT Press, 1984.

Haenchen, Ernst. *The Acts of the Apostles.* Translated by Bernard Noble and Gerald Shinn. Oxford: Blackwell's, 1971.

Hamm, M. Dennis. "Acts 3:1–10: The Healing of the Temple Beggar as Lucan Theology." *Biblica* 67 (1986): 305–19.

———. "Acts 3:12–26: Peter's Speech and the Healing of the Man Born Lame." *Perspectives in Religious Studies* 11 (1984): 199–217.

———. "The Freeing of the Bent Woman and the Restoration of Israel: Luke 13:10–17 as Narrative Theology." *Journal for the Study of the New Testament* 31 (1987): 23–44.

———. "Luke 19,8 Once Again: Does Zacchaeus Defend or Resolve?" *Journal of Biblical Literature* 107 (1988): 431–37.

———. "This Sign of Healing: Acts 3:1–10: A Study in Lucan Theology." Ph.D. dissertation, St. Louis University, 1975.

———. "Zacchaeus Revisited Once More: A Story of Vindication or Conversion?" *Biblica* 72 (1991): 249–52.

Harnack, Adolf. *Luke the Physician: The Author of the Third Gospel and the Acts of the Apostles.* Translated by J. R. Wilkinson. New York: G. P. Putnam's Sons, 1907.

Harrill, J. Albert. "Invective against Paul (2 Cor 10:10), the Physiognomics of the Ancient Slave Body, and the Greco-Roman Rhetoric of Manhood." In *Antiquity and Humanity: Essays on Ancient Religion and Philosophy: Presented to Hans Dieter Betz on His 70th Birthday,* edited by Adela Yarbro Collins and Margaret M. Mitchell, 189–213. Tübingen: Mohr Siebeck, 2001.

Harris, J. Rendel. "On the Stature of Our Lord." *Bulletin of the John Rylands Library* 10 (1926): 112–26.

Hartley, Lucy. *Physiognomy and the Meaning of Expression in Nineteenth-Century Culture.* Cambridge: Cambridge University Press, 2001.

Hawk, Daniel. "Saul as Sacrifice: The Tragedy of Israel's First Monarch." *Bible Review* 12, no. 6 (December 1993): 20–25, 56.

Hemer, Colin. *The Book of Acts in the Setting of Hellenistic History.* Tübingen: J. C. B. Mohr, 1989.

Henten, Jan Willem Can. *The Maccabean Martyrs as Saviours of the Jewish People: A Study of 2 and 4 Maccabees.* Supplements to the Journal for the Study of Judaism 57. Leiden: Brill, 1997.

Hobart, W. K. *The Medical Language of St. Luke.* Dublin: Hodges, Figgis, 1882. Reprinted, Grand Rapids: Baker, 1954.

Hock, Ronald F. "Homer in Greco-Roman Education." In *Mimesis and Intertextuality in Antiquity and Christianity,* edited by Dennis R. MacDonald, 56–77. Harrisburg, PA: Trinity Press International, 2001.

———. "Romancing the Parables." *Perspectives in Religious Studies* 29 (2002): 17–25.

Hoehner, Harold. *Herod Antipas.* Society for New Testament Studies Monograph Series 17. Cambridge: Cambridge University Press, 1972.

Holden, Lynn. *Forms of Deformity.* Sheffield: Sheffield Academic Press, 1991.

Hooker, Morna. *Jesus and the Servant: The Influence of the Servant Concept of Deutero-Isaiah in the New Testament.* London: SPCK, 1959.

Howe, E. Margaret. "Interpretations of Paul in the *Acts of Paul and Thecla*." In *Pauline Studies: Essays Presented to Professor F. F. Bruce on His 70th Birthday,* edited by Donald A. Hagner and Murray J. Harris, 33–49. Grand Rapids: Eerdmans, 1980.

Hughes, Joseph J. "Piso's Eyebrows." *Mnemosyne* 45 (1992): 234–37.

Humphries, Michael L. "The Physiognomy of the Blind: The Johannine Story of the Blind Man." In *Reimagining Christian Origins: A Colloquium Honoring Burton L. Mack,* edited by Elizabeth A. Castelli and Hal Taussig, 229–43. Valley Forge, PA: Trinity Press International, 1996.

Hurtado, Larry W. "The Origin of the *Nomina Sacra*: A Proposal." *Journal of Biblical Literature* 117 (1998): 655–73.

Hvalvik, Reider. "Barnabas 9.7–9 and the Author's Supposed Use of *Gematria*." *New Testament Studies* 33 (1987): 276–82.

Jeffrey, David L. "Wise as Serpents." In *A Dictionary of Biblical Tradition in English Literature,* edited by David L. Jeffrey, 839–40. Grand Rapids: Eerdmans, 1992.

Jeremias, Joachim. *Jerusalem in the Time of Jesus*. Philadelphia: Fortress, 1969.

Jervell, Jacob. *The Unknown Paul: Essay on Luke-Acts and Early Christian History*. Minneapolis: Augsburg, 1984.

John Chrysostom. "Homily X." In *The Homilies on the Acts of the Apostles*. Library of the Fathers of the Holy Catholic Church. Translated by J. Walker and T. Sheppard. Oxford: John Henry Parker, 1851.

Johnson, Luke Timothy. *The Literary Function of Possessions in Luke-Acts*. Society of Biblical Literature Dissertation Series 39. Missoula, MT: Scholars Press, 1977.

———. *The Acts of the Apostles*. Sacra Pagina 5. Collegeville, MN: Liturgical Press, 1992.

Jongeling, Bastiaan. "La préposition L dans 1 Samuel 16:7." In *Scripta signa vocis*, edited by H. L. J. Vanstiphout, 95–99. Groningen, Netherlands: Egbert Forsten, 1986.

Joosten, Jan. "1 Samuel 16:6,7 in the Peshitta Version." *Vetus Testamentum* 41 (1991): 226–33.

Kee, H. C. "Testament of the Twelve Patriarchs: A New Translation and Introduction." In *The Old Testament Pseudepigrapha*, edited by James Charlesworth, 1:775–928. London: Darton, Longman & Todd, 1983.

Kelber, Werner. *Mark's Story of Jesus*. Philadelphia: Fortress, 1979.

Kennedy, George A., trans. *Progymnasmata: Greek Textbooks of Prose Composition and Rhetoric*. Writings from the Greco-Roman World 10. Atlanta: Society of Biblical Literature, 2003.

Kessler, Martin. "Narrative Technique in 1 Sam 16:1–13." *Catholic Biblical Quarterly* 32 (1970): 543–54.

Kiilerich, B. "Physiognomics and the Iconography of Alexander." *Symbolae Osloenses* 63 (1988): 5–28.

Kouklanakis, Andrea. "Thersites, Odysseus, and the Social Order." In *Nine Essays on Homer*, edited by Miriam Carlisle and Olga Levaniouk, 35–53. Lanham, MD: Rowman & Littlefield, 1999.

———. "Thersites, Odysseus, and the Social Order." In *Nine Essays on Homer*, edited by Miriam Carlisle and Olga Levaniouk, 35–54. Lanham, MD: Rowman & Littlefield, 1999.

Kraus, F. R. *Die physiognomischen Omina der Babylonier*. Gräfenhainichen: C. Schulze, 1935.

———. *Texte zur babylonischen Physiognomatik*. Archiv für Orientforschung, Beiheft 3. Berlin, 1939.

Krien, G. "Der Ausdruck der antiken Theatermasken nach Angaben im Pollux-Katalog und in der pseudo-aristotelischen 'Physiognomik.'" *Jahreshefte des Österreichischen Archäologischen Instituts in Wien* (1955): 84–117.

Kühn, D. C. G., ed. *Galeni Opera Omnia*. 20 vols. Leipzig: Officina Libraria Car. Cnoblochii, 1821–1833.

Lavater, Johann Caspar. *Essays on Physiognomy: For the Promotion of the Knowledge and the Love of Mankind*. Translated by Thomas Holcroft. 3 vols. London: Printed by C. Whittingham for H. D. Symonds, 1789–1793.

———. *Physiognomische Fragmente zur Beförderung der Menschenkenntniss und Mensche liebe.* Leipzig and Winterthur, 1775–1778.

———. *The Physiognomist's Own Book: An Introduction to Pysiognomy Drawn from the Writings of Lavater.* Philadelphia: James Kay Jun. & Brother, 1841.

Luedemann, Gerd. *Early Christianity according to the Tradition in Acts: A Commentary.* Minneapolis: Fortress, 1989.

MacDowell, D. M. "Piso's Face." *Classical Review* 14 (1964): 9–10.

Malherbe, Abraham J. "A Physical Description of Paul." *Harvard Theological Review* 79 (1986): 170–75.

Malina, Bruce J., and Jerome H. Neyrey. "Honor and Shame in Luke-Acts: Pivotal Values of the Mediterranean World." In *The Social World of Luke-Acts: Models for Interpretation,* edited by Jerome H. Neyrey, 41–44. Peabody, MA: Hendrickson, 1991.

———. *Portraits of Paul: An Archaeology of Ancient Personality.* Louisville: Westminster John Knox Press, 1996.

Marconi, Gilberto. "History as a Hermeneutical Interpretation of the Difference between Acts 3:1–10 and 4:8–12." In *Luke and Acts,* edited by Gerald O'Collins and Gilberto Marconi, 167–80, 252–57. New York: Paulist, 1992.

Marrou, H. *A History of Education in Antiquity.* London: Sheed & Ward, 1956.

Marrow, S. B. "*Parrhēsia* and the New Testament." *Catholic Biblical Quarterly* 44 (1982): 431–46.

Marshall, I. Howard. *The Gospel of Luke: A Commentary on the Greek Text.* Exeter: Paternoster, 1978.

Martin, Clarice. "A Chamberlain's Journey and the Challenge of Interpretation for Liberation." *Semeia* 47 (1989): 105–35.

Martin, Dale B. *The Corinthian Body.* New Haven, CT: Yale University Press, 1995.

Mason, H. J. "The Distinction of Lucius in Apuleius' *Metamorphoses.*" *Phoenix* 37 (1983): 135–43.

———. "Physiognomy in Apuleius' *Metamorphoses* 2.2." *Classical Philology* 79 (1984): 307–9.

Meek, Kenneth. *Driving While Black.* New York: Random House, 2000.

Mesk, J. "Die Beispiele in Polemos Physiognomonik." *Wiener Studien* 50 (1932): 51–67.

Metzger, Bruce. *Manuscripts of the Greek Bible: An Introduction to Palaeography.* Oxford: Oxford University Press, 1981.

Milgrom, Jacob. *Leviticus 17–22: A New Translation with Introduction and Commentary.* Anchor Bible 3A. New York: Doubleday, 2000.

Milot, L. "Guérison d'une femme infirme un jour de sabbat (Luc 13.10–17)." *Sémiotique et Bible* 39 (1985): 23–33.

Misener, Geneva. "Iconistic Portraits." *Classical Philology* 19 (1924): 97–123.

Mitchell, Alan. "Zacchaeus Revisited: Luke 19, 8 as a Defense." *Biblica* 71 (1990): 153–76.

Mitchell, David T., and Sharon L. Snyder, eds. *The Body and Physical Difference: Discourses of Disability.* Ann Arbor: University of Michigan Press, 1997.

Montserrat, Dominic. *Sex and Society in Graeco-Roman Egypt.* London: Kegan Paul International, 1996.

Moore, Stephen D. "Are the Gospels Unified Naratives?" In *Society of Biblical Literature Seminar Paper* 26, edited by Kent Harold Richards, 493–58. Chico, CA: Scholars Press, 1987.

Moore, Stephen D., and Janice Capel Anderson. "Taking It Like a Man: Masculinity in 4 Maccabees." *Journal of Biblical Literature* 117 (1998): 249–73.

Mueller, J. R. *The Five Fragments of the Apocryphon of Ezekiel: A Critical Study.* Journal for the Study of the Pseudepigrapha: Supplement Series 5. Sheffield: Sheffield Academic Press, 1994.

Mueller, J. R., and S. E. Robinson. "Apocryphon of Ezekiel." In *The Old Testament Pseudepigrapha,* edited by James H. Charlesworth, 1:487–96. Garden City, NY: Doubleday, 1983.

Müller, I., ed. *Scripta Minora of Galen.* Leipzig: Teubner, 1891.

Müller, I., et al., eds. *Claudii Galeni Pergameni Scripta Minora.* Leipzig: Teubner, 1891.

Neale, David A. *None but the Sinners: Religious Categories in the Gospel of Luke.* Journal for the Study of the New Testament: Supplement Series 58. Sheffield: Sheffield Academic Press, 1991.

Neyrey, Jerome H. "The Symbolic Universe of Luke-Acts: 'They Turn the World Upside Down.'" In *The Social World of Luke-Acts: Models for Interpretation,* edited by Jerome H. Neyrey, 278–85. Peabody, MA: Hendrickson, 1991.

Nolland, John. *Luke 9:21–18:34.* Word Biblical Commentary 35B. Dallas: Word, 1993.

———. *Luke 18:35–24:53.* Word Biblical Commentary 35C. Dallas: Word, 1993.

Norris, Frederick W. "Early Christians and Animals." *Journal of Early Christian Studies* 8 (2000): 312–13.

Offermanns, D. *Der Physiologus nach den Handschriften G und M.* Beiträge zur klassichen Philologie 22. Meisenheim am Glan: Hain, 1966.

Olyan, Saul M. "'Anyone Blind or Lame Shall Not Enter the House': On the Interpretation of Second Samuel 5:8b." *Catholic Biblical Quarterly* 60 (1998): 218–27.

Opeku, F. "Physiognomy in Apuleius." In *Studies in Latin Literature and Roman History,* edited by Carl Deroux, 1:467–74. Brussels: Latomus, 1979.

O'Toole, Robert F. "Some Exegetical Reflections on Luke 13,10–17." *Biblica* 73 (1992): 84–107.

Pack, R. A. "Physiognomical Entrance Examinations." *Classical Journal* 31 (1935): 42–43.

Parsons, Mikeal C. "Isaiah 53 in Acts 8: A Reply to Morna Hooker." In *Isaiah 53 and Christian Origins,* edited by William Bellinger, Bruce Corley, and William Farmer, 104–19. Sheffield: Sheffield Academic Press, 1998.

———. "Luke and the Progymnasmata: A Preliminary Investigation into the Preliminary Exercises." In *Contextualizing Acts: Lukan Narrative and Greco-Roman Discourse,* edited by Todd Penner and Caroline Vander Stichele, 43–63. Atlanta: Scholars Press, 2004.

———. "The Place of Jerusalem on the Lukan Landscape: An Exercise in Theological Cartography." In *Literary Studies in Luke-Acts*, edited by Richard P. Thompson and Thomas E. Phillips, 155–72. Macon, GA: Mercer University Press, 1998.

———. *The Departure of Jesus in Luke-Acts: The Ascension Narratives in Context.* Journal for the Study of the New Testament: Supplement Series 21. Sheffield: Sheffield Academic Press, 1987.

———. "Acts." In *Acts and Pauline Writings*, edited by Watson Mills et al., Mercer Commentary on the Bible, 1–64. Macon, GA: Mercer University Press, 1997.

Patillon, Michel, ed. and trans. *Aelius Theon: Progymnasmata.* Collection des universités de France. Paris: Belles Lettres, 1997.

Penner, Todd. "Reconfiguring the Rhetorical Study of Acts: Reflections on the Method in and Learning of a Progymnastic Poetics." *Perspectives in Religious Studies* 30 (2003): 425–39.

Porter, Martin. *Windows of the Soul: Physiognomy in European Culture, 1470–1780.* Oxford: Oxford University Press, 2005.

Postlethwaite, Evan N. "Thersites in the *Iliad*." In *Homer*, edited by Ian McAuslan and Peter Walcot, 83–95. Oxford: Oxford University Press, 1998.

Preuschen, E. "Paulus als Antichrist." *Zeitschrift für die neutestamentliche Wissenschaft und die Kunde der älteren Kirche* 2 (1901): 169–201.

Raina, G. "Il verisimile in Menandro e nella Fisiognomica." In *Il meraviglioso e il verosimile tra antichità e medioevo*, edited by D. Lanza and O. Longo, 173–85. Florence: L. S. Olschki, 1989.

Ramsay, Sir William. *The Church in the Roman Empire before A.D. 170.* London: Hodder and Stoughton, 1903.

Raphael, Rebecca. "What Has Biblical Literature to Do with Disability Studies?" *SBL Forum.* www.sbl-site.org /Article.aspx?ArticleId=250.

Roberts, Colin H. *Manuscript, Society and Belief in Early Christian Egypt.* London: Oxford University Press, 1979.

———. "P.Yale 1 and the Early Christian Book." In *Essays in Honor of C. Bradford Welles*, edited by Alan E. Samuel, 25–28. New Haven, CT: American Society of Papyrologists, 1966.

Romm, James S. *The Edges of the Earth in Ancient Thought: Geography, Exploration, and Fiction.* Princeton, NJ: Princeton University Press, 1992.

Rose, Ashley S. "The 'Principles' of Divine Election: Wisdom in 1 Samuel 16." In *Rhetorical Criticism*, edited by J. J. Jackson and M. Kessler, 43–67. Pittsburgh: Pickwick, 1974.

Rosenstiehl, J.-M. "Le Portrait de l'Antichrist." In *Pseudépigraphes de l'Ancien Testament et Manuscrits de la Mer Morte*, edited by M. Philonenko, Cahiers d'Histoire et de Philosophie Religieuses 41, 45–60. Paris: Presses Universitaires de France, 1967.

Roth, S. John. *The Blind, the Lame, and the Poor: Character Types in Luke-Acts.* Journal for the Study of the New Testament: Supplement Series 144. Sheffield: Sheffield Academic Press, 1997.

Sandnes, Karl Olav. *Belly and Body in the Pauline Epistles.* Cambridge: Cambridge University Press, 2002.

Schiffman, Lawrence. *Reclaiming the Dead Sea Scrolls: The History of Judaism, the Background of Christianity, the Lost Library of Qumran.* Philadelphia: The Jewish Publication Society, 1994.

Schmid, J. *Das Evangelium nach Lukas.* 4th ed. Regensburger Neues Testament 3. Regensburg: Friedrich Pustet, 1977.

Schmithals, W. *Das Evangelium nach Lukas.* Zurich: Theologischer Verlag, 1980.

Schneider, G. *Das Evangelium nach Lukas.* Gütersloh: Gerd Mohn, 1977.

Schüssler Fiorenza, Elisabeth. "Lk 13:10–17: Interpretation of Liberation and Transformation." *Theology Digest* (1989): 303–19.

Seeley, David. *The Noble Death: Graeco-Roman Martyrology and Paul's Concept of Salvation.* Journal for the Study of the New Testament: Supplement Series 28. Sheffield: JSOT Press, 1990.

Seim, Turid Karlsen. "Abraham, Ancestor or Archetype? A Comparison of Abraham-Language in 4 Maccabees and Luke-Acts." In *Antiquity and Humanity: Essays on Ancient Religion and Philosophy; Presented to Hans Dieter Betz on His 70th Birthday,* edited by Adela Yarbro Collins and Margaret M. Mitchell, 27–42. Tübingen: Mohr Siebeck, 2001.

———. *The Double Message: Patterns of Gender in Luke and Acts.* Nashville: Abingdon, 1994.

Shookman, Ellis, ed. *The Faces of Physiognomy: Interdisciplinary Approaches to Johann Caspar Lavater.* Columbia, SC: Cambden House, 1993.

Siker, J. S. *Disinheriting the Jews: Abraham in Early Christian Controversy.* Louisville: Westminster John Knox Press, 1991.

Spencer, F. Scott. *Acts.* Readings: A New Biblical Commentary. Sheffield: Sheffield Academic Press, 1997.

———. "The Ethiopian Eunuch and His Bible: A Social-Science Analysis." *Biblical Theological Bulletin* 22 (1992): 155–65.

———. *The Portrait of Philip in Acts: A Study of Roles and Relations.* Journal for the Study of the New Testament: Supplement Series 67. Sheffield: JSOT Press, 1992.

Stein, O. "The Numeral 18." *Poona Orientalist* 1 (1936): 1–37; 2 (1937) 164–65.

Stempvoort, P. A. van. "The Interpretation of the Ascension in Luke and Acts." *New Testament Studies* 5 (1959): 32–33.

Strauss, M. L. *The Davidic Messiah in Luke-Acts: The Promise and Its Fulfillment in Lukan Christology.* Journal for the Study of the New Testament: Supplement Series 110. Sheffield: Sheffield Academic Press, 1995.

Swain, Simon. *Seeing the Face, Seeing the Soul: Polemon's Physiognomy from Classical Antiquity to Medieval Islam.* Oxford: Oxford University Press, 2006.

Talbert, Charles. *Reading Acts: A Literary and Theological Commentary on the Acts of the Apostles.* New York: Crossroad, 1997.

Terrien, Samuel. "The Omphalos Myth and Hebrew Religion." *Vetus Testamentum* 20 (1970): 315–38.

Testard, M. "Étude sur la composition dans le 'De officiis ministrorum' de saint Ambroise," In *Ambroise de Milan: XVIe centenaire de son élection épiscopale: Dix études*, edited by Y.-M. Duval, 155–97. Paris: Etudes Augustiniennes, 1974.

Threat and Humiliation: Racial Profiling, Domestic Security, and Human Rights in the United States. New York: Amnesty International USA Publications, 2004.

Tytler, Graeme. *Physiognomy in the European Novel: Faces and Fortunes*. Princeton, NJ: Princeton University Press, 1982.

Vogt, Tabine. *Physiognomonica*. Aristoteles Werke in deutscher Übersetzung 18.6. Berlin: Akademie, 1999.

Walaskay, Paul. "Acts 3:1–10." *Interpretation* 42 (1988): 171–75.

Walz, Christian. *Rhetores Graeci*. 9 vols. in 10. Stuttgart: J. G. Cotta, 1832–1836.

Watts, John. *Isaiah 34–66*. Word Biblical Commentary 25. Waco, TX: Word, 1987.

Weissenrieder, Annette. *Images of Illness in the Gospel of Luke: Insights of Ancient Medical Texts*. Wissenschaftliche Untersuchungen zum Neuen Testament 164. Tübingen: Mohr Siebeck, 2003.

Welles, C. Bradford. "The Yale Genesis Fragment." *The Yale University Library Gazette* 39:1 (1964): 1–8.

Wilkinson, John. "The Case of the Bent Woman in Luke 13:10–17." *Evangelical Quarterly* 49 (1977): 195–205.

———. *Health and Healing: Studies in New Testament Principles and Practice*. Edinburgh: Handsel, 1980.

Williams, Walter. "Racial Profiling." *Capitalism Magazine* (April 21, 2004). http://www.capmag.com/article.asp?ID=3639 (accessed October 2005).

Winterbottom, M. "The Text of Ambrose's *De Officiis*." *Journal of Theological Studies* 46 (1995): 559–66.

Wintermute, O. S. "Apocalypse of Elizah." In *The Old Testament Pseudepigrapha*, edited by James Charlesworth, 1:721–53. London: Darton, Longman & Todd, 1983.

Young, R. D. "The 'Woman with the Soul of Abraham': Traditions about the Mother of the Maccabean Martyrs." In *"Women Like This": New Perspectives on Jewish Women in the Greco-Roman World*, edited by A.-J. Levine, 67–81. Atlanta: Scholars Press, 1991.

Zahn, T. "Paulus der Apostel." *Realencyklopädie für protestantische Theologie und Kirche* 15 (1904): 61–88.

Zervos, G. T. "Apocalypse of Daniel." In *The Old Testament Pseudepigrapha*, edited by James Charlesworth, 1:755–70. London: Darton, Longman & Todd, 1983.

Name Index

Index of Ancient Sources

Index of Greek Words

Subject Index

Abraham, 78n17, 81–82
Abrahamic covenant, 15, 81–82, 83, 122, 123, 132, 141, 144n4, 145
Absalom, 40, 61
Achaia, 115
Achilles, 72, 129, 130, 147, 152
actors, 59
Acts of Paul and Thecla, 51–56, 98
Adam, 47, 76
Adamantius, 14
Aeneas, 91n21
Aesop's fables, 70n3
Africans, 78
Agamemnon, 74, 129, 150, 151
Ajax, 152
Americans with Disabilities Act, 144
anatomical method, 22–23, 68, 125, 127–29
  subverted by Luke, 133–36
animals, 21, 23, 57, 125
ankles, 110–13, 116
antichrist, physiognomy of, 46–47
antitemple polemic, 139
Aphthonius, 131
Arians, 60
Aristotelian philosophy, 20–21
arrogance, 30
astrology, 43, 64–65, 90
astronomy, 93
asymmetry, 47
Augustus, 29–31, 44, 99, 102

baldness, 55, 150
baptism, 133, 139

Barnabas, 92–93
belly, 50–51
bent woman (Luke 13), 82, 83–95, 122, 144
birth defects, 101
blemishes
  on animals, 48
  of priests, 40–41
blind, blindness, 47, 48n29, 101
  of Paul, 80
  and temple, 42
blind man (Luke 18), 98, 121
blond hair, 31–32
blood, 20
body, 25, 26, 59
  and soul, 13, 14, 22, 45, 59, 116, 120, 122
body language, 117
boldness, 54, 117
bowed legs, 55
bravery, 26
"brood of vipers," 76
Browne, Thomas, 13n7
bull, 44

caricature, 13n7
castration, 133, 134, 136
cattle, 30, 89
Celadus, 44–45
celibacy, 133
Cercopes, 104
character, and physique, 12, 15, 22, 26, 65, 127, 144–45
child of Abraham, 107
chiromancy, 44n14

187